The Seven Wonders of the World

Michael Ashley was born in Southall, Middlesex, in 1948. He has long had an interest in historical research in all its forms – by his early teens he had already compiled lists covering the rulers of all nations, past and present. In more recent years he has concentrated on research into science fiction and fantasy literature, having compiled several anthologies including a five-volume *History of the Science Fiction Magazine* and a two-volume *Best of British SF*. He also compiled *Who's Who in Horror & Fantasy Fiction* and has been a consultant and contributor to several science fiction encyclopedias and specialist periodicals. He now lives in Kent where he is working on a number of projects including a biography of Algernon Blackwood, a book on the Seven Champions of Christendom, and a Bibliography of British Science Fiction.

The Seven Wonders of the World

MICHAEL ASHLEY

FONTANA PAPERBACKS

First published by Fontana Paperbacks 1980

Set in Linotype Times

Made and printed in Great Britain by
William Collins Sons & Co Ltd, Glasgow

To Sue, the biggest wonder of them all,
and to Raz, who makes us all wonder

CONTENTS

Introduction 9

I. The Birth of the Wonders 15

II. Wonder of Wonders: The Pyramids of Egypt 35

III. Babylon the Great 84

IV. The God of the Games: The Statue of Zeus at Olympia 122

V. The Home of the Huntress: The Temple of Artemis at Ephesos 154

VI. Dignity in Death: The Mausoleum at Halikarnassos 183

VII. The Second Sun: The Colossus of Rhodes 207

VIII. The Working Wonder: The Pharos Lighthouse at Alexandria 230

Afterword 248

Appendices:

I. On The Seven Wonders of the World 252

II. The Forgotten Wonders 259

Selective Bibliography 279

Index 283

LIST OF FIGURES IN TEXT

1. The Seven Wonders of the World 17
2. The Locations of the Seven Wonders 23
3. Time Chart of the Seven Wonders 24
4. The Location of Egypt's significant pyramids 36-7
5. Simplified plan of the Giza Plateau 40
6. Cross-section of the Great Pyramid 45
7. Cross-sections of the other major pyramids 46
8. The transportation of the colossal statue of Djehutihotep 52
9. Comparative development of significant pyramids 64
10. Plan of Babylon in Nebuchadnezzar's day 86
11. The Hanging Gardens of Babylon 95
12. The Tower of Babel and the Temple of Marduk 97
13. The Assyro-Babylonian Empires 103
14. The Peloponnesos in 432 B.C. 124
15. The Sanctuary of Olympia in 432 B.C. 126
16. Plan and elevation of the Temple of Zeus 127
17. The Statue of Zeus according to Adler 131
18. The Greek colonies in Asia Minor 156
19. Plan of the Alexandrine Temple 158
20. Partial plan of Ephesos 176
21. Suggested plan of Halikarnassos 185
22. Suggested reconstructions of the Mausoleum 188
23. Mausoleum according to Waywell and Jeppesen 190-1
24. Partial plan of the City of Rhodes 209
25. The Colossus of Rhodes according to Maryon 211
26. Alexander's Empire by 305 B.C. 217
27. Plan of Ptolemaic Alexandria 237

LIST OF PLATES

1. The Pyramids at Giza from the south (*Egyptian Department of Antiquities, Cairo*).
2. The Pyramids of Djoser and Userkaf (*Hamlyn Picture Library*).
3. The Pyramids as depicted by Heemskerck.
4. The ruins of the Ishtar Gate, Babylon (*Radio Times Hulton Picture Library*).
5. Babylon as depicted by Kircher (*British Library*).
6. Babylon from the Ishtar Gate (*reconstruction by E. Unger*).
7. The Sanctuary at Olympia in Roman times (*reconstruction by R. Bohn, Radio Times Hulton Picture Library*).
8. The Statue of Zeus depicted by Heemskerck.
9. The Statue of the Ephesian Artemis (*Turkish Embassy, London*).
10. The Temple of Artemis at Ephesos (*Radio Times Hulton Picture Library*).
11. The Mausoleum depicted by Heemskerck.
12. The statue called 'Mausolos' (*Trustees of the British Museum*).
13. A suggested reconstruction of the Colossus of Rhodes (*Radio Times Hulton Picture Library*).
14. The Colossus of Rhodes depicted by Heemskerck.
15. A bas-relief depicting the sun-god Helios (*Rhodes Museum*).
16. The Pharos Lighthouse depicted by Heemskerck.
17. The Pharos Lighthouse based on the reconstruction by H. Thiersch (*Radio Times Hulton Picture Library*).
18. Fort Qait Bey on the site of the Pharos Lighthouse (*UAR State Information Service*).

INTRODUCTION

Several years ago, when I was working on a series of articles for an encyclopedia of science fiction, I found myself looking at a list of the Seven Wonders of the World. It wasn't the first time I'd read such a list – we've all seen them – but this time I found myself wondering more than usual about them. The names were so strange and alien. Of course we all know about the Pyramids, and I'd heard of the Hanging Gardens of Babylon and the Colossus of Rhodes, but did not know much about them. I knew even less about the Pharos Lighthouse, and as for the Statue of Zeus at Olympia, the Mausoleum at Halikarnassos and the Temple of Artemis at Ephesos, they meant little more than names.

So, I asked myself, as I sat there looking at this time-honoured list, what was so special about these works that they should be remembered, mostly in name alone, to this day? What were they, how did they come about, and what happened to them?

These thoughts stayed with me as I returned to my writing and, over the next two or three years, whilst I worked on other projects, I occasionally looked more into the background of the Seven Wonders. I became increasingly more fascinated with the story behind them even though, or perhaps because, little is readily available about them in print. I am no archaeologist, so at the outset I had no knowledge of the various academic journals available on the subject. But then, I told myself, neither do most other readers. All that is easily available in print about the Wonders are brief annotated and fairly lifeless lists copied with little variation from one reference work to another. They do little to enlighten the reader on the full meaning of the Seven Wonders and, more importantly, they are invariably inaccurate. I had discovered many years ago never to accept automatically anything in print, especially uncorroborated reported information, and this was particularly true about the Seven Wonders. General reference works would contain contradictory information without any apparent scope for resolving the dilemma. I can illustrate my point by referring to two much-lauded works available in virtually every library or bookshop, *The Book of Lists* (Bantam and Cassell, 1977) compiled by the Wallechinsky family, and the indefatigable *Guinness Book of Records* (25th edition, 1978) compiled by Norris McWhirter.

The Book of Lists begins its entry on page 166 and says: 'The list was created by a most respected Byzantine mathematician and traveller named Philon.' Page 123 of the *Guinness Book of Records* says 'The Seven Wonders of the World were first designated by Antipater of Sidon in the 2nd century B.C.' They can't both be right. I could further complicate the issue by saying that the *Guinness Book of Answers* (1978 edition) says that Antipater lived in the 2nd century A.D. It adds that the Mausoleum was built 'in *c* 325 B.C.', the Wallechinskies 'by 350 B.C.'. As for the Pharos, the Guinness book dates it at 270 B.C., the Wallechinskies in 200 B.C.

The reader is invited to check as many other sources as he wishes, and he is sure to find factual variations in all of them. In fact you'll probably find discrepancies in any number of facts you care to check. It's a researcher's hazard, and no book is immune to error.

One can make all kinds of excuses for these contradictions – printing errors, limited information available at the time of going to press, insufficient research – but it does not alter the fact that once it is in print it is there for all to see, and the public is unwarily and unwittingly misled.

It was this, as much as my growing interest in the Wonders themselves, that fired me into researching the subject in earnest. I found it necessary to unearth copies of the original works by the ancient Greek and Roman authorities who had seen the Wonders at first hand – and even these were contradictory!

Finally, after several years' cursory and over a year's concentrated research I felt I had at last put together the full story of the Seven Wonders. The trail was fraught with problems, for as archaeologists and historians will readily admit, in the cases where evidence is meagre, it is dangerous to assume anything, and a theory based on flimsy hypotheses is fragile indeed. In this book I have presented the facts as I have found them along with a variety of theories, but I leave room for the reader to make his own assessments about some of the conclusions. The world of which I write vanished over two thousand years ago – in the case of ancient Egypt over four thousand years ago – and we can only reconstruct it from incomplete archaeological evidence and the surviving fragments of writings by contemporaries whose motives for presenting the facts are at times questionable. Later writings about the Seven Wonders in the Middle Ages mix fact with fantasy and thus, although they may be better preserved, are of far less use to us. In fact, I still consider it surprising that we know as much about the ancient world as we do, and I have no hesitation in showering praises on the archaeologists whose patience and devotion have opened up the world of the past, and on the philologists and classical scholars whose sterling work on discovering and translating ancient writings have given us an insight into the minds of men long dead.

Without them this book could never have been written, and the Seven wonders would remain little more than names surrounded by myth.

I doubt that the information in this book will be new to devoted archaeologists, though I hope that they will find food for thought within its pages. The book is chiefly intended for the reader who, like myself, is interested in the ancient world but has neither the time nor the means to follow assiduously the many scholarly archaeological and historical journals.

I discovered that the real secret behind the Seven Wonders lay in their origins, which provide a fascinating and rich story of the fight for supremacy in the Near East and Mediterranean lands in the centuries before Christ. This story serves as a backcloth upon which to place the Wonders as landmarks of the rise and fall of powerful nations like Egypt, Babylonia, Persia and Greece. There is much to learn from the story of the Seven Wonders, and I hope you enjoy discovering it as much as I did.

Mike Ashley,
Walderslade, Kent,
December 1978

NOTE

I feel a brief comment on the spelling of the names of people and places is in order. Wherever possible I have adopted a policy of using the spelling as close to the original as possible, allowing for pronunciation and readability. This is most noticeable in the Greek names which we know more readily today from their Latinized equivalents such as Hercules instead of Herakles. Where there is no danger of confusion I have retained the original spellings, but in certain cases people and places are known too well by later versions of their names for me to complicate matters by introducing the original, as in the examples of Kurush for Cyrus or even Alexandros instead of Alexander. However, I have allowed for variant spellings in this volume's index, which I hope will aid the reader in the event of any confusion.

ACKNOWLEDGEMENTS

Although the final production and presentation of this book is my own, the research would have been a long and lonely task without the much welcomed advice and assistance of many people. A number I must mention and thank here especially Professor I. E. S. Edwards and Professor Kristian Jeppesen who unhesitatingly gave me the benefit of their formidable knowledge on the Pyramids and the Mausoleum respectively. I must also thank Miss Jean Blackwood, whose translations of a number of Latin texts are included here for the first time and without whose prompt assistance I would still be floundering. To Mrs Pamela Neads goes my thanks for her interest and aid in connection with the Colossus of Rhodes. Thanks also to B. F. Cook, Keeper of Greek and Roman Antiquities at the British Museum; the Joint Library of Hellenic and Roman Studies; the Archaeological Institute of the Dodecanese, Rhodes; the Egyptian and Turkish Embassies in London; the Maritime Museum, Alexandria; and the Service des Antiquités, Cairo. Also my thanks to Tim Shackleton of Fontana Paperbacks for his interest and advice on this project from the start, and, as always, my thanks to Miss Stewart and her colleagues at Chatham Reference Library for their unstinting and indispensable help. My thanks to them all.

CHAPTER I

THE BIRTH OF THE WONDERS

Most reference books, or at least those that go into any detail, will tell you that the idea of compiling a list of Seven Wonders of the World grew from the Greek's love of travel and their thirst for knowledge. In the years that followed the growth of Alexander the Great's Empire from Macedonia in the west to the River Indus in the east, Greek became the common language of the Mediterranean and Near East, and the Greeks were able to travel without hindrance throughout this region. With such freedom of movement travellers, with perhaps only limited time available, would want to know what sights most demanded to be seen, and writers were only too agreeable to oblige, contending with each other in producing lists of the most magnificent wonders.

Three centuries later, the peace of the Roman Empire allowed for even more extensive travel, and it was during these years that the majority of the important Greek and Latin histories and travel books were written: the works of Pliny the Elder (A.D. 23-79), whose *Historia Naturalis* is one of the most thorough works of antiquity; of Strabo (63 B.C.-A.D. 21) who wrote one of the most important works on geography of the period; of Vitruvius (*fl* 46-14 B.C.) whom the Emperor Augustus commissioned to compile a treatise on architecture and construction; of Plutarch (A.D. 46-120) whose *Parallel Lives* is unequalled amongst early biographies; and of Pausanias (*fl* A.D. 140-180), of Lucian of Samosata (*c* A.D. 125-190) and so many, many more.

Despite this profusion of names it is not to any of these writers that we turn for reference to the complete Seven Wonders of the World. In fact, only a few of them identify them specifically, and even then seldom in full. For instance, in *De Architectura* Vitruvius speaks of the Tomb of Mausolos as '. . . a work so remarkable that it is classed among the Seven Wonders of the World.'[1] Yet he does not name the other six. Pausanias in his *Guidebook of Greece* also singles out the Tomb for credit, but only to relate that the Romans have coined the term 'mausolea' for their own magnificent tombs, and he makes no mention of it ranking as one of the Seven Wonders.[2] Pliny does classify the Mausoleum as one of the Seven Wonders,[3] but not so the Temple of Artemis or the Pharos Lighthouse or even the mighty Pyramids, but here we can rely on Strabo who refers to them as '. . . the tombs of kings, of which three are noteworthy, and two of these are even numbered among the Seven Wonders of the World . . .'[4]

This is all rather hit-and-miss and highlights a strange situation. Only sparse mention is made of the phrase 'one of the Seven Wonders' in the writings of antiquity, as if not all authorities considered it of importance, yet today there is something almost sacred about these ancient marvels. Could it be that to the Greeks the classification of the Seven Wonders was not significant? Did it serve merely as a yardstick by which to compare other sights, or did it rank merely as a novelty poll much as today we enjoy such useless lists as 'the Ten Best Dressed Men' or 'the Ten People I'd Most Like to Invite to Dinner', conversation pieces and little more? The Seven Wonders were certainly known throughout the Greek and Roman worlds and thus served admirably as landmarks or as the pinnacles of beauty.[5]

There were in fact many varied compilations of the Seven Wonders, and although only a few of them survive to this day they are sufficient to show the diversity of subjects chosen: the Palace of Cyrus, the Labyrinth, Solomon's Temple, Alexander's Throne, the Capitolium, the Temple of Hadrian at Cyzicus, the Colosseum, the Altar to Zeus at Pergamon, and as many more. In Appendix II I shall take a closer look at seven of these 'also rans', but for the moment let us consider the origin of the Seven Wonders.

Reference books will tell you that the Seven Wonders originated with either Philon of Byzantium or Antipatros of Sidon. I shall return to these in due course, but I have found it advisable never to accept facts at their face value and so

THE SEVEN WONDERS OF THE WORLD

Date Completed	*Architect/ Sculptor*	*Date Destroyed*
c 2500 B.C.	Hemon and others	extant
c 600 B.C.	unknown	482 B.C.
c 432 B.C.	Phidias	462 A.D.
c 290 B.C.	Deinokrates, Skopas and others	262 A.D.
c 344 B.C.	Satyros and Pytheos	1522 A.D.
290 B.C.	Chares of Lindos	227 B.C.
c 280 B.C.	Sostratos of Knidos	1375 A.D.

Description and Location

1. The Pyramids at Giza
2. The Hanging Gardens of Babylon
3. The Statue of Zeus (Jove) at Olympia
4. The Temple of Artemis (Diana) at Ephesos (Fifth Construction)
5. The Tomb of Mausolos at Halikarnassos (the Mausoleum)
6. The Statue of Helios at Rhodes (the Colossus)
7. The Lighthouse at Pharos, Alexandria

I shall first look at the situation in the Greek world in the years before Philon and Antipatros and see what clues it might provide.

In the two centuries before Christ, Alexandria was the cultural centre of the Mediterranean, as well as a focal point of trade and consequently travel. Alexandria was the capital of Egypt, now newly ruled by the Ptolemies, and the first two of the dynasty, surnamed Soter and Philadelphos, were both great lovers of learning. They established a University at Alexandria and encouraged the pursuit of knowledge. Anyone who considered himself important came to the city to learn or to teach, and a tremendous amount of research was carried out through the auspices of the Ptolemies.

The Library also acted as an information centre, and it is quite conceivable that many travellers arriving at Alexandria from all parts of the Greek world would pay a visit there to learn what was new elsewhere in the world. The University Library had a large staff of cataloguers and researchers and it is not hard to imagine that they might have compiled an 'information sheet' of such places of interest for the tourist, much like today. Since no such list survives we can only conjecture, but such a situation is both feasible and logical. I would even go so far as to say the likeliest contender for supervising such a list would be the Kyrenian Eratosthenes (276-196 B.C.).

This Greek cannot be rated too highly – he was a genius ahead of his time. In an age when most of us think people believed the world to be flat, Eratosthenes calculated the circumference of the Earth to be a little over 25,000 miles, which is within 1% of error, a remarkable achievement. Eratosthenes was renowned in the ancient world for his universal knowledge and in 240 B.C. Ptolemy III summoned him back to Alexandria at tutor to his children. At about the same time he succeeded Kallimakhos as Chief Librarian. He wrote a treatise on geography and produced the best map of the age covering the known world from Britain to India, and from Ethiopia to the Caspian Sea. Could it be that within this treatise he set down the Seven Wonders of the World?

Alas none of his work survives, although it was frequently consulted by Strabo, whose *Geography*, written about 20 B.C.

in Alexandria, was one of the earliest to refer to the Seven Wonders as an already established list. Unless by some fluke Eratosthenes's work has survived to this day and remains to be discovered, we shall never know whether he actually did compile a list of Seven Wonders, but he lived and travelled at the one time when all the Wonders were in full glory. The most recent, the Pharos Lighthouse, had been completed only a few years before the scientist's birth, whilst the Colossus of Rhodes still welcomed visitors to the city, and would continue to do so until 227 B.C. Certainly one would think it had to be some contemporary of Eratosthenes who compiled the prime list of Wonders for it to include the Pharos and the Colossus. Any earlier and the Pharos was not even built, any later and the Colossus would be in ruins.

However, this is where our mystery begins. The accepted source of the Seven Wonders is, as I mentioned earlier, either of two writers, the engineer Philon of Byzantium, or the poet Antipatros of Sidon. In totally different ways these two list the same Seven Wonders, and *both* exclude the Pharos Lighthouse. Philon lived at about 150 B.C., Antipatros about fifty years later, and Philon certainly visited Alexandria. There is no doubt that the Pharos was one of the most impressive sights in the Mediterranean and its exclusion from either list is, at first thoughts, puzzling. In compiling his seven, Philon counts the Hanging Gardens and the Walls of Babylon separately, yet by his day Babylon was a shell of its former self, and the Hanging Gardens already legend. Why substitute two sights, all but vanished, for one magnificent structure on the doorstep of Egypt?

Let us first consider the nature of the Seven Wonders. It rapidly becomes apparent that the Pharos was the only functional Wonder – it served a purpose. That is not to say that the Pyramids or the Temple of Artemis did not also provide a service, but their roles were entirely passive and their inclusion amongst the Wonders was on their merits as works of artistic and technological skill. The Pharos however was not intended to be admired (although obviously it was) but rather to guide sailors. The ancients therefore would have excluded it because their Seven Wonders were established on artistic criteria. Certainly no writers of the time qualified their descriptions of the Pharos as being one of the Seven Wonders, and it is not included in any surviving list from the classical Graeco-Roman days. The earliest inclusion is in that by Bishop Gregory of Tours (A.D. 538-94), but since Gregory also included Noah's Ark we can dismiss his compilation as little more than fanciful.[6] In his day the light of learning was becoming very dim, and the Dark Ages had dawned.

But let us consider another explanation which also brings me to an entirely new theory on the origin of the Seven Wonders. The Pharos was the youngest of the Seven and therefore could not have been included if the prime list had pre-dated it. Suppose we assume that the list attributed to Philon and Antipatros was a copy of an earlier compilation selected perhaps two hundred years before, at the time of the founding of Alexandria, when Alexander the Great intended to restore Babylon to its former glory and make it the eastern capital of his Empire. Alexander ruled the greatest Empire the world had ever seen, and he knew it. He had already devastated the Persians and had intended to conquer the entire world, but it was proving to be larger than even Alexander had thought, and under pressure from his troops he had halted at the banks of the River Indus. At the time of his death Alexander was preparing a campaign to conquer Arabia and would naturally want to boost the morale of his troops. What better way than to glorify his Empire by drawing attention to its supreme Wonders, Wonders that Alexander alone had conquered. From the Pyramids in the south to the Statue of Zeus in the west and Babylon in the east, the Wonders clearly mark the extremities of Alexander's world. A compilation of the Wonders of that world would not only symbolize the greatness of Alexander's conquests, but also emphasize his mastery of them all.

Throughout this book you will find Alexander's name linked with the Wonders – as if by some mystic force his destiny and their own were entwined. Alexander was no fool – he wanted his achievements recorded for posterity, and he had taken an official historian along with him on his conquests. This was Kallisthenes, the nephew of Alexander's old tutor, Aristotle, and it was clearly more as a favour to Aristotle than out of respect for Kallisthenes that the historian was chosen, as Alexander hated him. When Kallisthenes was accused of creating unrest amongst the soldiers he was executed. However, others took his place, in particular two of Alexander's generals who later wrote important histories of the Conqueror: Aristobulos and Ptolemy Soter. Both generals lived to a great age and wrote their histories many years after Alexander's death, probably independently of each other in about 290 B.C., but there is no reason to doubt that they did not keep their own records earlier.

If Alexander did choose either of these to compile a 'Book of Wonders' to exalt his Empire, the likelier would be Aristobulos, a much-respected engineer and architect. Alexander's later biographer, Flavius Arrianus, frequently quotes from Aristobulos's history, which is now lost. Aristobulos regularly drew attention to the cities and countryside during the march of conquest, and he was entrusted with the restoration of the tomb of Cyrus the Great at Pasargadae. Clearly, as an architect, he would have been interested in the wonders of Ionia and Babylonia and doubtless referred to them in his book. Little is known about his life, but it has been surmised that he settled in the town of Kassandea in Macedonia where he died, aged 90, some time around 280 B.C.

The fact that no evidence survives to this day does not preclude its existence at one time, and it is perfectly feasible that Alexander suggested that Aristobulos compile a 'Book of Wonders' to glorify his Empire. Alexander's untimely death may have resulted in the projected book being abandoned, but the concept could have lived on, and Aristobulos worked it into his history.

If the 'Book of Wonders' idea seems far-fetched, the reader has only to consider that a conqueror would naturally want to know the nature of the empire he now rules. William of Normandy requested just such a book when he invaded England, the Domesday Book, and whilst this is a sober and scholarly work it reflects the nature of King William. Alexander on the other hand would have wanted something far more sensational, partly because he wanted to raise his troops' morale, but mostly because by the time of his greatest conquests Alexander had delusions of divinity.[7]

Might we suppose therefore that Alexander the Great first

suggested a 'Book of Wonders' to glorify his Empire, and that this concept was later explored and embellished by Aristobulos, and possibly even Ptolemy Soter, and later still by the Librarians at Alexandria until Philon's day. At this point Philon decided to take a closer look at the Wonders and singled out those Seven which best fitted his intentions. The resulting work was entitled *De Septem Orbis Spectaculis* (or *On the Seven Wonders of the World*), and so the legend was born.

The chart at the beginning of this chapter (Fig. 1) listed the popularly accepted Seven Wonders. Before going any further let us just familiarize ourselves with them. The reader might like to refer to Figures 2 and 3 which show the Wonders in their geographical and chronological contexts respectively. Figure 2 reveals just how far flung are the Wonders. Apart from a cluster of three along the coast of Asia Minor the remainder are at the extremities of the Greek world – the boundaries of Alexander's Empire. It would need the most ardent of travellers to even consider venturing to them all, a point highlighted, though somewhat exaggerated, by Philon in the opening paragraph to his treatise:

> Everyone knows of the renowned Seven Wonders of the World, but few have set eyes on them, for, in order to do so, you have to arrange a long journey to the land of the Persians on the far side of the Euphrates; you have to visit Egypt; you must then change direction and go to Elis in Greece. Then you must see Halikarnassos, a city state in Karia, and Ephesos in Ionia, and you have to sail to Rhodes, so that, being exhausted by lengthy wanderings over the Earth's surface, and growing tired from the effort of these journeys, you finally fulfil your heart's desire only when life is ebbing away, leaving you weak through the weight of years.[8]

It is passages like this that have caused scholars to doubt that the treatise was the work of Philon. It is not the style of a skilled engineer, but rather the florid prose of a sensationalist, but more of this in a moment. Journeying to all the Wonders might be tiring, but it was possible to visit the

Figure 2. The Locations of the Seven Wonders.

sites with ease within the space of a year in Philon's time.

Figure 3 is a simple time chart. On the left are set out dates relevant to the Seven Wonders, whilst on the right are a variety of other dates which help place the Wonders in their historical niche, even though some have no direct bearing on them. What strikes me most when looking at the chart is the antiquity of the Pyramids. Most of the other Wonders are grouped within the time span of two centuries, but the Pyramids are at the very dawn of civilization. Indeed, the Pyramids were as ancient to the Librarians at Alexandria, as the Alexandrians are to us today. Yet, after all those thousands of years, the Pyramids are still with us, as mysterious and awesome as ever, whilst all the other Wonders have long since vanished.

The selection of the Pyramids as a World Wonder was inevitable, but the Greek world was overflowing with marvels created by man as the authorities of old readily emphasized. In glorifying their world it would seem logical to boast as

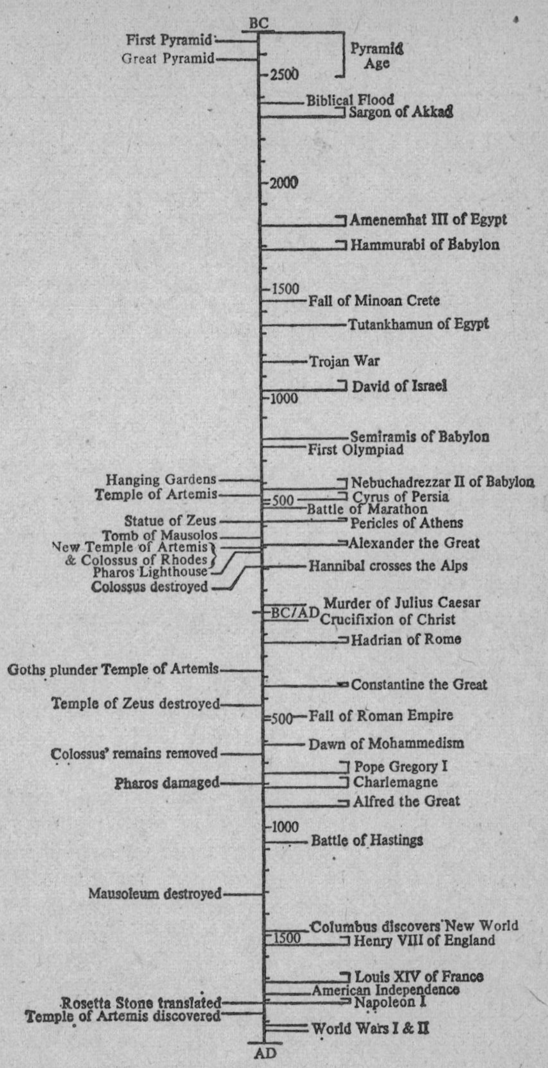

The left-hand side lists dates relevant to the Seven Wonders, whilst the right-hand list gives dates of other important events to help place the Wonders in their true sequence.

Figure 3. Time Chart of the Seven Wonders.

many Wonders as possible, so why did they feel it necessary to restrict themselves to seven?

The number seven had long been considered significant by the ancients. Thomas Davidson (1856-1923), one-time Presbyterian chaplain at Vienna and Brussels, points out that:

> The number seven is an image of God and is impressed on the Universe as well as on the bodily and mental constitution of man. Up to number ten, only seven neither produces nor is produced – not being formed from any other number by multiplication. Everything in the cosmos is enamoured of seven – the idea of the planets – as unity is of the fixed sphere.[9]

This concept was one preached by the famous Greek philosopher and mathematician Pythagoras (582-497 B.C.). He maintained that all numbers had a special meaning, an idea he had gleaned from his travels in Egypt and Babylonia. The Babylonians – or more specifically the Chaldaeans – were early experts in astronomy and they attached much magical significance to the stars and planets and hence, whilst founding a science, they also developed astrology. To them the heavens consisted of seven prime planets or spheres – the Sun, Moon, Mars, Venus, Mercury, Jupiter and Saturn – and thereby seven signified completeness.

It was not solely a Babylonian belief. The Jews preached that God made the Earth in six days and rested on the seventh, the basis of the seven day week. The Bible frequently uses the significance of seven: Joshua marched around Jericho seven times, for instance, accompanied by seven priests. There is the story in 2 Kings 5 where the leper Naaman has to bathe seven times in the River Jordan to be cleansed. Then there is Joseph's interpretation of the Pharaoh's dream of seven fat years and seven lean. Noah and his family entered the ark seven days before the Deluge, and it is interesting to note that whilst Noah took the animals into the ark 'two by two', Jehovah instructed him to take in seven of each clean animal – that is, animals suitable for sacrifice (Genesis 7.2-9).

The Romans were equally aware of the significance of the number seven. The celebrated writer Marcus Varro

(116-28 B.C.), dubbed 'the most learned of the Romans' and responsible for no less than 490 books, drew special attention to the constant recurrence of the number seven in nature in his book *Hebdomades* (or *On Portraits*), now unfortunately lost. His observations ranged from the knowledge that the human embryo is capable of surviving outside the womb after the seventh month of pregnancy to the fact that the most prominent constellation in the night sky, the Great Bear, consists of seven stars.

The Greeks and Romans used the number seven on many occasions to signify completeness or consolidated strength. There were the Seven Sages renowned for their wise sayings such as 'Too many workers spoil the work', the basis of a well-known modern proverb and originated by Bias of Priene in about 570 B.C. The city of Rome was built on seven hills, and tradition states that in its early years it was ruled by seven kings. When Constantine the Great divided the Roman Empire into East and West he chose Byzantium as the eastern capital (and renamed it Constantinople) partly because it also stood on seven hills. In Greek legend we have the story of the Seven Heroes against Thebes, a siege intended to restore the rightful king to the throne. Another legend tells how every year the Athenians sent seven youths and seven maidens to Crete as sacrifice to the Minotaur, a yoke they had to bear until Theseus became one of the seven and slew the beast.

To this day the number seven has retained its importance, especially in magical circles. The French occultist Eliphas Levi (1810-70) wrote:

> The number Seven represents magical power in all its fullness; it is the mind reinforced by all elementary potencies, it is the soul served by Nature.[10]

Groups of seven will be found in fact and fantasy throughout history. There are the Seven Churches of Christendom[11] and the Seven Champions of Christendom.[12] We have the Seven Deadly Sins and the Seven Seas. Dante's Hell had seven levels, and there is the ancient folk tale of Snow White and the Seven Dwarfs. The film industry has given us the epic of *The Magnificent Seven*, itself based on a Japanese film *The Seven Samurai*, and I'm sure the reader can call to mind scores of books and films with 'seven' in the title. And if you should think this is all so much coincidence the concept of seven representing completeness is clearly supported by Nature. Light is made up of seven colours of the spectrum – red, orange, yellow, green, blue, indigo and violet – a point clear to anyone who has ever seen a rainbow.

Considering all things, it was inevitable that the list of Wonders would consist of Seven – that was complete and perfect. Any more or less would have decreased their importance.

What of the men who preserved the memory of the Wonders for posterity? As I mentioned earlier, the two names most closely associated with the list are Antipatros of Sidon and Philon of Byzantium, but there were many other compilers, most of whom drew upon earlier, now lost, versions. These included England's own Venerable Bede, though he lived over eight centuries after Philon. A selection of these other lists will be found in Appendix II at the back of this book.

Philon's list is, by chance, the oldest surviving version and is far more detailed than that of Antipatros. Antipatros was a noted poet who lived about 100 B.C., and possibly survived until as late as 60 B.C., since he died at a great age. He was skilled in the writing of epigrams which, in the centuries after Alexander, was regarded by the *cognoscenti* of the Greek world as the essential talent of the true scholar. An epigram was a brief and succinct way of expressing one's sentiments. They became so fashionable that from around 200 B.C. onwards various people assembled books of epigrams, and out of this grew the renowned *Greek Anthology*.

The best way to illustrate an epigram is to quote Antipatros.

I have seen the Walls of rock-like Babylon,
  that chariots can run upon,
And the Zeus on the Alpheus, and the Hanging Gardens,
  and the Great Statue of the Sun,
And the huge labour of the Pyramids,
  and the mighty Tomb of Mausolos;

But when I looked at the House of Artemis soaring to the clouds, those others were dimmed;
Apart from Mount Olympus, the sun never looked upon its like.[13]

Knowing when Antipatros lived he could not have seen the Hanging Gardens or the Colossus of Rhodes in their prime, and he possibly never saw the other Wonders, but that is not the point. They were sufficiently well known by his day for him simply to enumerate them, without description, to convey his impression of the superiority of the Temple of Artemis. Clearly, therefore, Antipatros could not have originated the list.

Antipatros came from the Phoenician town of Sidon, on the coast of modern-day Lebanon. He was known to the great Roman statesman Cicero (106-43 B.C.) who referred to him in *De Oratore* (written about 55 B.C.) in the following complimentary way:

> . . . the great Antipatros of Sidon . . . had a habit of pouring out hexameters and other verse of various forms and metres, impromptu; and as he had a quick wit and a good memory, made himself such an adept by practice, that when he deliberately decided to throw his ideas into verse, words followed automatically . . .[14]

This talented poet was very popular throughout the Mediterranean, but especially in Rome, and we can imagine that it was he who popularized the concept of the Seven Wonders far and wide. How unfortunate therefore that we cannot prove conclusively that it was this Antipatros who was responsible for the epigram. The Cambridge University Press edition of *The Greek Anthology*, from which the above verse was quoted, attributes it to Antipatros of Thessalonika, a rather obscure poet who lived a century after the Sidonian in the reign of the Emperor Augustus. Authorities have admitted that few of the epigrams can be identified with any certainty, and it is only assumed on the basis that this particular anthology originated with Philip of Thessalonika in the first century A.D. that he would attribute verse to fellow citizens wherever possible.

Of more importance is the source assigned to Philon of Byzantium. Byzantium stood on the north side of the Bosporos, and after several name changes still exists today as Istanbul. It was an important free city at the time of Philon and remained so until the reign of Emperor Vespasian (A.D. 69-79) abolished its powers. For Philon travel was unrestricted throughout the eastern Mediterranean and he made good use of this to advance his scientific knowledge. He spent many years in Alexandria and quite probably visited the sites of all the Wonders, including Babylon. It is known that a very good road linked the two cities since it was along it that Alexander the Great's funeral train came in 322 B.C.

Philon wrote a number of works on a variety of engineering matters, but all that survives today are fragments of *The Elements of Mechanics*. In this he expounded on the formation of harbours, on levers and catapults, on siegecraft and the defence of cities and even on a forerunner of the air-gun. A number of inventions are attributed to him, though he may only have perfected machines originated by his predecessors, especially the Alexandrian Ktesibios, who lived about fifty years earlier and was the inventor of the clepsydra, or water-clock. Philon may have been the inventor of the water-wheel which used the power of running water to raise buckets of water to the tops of towers.

As the earlier quote showed, *De Septem Orbis Spectaculis* is not typical of Philon's technical approach. It is an uneven amalgam of observed detail and embellished fancy, and as a consequence the great German scholar Johann Frabricius (1668-1736) attributed the work to the all-but-unknown writer Philon Herakleiotes. A more probable explanation however is that during his travels Philon made notes about the Wonders with a possible view to writing a treatise at a later date. Probably he never did, and his notes passed to another, unknown writer, who added the introduction and generally exaggerated the script with vivid and picturesque rhetoric.

Whoever its writer, it is the only detailed work of antiquity about the Seven Wonders, and the reader will find it reprinted in full as Appendix I to this book. I have also chosen to preface each of the chapters with a relevant extract. Unfortunately the paragraph covering the Mausoleum has been lost in the course of time, and Philon did not cover the Pharos, so I have located substitutes for this purpose.

My main problem however was finding an English translation. The original manuscript of *De Septem Orbis Spectaculis* was for centuries (until 1816) kept in the Vatican Library. It had, of course, been written in Greek, but in 1640, the theologian and scholar Leo Allatius (1586-1669) attempted a loose Latin translation. Twenty years later the French ambassador to the Pope, Dionysius Boessius, produced a more polished version, but when it was published in *Miscella* in 1661, the text was full of typographical errors. A further forty years passed and the Dutch scholar Jakob Gronovius (1645-1716) included both translations in his *Thesaurus Antiquitatum Graecarum* (1697-1702), but it was not until this edition was reprinted by the Swiss philologist Johann Orelli (1770-1826) in 1816 that the definitive volume appeared. Orelli bolstered the text with further passages on the Wonders from the Greek and Roman writers to give a complete picture of how the ancient world viewed the Seven Wonders.

The final link in the chain is the version reprinted by the German philologist Rudolf Hercher (1821-78), and it was this edition that I was fortunate enough to have translated.

As these works were only studied by specialist scholars, they were clearly not the sources from which we all know the Wonders. Our preconceived mental pictures of them are as a result of the oft-reprinted paintings and engravings made by artists over the centuries since the Middle Ages, when the printing and painting revolution brought about a general awareness of the heritage of the ancient world. The man behind these paintings was almost certainly Marten van Heemskerck (1498-1574) who produced a series of engravings depicting the Seven Wonders, and which were promptly imitated by Philipp Galle (1537-1612) and Marten de Vos (1531-1603). Galle was the founder of the family of noted Dutch engravers whose work adorned numerous books over the next few generations. Heemskerck's pictures captured the imagination of the public and were frequently copied. It is strange that although today's archaeologists have discovered much about the

Seven Wonders, in our minds we still picture the romantic visions now four hundred years old. This is especially true of the Colossus of Rhodes. At its very mention most readers would picture a giant man, torch in hand, standing astride a harbour, just as it was depicted by Heemskerck and later artists following a popular tradition of unknown origin. Similarly, at the mention of the Hanging Gardens of Babylon, many would imagine some soaring Tower of Babel, groaning under the weight of countless, nameless blossoms. Although these impressions could not be more erroneous, they persist, because of their frequent reproduction down through the centuries in decorating books, tapestries and murals. This book is no exception, for engravings by Heemskerck and others have been included in the Plates.

The first man to debunk some of the misconceptions about the Wonders was the German Jesuit, Athanasius Kircher (1601-80). Today he is remembered mostly as the inventor of the magic-lantern, the forerunner of the film projector, but his knowledge was not confined to any single field. He originally taught mathematics and Hebrew at the College of Rome, but in 1643 turned to the study of archaeology, microscopy, geology, and even attempted a translation of the Egyptian hieroglyphs. Kircher wrote a work on the Seven Wonders which almost certainly interested the Austrian architect Johann Fischer von Erlach (1656-1723). He was fascinated by the idea of reviving the classical style as is clear from his masterpiece, the Church of St Charles in Vienna. From 1705 to 1712 he toured Europe assembling data for his *Entwurff einer historischen Architektur.* Finally published in 1721 it was the first attempt at an illustrated history of architecture. This was how he introduced the book:

> Those persons who have honoured me with their acquaintance know that I undertook this work only as a kind of amusement at a time when the Wars with which his Imperial Majesty was taken up left little time or employment for civil architecture.
>
> As the author's main aim has been to represent in a true light the chief of those famous edifices which the rust of time has eaten up, he has been attentive only to the most

authentic testimonies such as contemporary historians, and ancient medals which have retained their images . . .

As for such modern designs as have hitherto been extant, some of which are the bare productions of wild rambling fancy, the author has had very little regard to them. This the judicious reader will soon perceive; if he but compare the Seven Wonders of the World as here laid down with other descriptions of them which are to be found and of which the greater part would hardly be suspected for what they are designed were it not for their titles.[15]

Considering that Fischer von Erlach only had ancient records to assist him, and no archaeological evidence, his reconstructions were comparatively accurate, granting the usual howler about the Colossus. A few later architects followed in his footsteps, especially Karl Friedrich Schinkel (1781-1841), but it was von Erlach's designs that would prove the most immortal, and again influence our conceptions of the Seven Wonders.

Due to these artists and architects the general reader has a misimpression of the Seven Wonders, which the sterling work of the archaeologists has done little to amend. So I hope that this book will in some way alter that situation.

The following chapter are arranged in the order that the Wonders were created to sustain a historical narrative. They are sub-divided to allow for more immediate reference: the first section describes the Wonders and the world in which they existed, whilst the second part looks into the story behind the Wonders, the reasons for their existence and what became of them and the men involved. Where necessary a third section covers the rediscovery of the Wonders and looks at the men who have painstakingly restored the gaps in our knowledge. In the last one hundred or so years, archaeologists have succeeded in adding substance to the ancient descriptions of the Seven Wonders, but have far from solved all the mysteries that surround them. This is particularly true of the Pyramids, which, after over a century of sound scientific research still retain much of the enigma of their origin and purpose. As they are the most ancient of the Seven Wonders, it is to them that I turn first.

NOTES ON CHAPTER I

1. *De Architectura* Book 2. Chapter 8
2. Pausanias VIII. 16.4
3. *Natural History* XXXVI.4 (30)
4. *Geography* 17.1.33
5. That they were renowned as landmarks is clear from Lucian's satirical dialogue *Icaro-Menippos* composed *c* A.D. 160. Lucian tells of the Greek philosopher Menippos who lived about 250 B.C., and who relates to a friend that he has visited the Moon. Looking back towards the Earth Menippos states: '. . . when I suddenly peered down I was long uncertain where the big mountains and the great sea were, and if I had not spied the Colossus of Rhodes and the lighthouse on Pharos, I vow I shouldn't have known the earth at all.'
   That they were renowned as pinnacles of beauty is clear from Antipatros's epigram on page 27, and also the Latin elegies of Propertius (*c* 50-15 B.C.). The following elegy composed in about 22 B.C. signifies his feelings for the Roman courtesan Cynthia:
   My songs shall be so many memorials of thy beauty. For neither the Pyramids built skyward at such cost, nor the House of Jove at Elis that matches heaven, nor the wealth of Mausolos's tomb are exempt from the end imposed by death. Their glory is stolen away by fire or rain, or the strikes of time whelm them to ruin crushed by their own weight. But the fame that my wit hath won shall never perish; for wit renown endureth deathless. (Book 3.2)
6. Bishop Gregory's List of Wonders is reprinted in Appendix II.
7. This theory is supported by some circumstantial evidence reported by Diodorus (Book XVIII.4). Alexander intended to glorify his Empire with many new wonders and sent a letter to his general Krateros outlining his schemes. In particular he stipulated a Temple to Athene at Ilium 'that could never be surpassed by any other' and a tomb to his father Philip II 'to match the greatest of the pyramids of Egypt'. After Alexander's death his regent Perdikkas discovered the letter and realizing the extravagance of the schemes quashed them all. Nevertheless it shows that Alexander desired to produce marvels almost solely for their own sake rather than for any religious or practical purpose.
8. Philon's treatise is reprinted in full in Appendix I.
9. *The Encyclopedia of Religion and Ethics* edited by James Hastings (T. & T. Clarke, 1917)

10. *The Sorcerer's Handbook* edited by Wade Baskin (P. Owen, 1974)
11. The Seven Churches of Christendom (or of Asia) were those to whom the apostle John addressed his epistles in chapters 2 and 3 of *Revelation*, namely: Ephesos (2.1), Smyrna (2.8), Pergamon (2.12), Thyatira (2.18), Sardis (3.1), Philadelphia (3.7) and Laodicea (3.14)
12. The Seven Champions of Christendom were the patron saints of seven of the European countries involved in the Crusades: St George (England), St Andrew (Scotland), St Patrick (Ireland), St David (Wales), St Denis (France), St James (Spain) and St Antony (Italy)
13. *The Greek Anthology*: *the Garland of Philip* edited by A. S. F. Gow and D. L. Page (Cambridge University Press, 1968) Volume 2, Page 92. Poem XCI (AP 9.58)
14. *De Oratore* Bk 3.50 (194)
15. *Civil and Historical Architecture* (a translation of Fischer von Erlach's *Entwurff einer Historischen Architektur* by T. Lediard) London, 1737.

CHAPTER II

WONDER OF WONDERS: THE PYRAMIDS OF EGYPT

The construction of the Pyramids at Memphis is beyond the strength of men and their description is beyond belief, for they are mountains placed on top of mountains, and it is not easy for the mind to grasp how the huge masses of hewn stone could have been raised; and all have doubts concerning the huge force of the mechanical devices needed to bring the massive structures together.

Thus Philon begins his description of the awesome Pyramids of Egypt. To imagine Egypt without the Pyramids is like picturing the New York skyline without skyscrapers or London without the Tower. Yet there was once a time when the land west of the River Nile bore no trace of these 'mountains on top of mountains', but it is so far back in time that one must return almost to the dawn of recorded history.

Although Egyptologists disagree as to the date, the general opinion is that the first Pyramid was raised above the Egyptian skyline near Memphis, during the reign of King Djoser in about 2660 B.C., over forty-six centuries ago. To put that in some perspective, Djoser's Pyramid is two-and-a-half times the age of the original Colosseum, and seventeen times older than St Paul's Cathedral. The Pyramid had already been standing for 1500 years when Odysseus began his wanderings, and for over 2000 years before Nebuchadnezzar built his Hanging Gardens. Scarred and ensorcelled by the passage of time, the Pyramids still stand proudly in Egypt like some great Lords looking out over a people whose history they have witnessed and whose future they might well outlive.

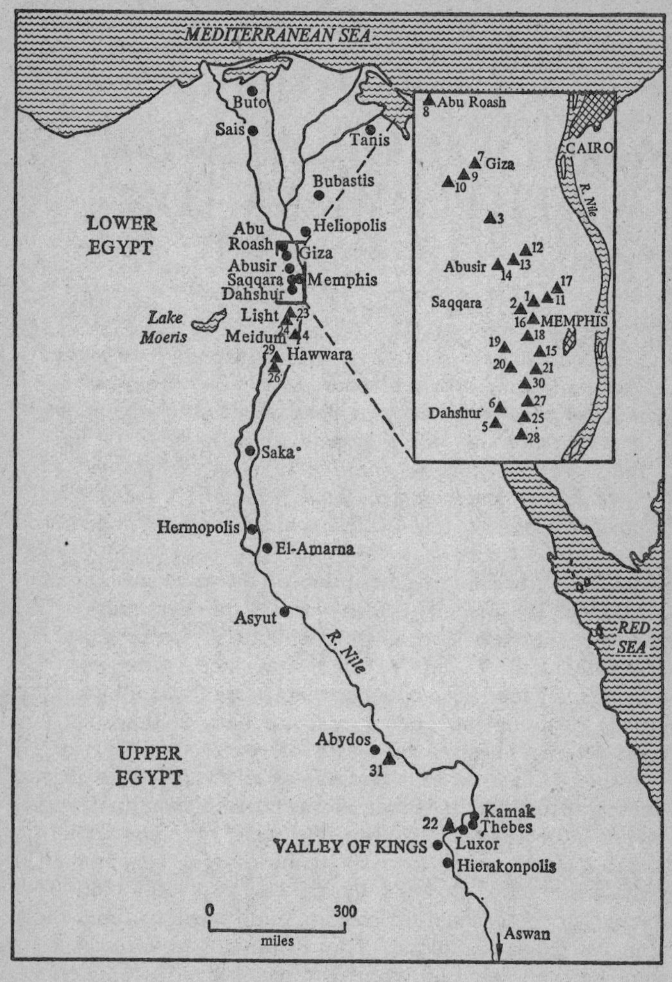
MEDITERRANEAN SEA
Buto
Sais
Tanis
Bubastis
Heliopolis
LOWER EGYPT
Abu Roash
Giza
Abusir
Saqqara
Memphis
Dahshur
Lake Moeris
Lisht
Meidum
Hawwara
Saka
Hermopolis
El-Amarna
Asyut
R. Nile
Abydos
UPPER EGYPT
Karnak
Thebes
Luxor
VALLEY OF KINGS
Hierakonpolis
Aswan
0
300
miles
RED SEA
CAIRO
MEMPHIS

.ey to Plan.

No. on Map	Pyramid Identification	Possible Date of Reign	Dimensions* Base	Height (if known)	Location
		B.C.	ft.	ft.	
1.	'Step' Pyramid of Djoser	2686–2657	411×358	204	Saqqara
2.	Sekhemkhet	2657–2651	395	230	Saqqara
3.	'Layer' Pyramid of Khaba	2651–2645	276	?	Zawiyet el-Aryan
4.	'False' Pyramid (Huni?)	2637–2613	473	315	Meidûm
5.	'Bent' Pyramid of Snofru	2613–2589	620	336	Dahshur
6.	'Red' Pyramid of Snofru	2613–2589	719	340	Dahshur
7.	'Great' Pyramid of Khufu	2589–2566	756	481	Giza
8.	Djedefre	2566–2558	320	?	Abu Roash
9.	'Second' Pyramid of Khafre	2558–2526	708	471	Giza
10.	Menkaure	2526–2498	356	218	Giza
11.	Userkaf	2494–2487	247	?	Saqqara
12.	Sahure	2487–2475	257	162	Abusir
13.	Neferirkare	2475–2455	360	228	Abusir
14.	Niuserre	2427–2416	274	?	Abusir
15.	Djedkare Izezi	2408–2376	265	?	Saqqara
16.	Unas	2376–2345	220	62	Saqqara
17.	Teti	2345–2315	210	59	Saqqara
18.	Pepi I	2310–2290	250	?	Saqqara
19.	Merenre I	2290–2283	263	?	Saqqara
20.	Pepi II	2283–2188	258	171	Saqqara
21.	Ibi	2185–2182	102	?	Saqqara
22.	Mentuhotep I	2061–2010	70	65	Deir el-Bahri
23.	Amenemhat I	1991–1962	296	?	Lisht
24.	Sesostris I	1971–1928	352	200	Lisht
25.	Amenemhat II	1929–1895	296	?	Dahshur
26.	Sesostris II	1897–1877	347	?	Illahun
27.	Sesostris III	1878–1843	350	?	Dahshur
28.	Amenemhat III	1842–1797	342	?	Dahshur
29.	Amenemhat III	1842–1797	334	?	Hawwara
30.	Khendjer	c. 1760	170	?	Saqqara
31.	Amosis	1575–1550	?	30+	Abydos

*In many instances the pyramids remain to be properly surveyed and at best their dimensions, especially their height, can only be calculated theoretically

The key to the right supplies additional data on the pyramids as regards dimensions, location and possible date of construction.

Figure 4. Chart showing location of Egypt's significant Pyramids.

THE MOUNTAINS OF STONE

There are pyramids dotted .long much of the lower stretches of the River Nile, but their greatest concentration is in a fifty-mile stretch of the west bank just south of Cairo. Figure 4 shows the locations of the major surviving pyramids which at one time numbered in excess of eighty. Today, as in Philon's time, the most impressive are in the vicinity of Memphis, the original capital of United Egypt, but more specifically the group at Giza which includes the two numbered by Strabo amongst the Seven Wonders, the Great Pyramid of Khufu, and the Pyramid of Khafre.

The pyramids are approached today along a broad boulevard that stretches five miles westward from Cairo, across the Nile, through the suburb of Giza, past the outlying villas and fertile fields and into the desert. There the pyramids await the traveller, clearly visible along his route. In Philon's day there was no Cairo; that grew from Arab settlements in the seventh century. Then the administrative centre was at Alexandria, over one hundred miles to the north, but the pyramids were easily accessible by boat along the mighty Nile. During the three summer months the Nile flooded and the waters lapped around the very base of the Pyramid plateau.[1]

The pyramids at Giza were built for three kings of the Fourth Dynasty during the twenty-fifth century B.C. Better known by the later Greek versions of their names – Cheops, Chephren and Mycerinus – the kings are more correctly Khufu, Khafre and Menkaure. The site selected by Khufu was the farthest point north that pyramids had yet been built, but it was a sensible site, not only because it was safe from the flood waters but also because here the pyramids dominated the area.

Today the plateau is still dominated by the three pyramids together with that bizarre enigma of the ancient world, the Great Sphinx. All around are the excavated ruins of temples and tombs, reminding us that the pyramids did not stand in isolation. Over four thousand years ago they were the focal point of a complicated series of buildings. A typical complex consisted of the main pyramid surrounded by a small enclosure wall which joined at a Mortuary or Offering Temple. This was then linked to a Valley Temple by way of a long, covered causeway. The main pyramid would often have one or more subsidiary pyramids, usually for the king's wives; whilst outside the enclosure wall would be strategically placed tombs of court officials and members of the royal family (frequently one and the same). These tombs are better known by their Arabic name *mastabas*, so called because they resemble the bench-like seats outside modern-day Arab homes. The Giza plateau, and in fact the whole area around Memphis, is littered with *mastabas*, and it is they that have provided so much information about the ancient Egyptian customs in life, and more especially, death.

Before looking at the purpose of the pyramids and the beliefs of the ancient Egyptians, let us first explore the Giza Pyramids as they originally appeared.

Figure 5 shows a plan of the Giza Plateau reconstructed from modern excavations. The pyramids range diagonally from the north-east to the south-west, in order: Khufu's, Khafre's and Menkaure's. Khufu's is known as the Great Pyramid, measuring originally just over 481 feet high – nearly three times the height of Nelson's Column and about the same as St Paul's Cathedral. Second in line is Khafre's Pyramid, only ten feet less in height. However Khafre had his built on slightly higher ground so that when viewed from the south – especially from the Nile downstream from Memphis – it appears the greater. Third, squatting like a child before its parents, is Menkaure's Pyramid, only 204 feet high.

Menkaure's complex shows signs of hurried completion, for reasons we shall come to later. The foundations for the temples and causeway were of stone, but they were completed with crude brick. Had the pyramid been finished to the degree of perfection originally intended then it would have been a most worthy companion for the two giants, but today it is a rather poor relic and considered second-rate by many. Yet even a second-rate pyramid would prove too much for later conquerors. In 1215 Khalif Malek al Azis Othman ordered that the pyramids be dismantled but after eight months of constant work on Menkaure's Pyramid alone, his men had made so little impression that activity ceased.

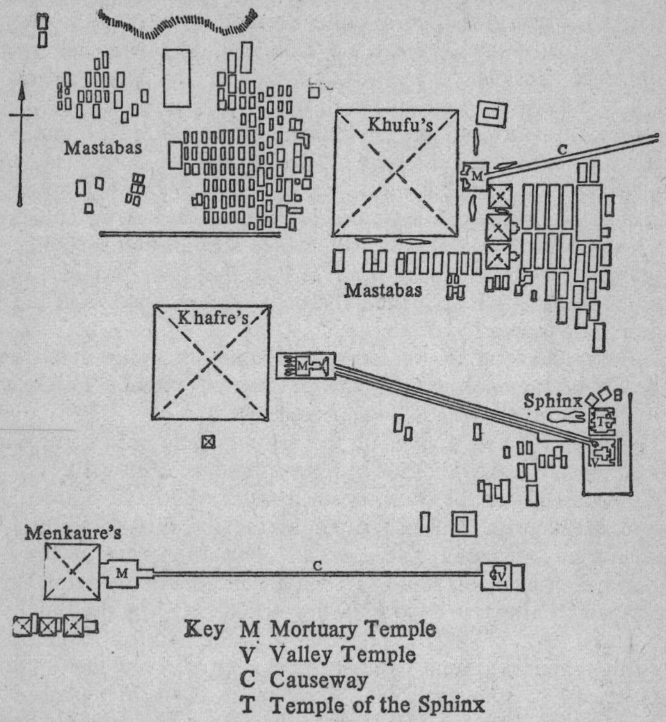

Figure 5. Simplified plan of the Giza Plateau showing the major pyramids and their attendant tombs and temples.

Just to the south of Menkaure's Pyramid are three small pyramids attributed to his queens, although their individual identities have not been ascertained.

Outwardly, Khafre's Pyramid complex is certainly the most outstanding. Its Valley Temple has been classed as one of the most remarkable buildings of the Old Kingdom.[2] Measuring 147 feet square and 43 feet high, it consisted of thick limestone walls faced with blocks of red granite quarried at Aswan.

Passing from the Temple to the Causeway one would see towering on the right the Great Sphinx. This was not included by Philon in his description of the Wonders, nor for that matter by his contemporaries, but by general agreement today it is linked with the pyramids. Pliny, who regarded the pyramids as 'a superfluous and foolish display of wealth'[3] thought the Sphinx deserved 'to be described even more than they'.[4] For much of its existence the Sphinx had been partially or totally buried by the drifting sand. A stone plaque set between its front paws records how Tuthmosis IV (*c* 1410 B.C.), before he became the Pharaoh, was out hunting one day and rested in the shadow of the Sphinx. Tuthmosis fell asleep and in his dream Har-em-akhet, the god of the Sphinx, came to him saying that if the prince cleared the sand from around the Sphinx and restored the statue, he would inherit the Double Crown of Egypt. Tuthmosis promptly organized the restoration and soon after succeeded Amenhotep II as king.

Over the ensuing centuries the sand has frequently reclaimed the Sphinx and thus helped enshroud it in mystery. Now fully excavated it can be seen in its complete majesty, though at the sacrifice of some of that romantic enigma. The huge statue is of a recumbent lion with the head carved in the likeness of a man, purportedly King Khafre himself. The overall length is about 240 feet and it reaches 66 feet at the highest point. The general opinion is that it was fashioned from a knoll of rock left by the pyramid builders, finished with limestone blocks and plaster and finally painted with ruddle. Authorities disagree on the time of its construction, some suppose it was a later addition, others that it pre-dates the pyramids. The features may originally have been those of the sun-god Atum, subsequently sculptured to resemble Khafre's since it was believed that the king became the sun-god after death. Then again this sculpturing may have happened in reverse – how can one be sure over such an expanse of time? The Egyptians regarded the lion as the guardian of the Gates of the Underworld, and sphinxes on a much smaller scale are common in many of the later tombs.

From the Great Sphinx one has an unequalled view of the Pyramids of Khafre and Khufu. Originally they would have gleamed as the sun reflected from the outer casing of fine limestone blocks brought from the quarries of Tura, a few hiles upriver. Today, apart from at the apex of Khafre's Pyramid, that casing has gone, leaving a rough staircase of limestone blocks. It was not time that dimmed the glory of the Pyramids but man, who plundered the easily available stone for his own building purposes over the centuries. In Philon's time the Pyramids could still be seen in their original glory:

> The whole of the work of joining the stones together has been so cleverly and elegantly accomplished that the whole monument seems to have sprung from one hewn stone. Different kinds of stone are joined together in turns, for here is pure marble whilst there is black Ethiopian stone. The stone which they call blood-like is not present. The one that is brought from Arabia is there, changing colour, translucently fresh and green. Some take on a radiant glossy blue colour, and there are others which, like the apple tree, turn golden. Some are a purple colour, not dissimilar to those stained with the marine purple dye of sea-shells. For the rest, delight is enhanced by astonishment, excellence of artistic inspiration by admiration, and distinction by extravagance.

Allowing for the poetic extravagance of Philon's copyist, we might imagine that the pyramids were painted in some way, a matter which has never been satisfactorily resolved. However, Philon was to some extent embellishing the report of the pyramids by Herodotus, the first European to record his visit to Egypt. Dubbed 'the Father of History' Herodotus toured the country some time after 460 B.C. Referring to Khafre's Pyramid he states that the foundations were built from 'the many-coloured stone of Ethiopia'.[5] This was in fact the red granite brought from the Aswan quarries six hundred miles upriver.

The temples and causeway were also still visible, and although Philon ignored them, Herodotus did not:

> It took ten years' oppression of the people to make the causeway for the conveyance of the stones, a work not much

inferior in my judgement to the Pyramid itself. This causeway is five furlongs in length, ten fathoms wide, and in height, at the highest point, eight fathoms. It is built of polished stone and is covered with carvings of animals.[6]

The Valley Building and the start of the Great Pyramid's causeway are today lost beneath the village of Kafr es-Samman, but remains of the Mortuary Temple have brought to light carvings similar to those described by Herodotus.

The dimensions of Khufu's and Khafre's Pyramids are colossal. As I have said their heights were respectively 481 and 471 feet, whilst their base measurements were 756 feet and 708 feet per side. Khufu's Pyramid therefore covers an area a little over 13 acres, and Khafre's 11½ acres. The volume of Khufu's Pyramid can be calculated at 91.6 million cubic feet, that of Khafre's 78.7 million. Their weight is less easy to assess due to the different stones, and because their centres were outcrops of local rock. However, Khufu's has been estimated to weigh about 5.3 million tons and Khafre's 4.6 million. The builders of Khufu's Pyramid moved some 2.3 million blocks, and the casing stones, all weighing between 2½ and 15 tons, were set in place with a precision of one-fiftieth of an inch! Whichever way you look at them, they are truly awesome.

Over the years various people have enjoyed interpreting these statistics into comparative terms, especially with the Great Pyramid. Napoleon Bonaparte is supposed to have calculated that all three pyramids contained enough stone to build a ten-feet-high wall, one foot wide, all round France. Someone showed that there is space within the Great Pyramid to fit the Houses of Parliament and St Paul's Cathedral and still have room to spare. Others have manipulated the dimensions to calculate more abstruse comparisons, and I shall return to these later.

What has intrigued people most about the Great Pyramid, apart from its sheer size, is the inner system of corridors and chambers. For centuries, because the entrance was covered by sand, Khafre's Pyramid was thought to be inaccessible, whereas Khufu's mysterious interior had been known since the days of Herodotus. He reported a story now known to be mere fabrication but which for years lured explorers to the Pyramid. He related that Khufu was buried deep within the Pyramid in a vault upon an island surrounded by water from the Nile.[7] When Pliny the Elder explored the pyramids in the first century A.D., he added fuel to the legend by referring to a 'well, eighty-six cubits deep, which communicates to the river'.[8] This 'well' became the subject of many fantastic stories. Writing nine centuries after Pliny, the Arab traveller Abul Hassan Ali Masûdi recorded how one man was lowered down the well '. . . by means of a rope which broke at a depth of one hundred fathoms, and the man fell to the bottom; he was three hours falling . . .'.[9] The true significance of the well was not discovered until 1817, another nine hundred years after Masûdi. The reader may well be pondering upon the reason for a well within the Great Pyramid, so let us explore the interior.

Figure 6 shows a cross-section of the Great Pyramid looking west, that is, from the Causeway. The entrance is situated in the north face, at a vertical height of 55 feet from the ground, or nearly 90 feet climbing the blocks. It is about 24 feet nearer the eastern side and not central, a fact that misled many early explorers until soldiers under the Khalif al-Ma'mûn forced their way through the rock with battering-rams. Ma'mûn was the son and successor of the notorious Khalif Harûn-al-Raschid of *Arabian Nights* fame, and he ruled Baghdad from A.D. 809-813. The entrance forced by his men is still visible today and is called, appropriately, 'Ma'mûn's Hole'.

Leading from the true entrance is a low corridor just under four feet high and three feet five inches wide, known as the Descending Gallery. It slopes down at an angle of 26° 31′, or a gradient 1:2. After sixty feet it divides. The downward continuation, at the same gradient, was, until recently, blocked, although it had been explored by Giovanni Caviglia in 1817. It leads to an unfinished underground chamber, similar to those which will be found under the other Giza pyramids (see Fig. 7).

The main passage now continues upwards, also at a gradient of 1:2, and is called, naturally, the Ascending Gallery. The entrance to this passage had once been sealed but the batter-

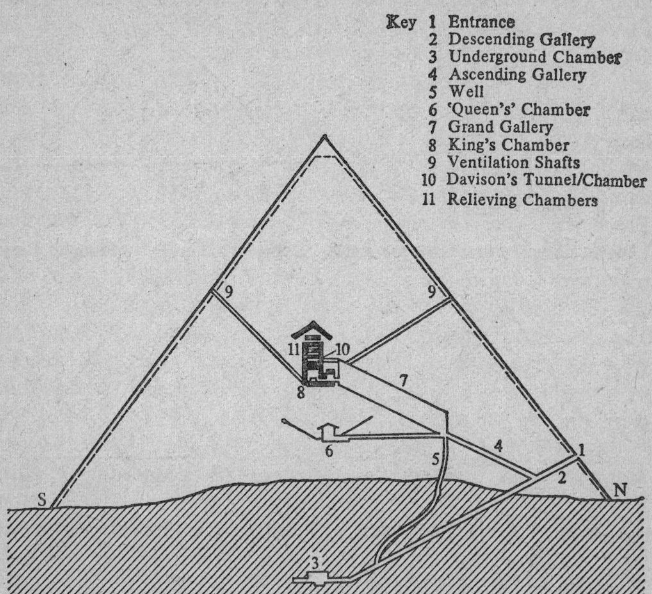

Figure 6. Cross-section of the Great Pyramid of Khufu as seen from the east.

ing by Ma'mûn's men at the entrance dislodged the stone plug, and the muffled sound of its fall alerted the Arabs to locate the true entrance. The Ascending Gallery is still blocked by three granite plugs, but determined tomb robbers had tunnelled past these through the surrounding softer limestone.

After 129 feet of cramped passageway, the Ascending Gallery also divides. Farther along it blossoms into the Grand Gallery, whilst stretching forward horizontally is another low corridor. After about forty feet this enters a roughly-finished room erroneously called the 'Queen's Chamber' by the Arabs who assumed Khufu's principal queen was buried here. This room is approximately 19 feet by 17 feet, and its pointed roof reaches a height of 20½ feet.

At the point where the Ascending Gallery divides into the

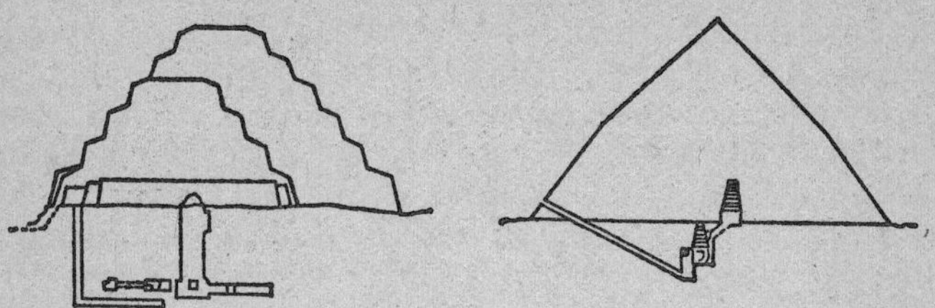

1 Djoser's Step Pyramid looking south 2 Snofru's Bent Pyramid looking east

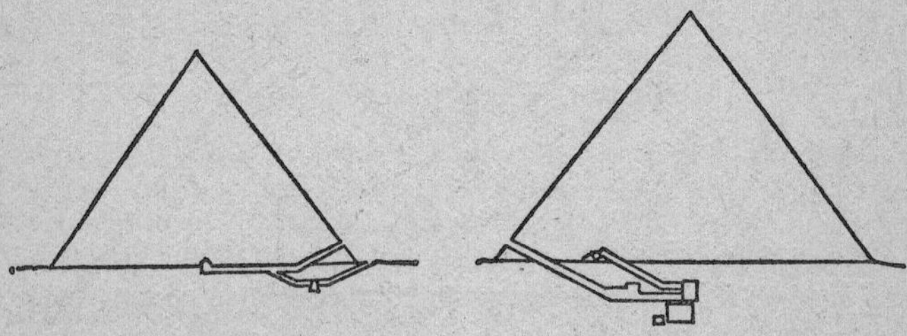

3 Khafre's Pyramid looking west 4 Menkaure's Pyramid looking east

Figure 7. Cross-sections of four important Pyramids.

Queen's Chamber passageway and the Grand Gallery is the 'well'. When Caviglia explored it he deduced it was the escape route used by workmen after they had interred the King and sent the stone plugs down to block the Ascending Gallery. It meanders down several hundred feet to join the original extension of the Descending Gallery.

The Grand Gallery has been called one of 'the most celebrated architectural works which have survived from the Old Kingdom'[10] by Professor I. E. S. Edwards, former Keeper of Egyptian Antiquities at the British Museum. 28 feet high and 7 feet wide, it slopes up at the 1:2 gradient for 153 feet. Its ceiling shows how the ancient architects overcame the problem of roofing such a long passage which had to sustain enormous pressures from the stones above. From a height of 7½ feet, on both sides of the Gallery, the succeeding courses of stone project inwards by some three inches each. This overlapping, or corbelling, continues for seven courses, leaving a space of three and a half feet to be covered by roofing slabs laid at a slightly steeper gradient than the Gallery, and notching into the tops of the walls.

The floor of the Grand Gallery is not flat. A channel two feet deep and three and a half feet wide runs along the centre, flanked by two ramps of equal width. It was in this channel that the stone plugs were stored prior to their introduction to the Ascending Gallery. A wooden platform laid over them allowed the funeral procession an uninterrupted access to the Gallery.

The King's Chamber is entered from the top of the Grand Gallery through a low passage and beyond a small anteroom. Unique amongst all tombs, the King's Chamber is situated in the very heart of the Pyramid. It measures a little over 34 feet by 17 feet, with a height of 19 feet. The whole is built of granite slabs, pink and polished, including the flat ceiling where the nine slabs weigh in total about 400 tons.

To the right of the Chamber entrance is the empty granite sarcophagus that once contained the coffin and remains of King Khufu. It measures less than four feet high by four feet wide and seven feet long, and, as many explorers delighted to discover, when struck it resounds like a bell. The sarcophagus is just one inch wider than the Ascending Gallery from which the great Egyptologist Flinders Petrie deduced that it was placed in position whilst the Pyramid was under construction.

The architects devised a unique method to relieve the roof of the King's Chamber from the colossal weight above. They erected a series of four additional layers of granite supported at both ends to create four 'relieving chambers', plus a fifth which culminates in a sloping roof. The first of these was discovered by an adventurous Welshman called Nathaniel Davison in 1763, and it has been called Davison's Chamber ever since. He reached it by means of a narrow tunnel leading from the top of the Grand Gallery. These chambers have since more than adequately fulfilled their purpose, as in the centuries since the Pyramid's completion one or more earthquakes have cracked the ceiling slabs, but the King's Chamber remains intact.

Two tiny shafts slant upwards from the north and south

walls of the King's Chamber and penetrate the outer walls of the Pyramid. They are called, for want of a better term, 'ventilation shafts', but their true purpose has never been explained satisfactorily.[11] Two similar shafts leave the Queen's Chamber at the same angle and were presumably originally intended for the same purpose, but they were abandoned along with the work on the Queen's Chamber.

Such, externally and internally, is the Great Pyramid. Its exploration brings an inevitable flood of questions. How and why was it built? Why all the many chambers and passages? How long did it take? I shall leave the question of why it was built until the next section, which discusses the whole story of the development of pyramid building and the Egyptians' religious beliefs. But how was it built? That is a question that has plagued explorers for centuries.

It is a point to remember at the outset that the ancient Egyptians were not primitive natives, but a controlled society with several centuries of cultural development behind them, as well as a number of generations of pyramid builders. Today our minds and senses have been dulled by centuries of so-called civilization, and it is easy to cast aside our ancestors with a short-sighted sneer of snobbery and assume they were incapable of anything but hunting and worshipping obscure gods. It comes as a shock to realize that the ancient Egyptians were superior to us in many ways, especially ability and ingenuity. We take for granted problems that they had to strive to master, and in so doing we have forgotten how to accomplish the simplest of tasks without resorting to one of the numerous aids of modern technology. The ancient Egyptians may not have been as intelligent as us in terms of scientific knowledge, but they were no less wise in their ability to use what they did know. Twentieth-century man still has much to re-learn.

In addition, the Great Pyramid did not sprout like Pegasus, fully-fledged from the desert sands. It marked the zenith of architectural and sculptural skill combined with the complete control of manual and financial resources – in other words the height of power of the Old Kingdom pharaohs. Here was a period of wealth and supremacy that had risen as steeply as one side of a pyramid from the days of King

Djoser to the reign of Khafre, and which declined as rapidly in the years to the end of the Sixth Dynasty and Egypt's entry into the Dark Ages. Only a few centuries after the Pyramids at Giza had been completed, Egyptians of the Tenth and Eleventh Dynasties looked upon them as the work of gods, and the secret of their precise construction was forgotten. It might seem impossible to us that such skill could be lost in the space of a few decades, but history is littered with examples of technological advances being rediscovered centuries after the original breakthrough. Take, for instance, the example in Chapter I where Eratosthenes calculated the circumference of the Earth to within fifty miles of the correct figure, yet a thousand years later it was generally believed that the world was flat. The pyramid builders left little record of their efforts and so the following account is that most accepted amongst Egyptologists who, over the years, have deduced the ancient methods from minute clues salvaged from four thousand years of desert.

Khufu's Pyramid was the first to be raised at Giza. Earlier examples were at Saqqara, Dahshur and Meidûm. Consequently, when the architects and surveyors came to Giza, the plateau had to be prepared from scratch. The first task was to level the site, which in the case of the Great Pyramid, comprised an area of thirteen acres, equal to five-and-a-half football pitches. Nevertheless the perimeter was levelled so accurately that it varies by only half-an-inch. It was not necessary for the inner floor of the pyramid to be quite so level, and in fact an outcrop of rock was usually left for later use. Even so, how did the ancient surveyors obtain such accuracy over so large an area?

Irrigation was essential to the Egyptians and generations of farmers became expert canal builders. They well knew how water finds its own level. They adapted this knowledge and first constructed a small mud-brick enclosure around the pyramid base and filled it with water. The workmen then excavated a series of small trenches until the base of each trench was the same depth below the surface of the water. With these accurate guidelines the water could be released and the rock between the trenches levelled.

The base of the pyramid also had to be aligned with the

four cardinal points. Essentially it was only necessary to fix one point and then align the remaining sides with an accurate ninety-degree measure. The Egyptians had become skilled surveyors through the necessity to re-plot the precious farms whose boundaries had been eradicated annually by the Nile flood. The compass was unknown to the Egyptians, but they were observers of the skies – though not as accomplished as the Babylonians. The most logical method for ascertaining due east would be to observe the rising of the Sun on the days of the spring and autumn equinoxes, and this may have sufficed for most surveys. But the alignment of the Great Pyramid is more accurate than this method would allow. The greatest error in their surveying is on the east side which veers west of true north by 5′ 30″, one-eleventh of a degree! The south side is south of due west by only 1′ 57″! To gain such accuracy the surveyors must have aligned on true north. This could only have been accomplished by accurately observing the rising and setting of a number of stars and plotting the points on a false horizon, such as an artificial wall. True north is midway between these points.

While the levelling and surveying of the site were being carried out, the stones were being cut and hauled. The bulk of the stone was quarried locally, but the special-quality fine limestone came from the Muqattam Hills at Tura. The cutting of these blocks was not as troublesome as their transportation. The Egyptians of the Old Kingdom possessed copper tools so that saws and chisels, assisted by the high abrasive quality of the plentiful quartz sand, would easily cut through stone. It was only necessary to cut sufficient room to take a wooden wedge. These were then moistened so that they expanded and split the stone along the line of least resistance. Such methods have been reconstructed successfully today. The cutting of the granite at Aswan was more of a problem as granite is far harder, too hard for the copper tools. So the Egyptians used a rock harder than granite – dolerite, a greenish variety of basalt. Once they had made a small cavity the wedge method could again be applied. The shaping of the granite was more easy. When heated over a fire and rapidly cooled with cold water the outer face of a granite block becomes brittle and can be easily worked with copper tools.

The transportation of these blocks was another problem entirely. The huge granite blocks had to be brought six hundred miles downriver from Aswan to Giza, a tremendous feat in itself. Since the blocks were mostly transported at the time of the Nile floods, the workers had to contend with the swollen, rushing waters whilst trying to steer the heavy blocks downriver on huge barges. One wonders just how many blocks now lie on the bottom of the Nile bed.

Once the blocks were on board the barge at least the river took care of the journey. But how were the blocks moved on land? All manner of grandiose schemes have been suggested, but none seems better than the simplest. Without the advantage of the wheel, these blocks were hauled over land on wooden sledges by teams of men – the number varying with the weight of the stone. Egyptian engravings have been found illustrating this very method, as in Figure 8 overleaf. This depicts a sixty-ton statue being moved by 172 men, a figure in accord with modern calculations. The engraving also shows men pouring water, or possibly milk (a better lubricant), between the sledge and the surface rock to lessen the friction. Calculations show it would need only about eight men to move the smaller blocks and up to 144 for the heaviest. This enables us to assess the total manpower required to build the Great Pyramid. Herodotus in his account records that he was told 100,000 men were needed,[12] but more recent calculations, such as those by Professor Kurt Mendelssohn, estimate nearer 70,000.[13]. This army was almost certainly split into several large groups of workers, and then probably sub-divided into more manageable gangs of fifteen to twenty as and when required, several gangs combining for the large blocks.

If we accept the estimate that the Great Pyramid contained 2.3 million blocks, it would mean each gang was responsible for between 550 and 600 stones. The unknown quantity is the time factor. Both Herodotus and Pliny reported that the Great Pyramid took twenty years. We know that the work of shipping and transporting the blocks took place predominantly during the three months of the Nile flood. If the figure of

Figure 8. The transport of the Colossal statue of Djehutihotep, a nobleman of the Twelfth Dynasty.

twenty years is correct (although dates recorded on the Red Pyramid at Dahshur imply construction was considerably faster than this), then we have a period of sixty months in which every gang moved some six hundred blocks. That is ten blocks a month, or one transported from quarry to site every three days, a not unreasonable assumption when we remember that the bulk of the stone was quarried locally.

In addition to the 70,000 manual workers would be the quarrymen and skilled masons, sculptors and surveyors, perhaps numbering 10,000. Their work was not confined to the Pyramid, since the causeway, temples and possible subsidiary pyramids had all to be completed on time. Work was streamlined, however. As Khufu's Pyramid tapered to the apex, thus requiring less stone, so work commenced on Khafre's Pyramid to keep employment even. However, as the heavy work was seasonal, the important task was to get the blocks to the site during the Nile floods, so that for the remaining nine months the skilled workers with a smaller manual support force could concentrate on the problem in hand – to raise the pyramid.

With the blocks on site, how were they positioned? The first layer was relatively simple, although care had to be taken to ensure the outer edges were correctly aligned. Socket stones were embedded in the rock in each corner to provide accuracy and stability.

To raise the blocks to each successive course the Egyptians built a large supply ramp of brick and earth, which grew higher and more wedge-shaped with each layer. In order to keep the gradient constant the ramp also grew longer. Evidence of these ramps has been found at other sites showing gradients of between 1:8 and 1:12. On this basis we can imagine that as Khufu's Pyramid reached its zenith, the ramp along which the treasured capstone was hauled was about three-quarters of a mile long, which agrees with Herodotus's report that the Causeway was five furlongs.[14]

Herodotus also records that the blocks were raised by 'machines', rather like cranes, which swivelled at the base and heaved the stones up from the lower course to the one above. Unfortunately no traces of such machines have been found, nor is there reference to them in Egyptian carvings. Cranes or hoists as we know them did not come into use until about the sixth century B.C. It seems likely that Herodotus was receiving an account from Egyptians who themselves had long forgotten how the pyramids were raised and had concocted their own feasible explanation. The concept of ramps was first reported by Diodorus of Sicily, a historian of the first century B.C. whose work is usually noted, ironically, for its transmission of erroneous accounts.

Having hauled the blocks along the ramps they nevertheless had to be positioned, and here the Egyptians did resort to a 'machine' – the simple lever. Flinders Petrie deduced that they used long iron crowbars which raised one side of the block sufficiently to insert a wooden baulk beneath. Then the other side was raised in the same way and a second wedge inserted. The process was now repeated, rocking the stone from side to side and raising it progressively with wooden blocks.

When the central core had reached the intended height a

marker post was set at the top to enable the surveyors to sight accurately from the four edges and ensure a true pyramid shape had been achieved. The capstone, or pyramidon, was then set in place, probably at dawn so that the priests could ceremonially initiate the pyramid with the first rays of the rising sun. The capstone was almost certainly encased in a layer of gold to reflect these rays, and was probably enscribed with ritual markings. Then the fine Tura limestone dressing was applied, starting from the top and working down. This way the ramp was dismantled stage by stage and was entirely dispersed when the final layer was dressed. It was almost certainly transported to the next pyramid which would be in its early stages.

I have left until now the matter of the Great Pyramid's internal chambers, and the reader might like to refer again to Figure 6 (p. 45). One would imagine these corridors were built as the Pyramid rose, but this was not entirely the case. Khufu's original plan was to have a burial chamber beneath the Pyramid, as was traditional. The descending shaft was hewn from the rock and the chamber commenced. Then Khufu changed his mind and ordered an internal chamber. The lower courses of the Pyramid were already laid, hence the new Ascending Gallery had at first to be hewn through the limestone blocks. This tunnel originally led to the Queen's Chamber, but this was also abandoned before completion, perhaps because it was not in the heart of the Pyramid, and the unequalled Grand Gallery commenced. The motive behind Khufu's changes is not known for sure, but it almost certainly had a religious significance, a matter I shall explore shortly.

Khufu was the king, and his Pyramid was given the name 'the Horizon of Khufu', but it was not he who masterminded the Great Pyramid. Do we know the name of the architect/surveyor/engineer who was responsible for the overall design and construction of the greatest stone building on Earth?

We cannot be sure, but it is likely that the man in overall control of the construction work was the king's vizier, Prince Hemon, grandson of King Snofru and nephew of Khufu. We know little else about him except that he was probably also in charge of the building of Khafre's Pyramid, at least in its early stages. It would be foolish to think he worked alone, and connected with him are his father, Ka-nefer, and uncle, Ankh-af, both of whom would have learned much about pyramid building during the reign of Snofru. But it was Hemon who was Khufu's vizier, and it was he who would have to face the wrath of the king should anything go wrong. Now, four-and-a-half thousand years later we know that Hemon succeeded like no other architect before or since. He built the First and the Greatest Wonder of the World – a monument that has never been equalled.

THE STORY BEHIND THE PYRAMIDS

Having seen the probable way in which the pyramids were built we are left with the puzzle of why the ancient Egyptians went to such enormous lengths. What did they hope to achieve in spending twenty years on building a mountain?

Let me just say that I am now entering upon a subject that is almost taboo. Egyptologists are wary of anyone who broaches the subject of pyramid origins, because the matter is far from being resolved, and the Egyptologist has suffered from the sensational aspects of the pyramid as broadcast by the pyramidologists, whom I shall discuss later. I see no reason to doubt the experts' view that the pyramids were intended as tombs and nothing else.

So, to begin, the development of the pyramid cannot be viewed without first looking at the background of Egyptian religion and politics which, to a great extent, were one and the same.

The religious beliefs are as complicated as they are vague, being a conglomeration of early tribal religions. In Egypt's pre-dynastic days the society was predominantly tribal, and every tribe had its own chief god or gods. Even as a more centralized Egypt evolved with the union of the Kingdoms of Upper and Lower Egypt, the nations still retained their tribal aspects with the regions divided into provinces called nomes, ruled by nomarchs. These nomes kept their individual gods, and there was no attempt to change this situation.

In about 3100 B.C. (though some authorities place it as late as 2850 B.C.), King Menes of Upper Egypt, who resided at Nekhen (later called Hierakonopolis), conquered Lower Egypt, which had its capital at Pe (or Buto), and established himself as sole ruler of Egypt from the Nile Delta to the cataracts at Aswan. Menes built for himself a new capital at Memphis on the border of the two kingdoms, and it is from his reign that the First Dynasty is reckoned.

The local deity of Nekhen, and hence of Menes, had been Horus, the falcon-god. The Horus legend is perhaps the most famous of all Egyptian myths, and it is worth summarizing here. Horus was the posthumous son of Osiris, king of the Delta. Seth, the brother of Osiris, killed the king and usurped the throne. Osiris's body was cast into the Nile but was recovered by his widow Isis. Learning of this Seth captured the body, had it chopped into sixteen pieces, and scattered these parts throughout Egypt. Undaunted, Isis and her sister, Nephthys, recovered all but one of the parts, and reassembled the king. Thereafter Osiris remained as lord of the Underworld. Horus vowed to avenge his father and an epic struggle for power began. The result was finally decided by a tribunal of the gods in which Horus was recognized as the legitimate ruler of Egypt. Seth was thereafter Lord of the Heavens.

There is much to support the belief that this legend contains a grain of truth, and that in pre-dynastic days a king of Upper Egypt, called Seth, conquered the Delta and deposed Osiris, but that there was a counter-revolution and Horus was triumphant. This same story of revolt and counter-revolt repeats itself throughout Egypt's history. By the time of Menes, the king had become regarded as the personification of Horus and thus ruler by divine recognition. This was signified in the *serekh* or royal insignia, a representation of the palace (or *per-o* in Egyptian from which the Hebrews derived pharaoh) incorporating the king's most important Horus-name. The rulers of the Double Kingdom had a number of names besides a personal one, and this has resulted in considerable confusion among Egyptologists in identifying just who was whom. The *serekh* was surmounted by the falcon-symbol of the god Horus, thus identifying the king.

Horus was not the only important deity. The local god of

Memphis was Ptah, an ancient deity regarded as the creator of all things. Meanwhile at On (called Heliopolis by the Greeks) there was a thriving sun-cult with an advanced pantheon of gods. The principal deity was Re, but the cosmogony included Osiris, Isis and Seth. Here we see the Egyptian conservatism at work. Rather than discard gods, and in an attempt to satisfy everyone, all were incorporated into one big family, usually resulting in complete confusion.

The Heliopolitan priesthood had not ignored Horus. Along with Re he symbolized a separate aspect of the sun-god, and it is not difficult to imagine the high-soaring falcon as one with the sun as lord of the skies.

It was a short step from here to the king also being associated with the sun. He was, after all, Horus incarnate. If Horus was also the sun-god, then clearly, after death, the king returned to his spiritual self as the solar deity. The king must therefore also be the personification of Re. This development did not happen overnight, but we can almost imagine how it was engineered during many generations by the priests of Heliopolis, who in reality ruled Egypt. It was not a smooth transition either, but the road to the pyramids lay ahead.

Before following that road, let us see how the two seemingly opposed religious beliefs affected the Egyptian burial customs.

The common factor between the Osiris and Re religions was their confirmation of rebirth. Osiris was brought back to life by Isis and became Lord of the Dead. Re, the sun, died each night as he was consumed by the sky-goddess Nut, but each morning was reborn. The Egyptians therefore firmly believed in a life after death. They also believed that the body had a spirit-self in addition to the physical being. The exact interpretation of their beliefs is not clear, but it would seem that the body possessed a *ka*, or second spirit, thought by differing authorities to signify a guardian angel, the soul, or the body's double. After death the spiritual entity of the body became the *ba* which was free to roam between the Underworld and the dead body. The entry to the Underworld was through the pit in the grave, and it was to this pit that the *ba* returned after its sojourns in the land beyond.

The critical factor here was that for the *ba* to survive it was essential for the body to be preserved from decay and supplied with all the everyday needs of life. The *ba* was not immortal, and if the body was neglected, the *ba* died. To Egyptians the after-life was the whole purpose of mortal existence, and this was why they spent so much of their lives preparing such grandiose tombs equipped with all their belongings, and why offerings of food were regularly made. Tombs had to be substantial as they were expected to last forever.

Unfortunately the graves were frequently pillaged for their treasures.[15] Naturally, this mostly affected the rich who would fear that after death the desecration of their tombs would spell doom for their *ba*. The poor had as much to fear for their simple graves covered with an earth mound were soon rapidly eroded by the elements, exposing the body to rapid decay. There was clearly a need for something more substantial to keep out both weather and thief.

Thus the *mastaba* came into being, a mud-brick superstructure built over the grave-pit. The *mastaba* was not solid but composed of a number of chambers duplicating the deceased's former home. Amongst the rich these *mastabas* were large, with an elaborate maze of rooms. There were no corridors since the *ba*, as a spirit, could pass through brick. The body was placed in the pit beneath the central chamber and surrounding rooms would contain the personal belongings. There was no entrance to the *mastaba* other than an offering room where relatives left food. In later tombs where the burial pit and the offering chamber were some distance apart there was another room beyond the chamber called a *serdab*, which is Arabic for cellar. This room had no means of entrance, but a slit through which a seated statue of the deceased could look. The Egyptians believed the *ba*, recognizing its likeness in the statue, would enter it and partake of the essence of the food. In case later generations forgot to venerate their ancestors, the ingenious Egyptians included carvings on the walls of the inner chambers depicting the offerings, so that the *ba* was ensured survival as long as the *mastaba* lasted. These reliefs have been an invaluable source of information about the ancient Egyptian way of life.

It is generally accepted that the *mastaba* was the basis for the pyramid, and the transition came about in the reign of King Djoser in the Third Dynasty.

Djoser came to the throne in about 2686 B.C., and he had the good fortune to ascend at a time of peace. In the centuries since Menes had united the two kingdoms there had been a constant rivalry between them. An uprising brought an end to the First Dynasty, and a religious schism in the Second Dynasty resulted in civil war when many of the earlier tombs were burned. Peace was not restored until the powerful figure of Kha-sekhem came on the scene. He reconquered lower Egypt and reached a compromise with the priests. Thereafter his *serekh* bore both the Horus and rival Seth symbols, and he changed his name to Kha-sekhemui, which means 'the two gods at peace in him'. He solidified his position by selecting Princess Nemathap of Lower Egypt as his Great Queen instead of the princess of Upper Egypt who was the natural choice.[16]

The fruit of the marriage was Djoser. It is possible that an elder brother Senakht ruled for a while, but the records are vague here, and if he reigned at all it was not significant. Egypt's rise to glory began with Djoser and his association with his chief minister Imhotep.

The pedestal of a long-lost statue of Imhotep tells us that he was 'Chancellor of the King of Lower Egypt: First after the King of Upper Egypt: Administrator of the Great Palace: Hereditary Nobleman: High Priest of Heliopolis: Builder, Sculptor and Maker of Vases in Chief.' It makes him sound a jack-of-all-trades, but unlike that proverbial figure, Imhotep was Master of All. Centuries later the Egyptians came to worship him as a demi-god whilst the Greeks adopted him as Asklepios, the god of medicine. His father, Ka-nefer, was Director of Works of Upper and Lower Egypt, a position later equated with the vizier, or Prime Minister.

The significant part of that inscription is that Imhotep was the High Priest of Heliopolis. By the time of Djoser, the Re religion had reached a position of pre-eminence and the king was accepted as the sun-god in human form. Imhotep was therefore in a very influential position, a status he was to use to the full.

The following theory for the origin of the pyramids is one advanced by Kurt Mendelssohn in his book *The Riddle of the Pyramids*, and its logicality and simplicity have much to recommend it. However, it does not have the support of all Egyptologists, and I present it here purely as a theory along with others wherever relevant and remind readers that the mystery of the pyramids is, as yet, far from being solved. As Professor I. E. S. Edwards remarked to me in a recent letter, 'Something of interest and importance seems to come to light almost every year and theories and ideas have to be revised accordingly.'

Egypt was now at peace, but there was no reason to assume it would last forever. Earlier tombs had been desecrated, and Djoser, as the first king of a local dynasty, must have feared that further rebellions might have followed his death with the possible destruction of his tomb and his *ba*. There was a need therefore for something even more solid than before. It would also have occurred to Imhotep and Djoser that unrest was most liable to erupt during the three months of the Nile flood when the majority of Egypt's agriculturally-based populace was idle, an ideal time for rebel-rousers to stir up discontent. If work could be found for the idle there was less chance of a revolution. Is it too much to assume that Imhotep linked these two requirements – a substantial tomb and work for the idle – and came up with a pyramid? Well, not quite like that, but all ideas spring from a seed sown at some time.

At the outset Imhotep planned for Djoser a grand *mastaba*, built on the site of the Memphis necropolis at Saqqara. It measured about 207 feet square by 26 feet high and was built entirely of stone. All previous *mastabas* had been rectangular, that of Kha-sekhemui measuring 223 feet by 54 feet, and that was built of mud-brick except for a stone central chamber. This might also have been the work of Imhotep or his father.

The change in design to a square *mastaba* had caused some Egyptologists to speculate that Imhotep was not merely constructing another *mastaba*-covering for the grave, but was representing in stone the 'primeval mound'. On early graves the covering was a simple earth-mound, which was square, and was believed to represent the first land to appear above the waters of chaos when the Earth was formed. This mound continued to appear on all graves, even when they were shielded by *mastabas*. Possibly Imhotep was here combining basic principles.

Having felt his way working with stone on this scale, Imhotep extended the *mastaba* by fourteen feet all round, though only twenty-four feet in height. Small though this addition may sound it increased the size of the *mastaba* by over 26% bringing the total volume to nearly one-and-a-half million cubic feet of stone – and this at a first attempt!

Experimenting further, Imhotep extended the eastern side by a further twenty-eight feet, and then by an additional nine-and-a-half feet all round, making the total dimensions 282 by 254 feet. It was at this point that history was made. Above the base *mastaba* Imhotep added a second, then a third and a fourth layer, each progressively smaller, reaching a height of about 140 feet. The Step Pyramid was born.

It was not the end. By now Imhotep's gangs had shifted over 200,000 tons of stone to Saqqara for the pyramid alone, but this was not the only project in hand. As the pyramid rose, so work began on the first pyramid complex. Though not of the same design as the Giza complexes, it still consisted of a large enclosure wall running for nearly 1800 feet from north to south and about 912 feet from east to west. The infant pyramid was at the centre of the enclosure with the mortuary temple on the northern inner side, and a row of palaces along the eastern flank. In brief the pyramid complex was the *mastaba* – on a grand scale – and the pyramid was the central mound. There was something eerie about these buildings; they had all the appearances of a royal court, including a throne room, but nothing was intended for the living. It was a palace for the dead.

Beneath the pyramid was a complicated series of tunnels and chambers. Here Djoser saw fit to bury the remains of the previous kings and their families whose tombs had been desecrated during the civil war.

Imhotep had not finished yet. The pyramid, now at its fourth stage, was extended to the north and west so that it measured 411 by 358 feet, with the greater length on the east-west axis. Two more layers were added bringing the total height to 204 feet, and containing 850,000 tons of stone, about one-sixth of that used in the Great Pyramid. As an experiment the first pyramid, called the Step Pyramid because of its staggered layers, was an impressive sight, gleaming with its covering of Tura limestone and rising majestically above the enclosure wall dominating the heights of Saqqara. How proud Djoser, Imhotep and the builders must have felt. Here was a tomb fit for a king – and a god. As testament to Imhotep's skill and ability the Step Pyramid still stands to this day, over 4650 years later. If no further pyramids had been built in Egypt we can be sure that Djoser's would still rank today as a Wonder of the World.

Whether we view the multi-layered tomb as a secure protection for the grave, a means of employing the idle masses, or both, it does not explain the pyramidal shape. What was the significance of that?

The principle behind the pyramid concept is based within the Re religion. The symbol of Re was called a *ben-ben* and it was a pyramid design, which Professor I. E. S. Edwards surmises was suggested by the shape formed by the sun's rays when it filters through a small slit in the clouds.[17] Since the king was the personification of Re, it followed that his tomb should be the Re symbol. There are other factors in support of the pyramid shape, one being a line from the famous Pyramid Texts – hieroglyphic inscriptions found in the pyramids of the Fifth and Sixth Dynasties. It says: '. . . a staircase to heaven is laid for him so that he may climb to heaven thereby.' A later text also supports the shape of the true pyramid: 'I have trodden those thy rays as a ramp under my feet whereon I mount up to that my mother, the living Uraeus on the brow of Re.'

There are further ramifications in the change from step pyramid to true pyramid, but considering the tremendous undertaking, one could not expect Imhotep to accomplish everything at once. The next few generations would see a striving for perfection in the pyramid shape together with the infusion of astral or star-worship into the Re cult. The polar stars became venerated like the sun, and for this reason later pyramids were orientated towards the north instead of the east.

Could Imhotep realize just what he had started when he

raised the first pyramid at Saqqara, and that over four thousand years later men would still wonder and marvel at his purpose? Not only did he overcome astonishing structural problems, but he also seemed to have solved the problem of social unrest. During the century of major pyramid building there is no record of civil uprising. A misconception has arisen that the builders were slaves, but apart from a few prisoners-of-war, the gangs were composed of farm labourers who were temporarily unemployed. To them it was a privilege to work on these colossal religious projects and furthermore they were assured food and security. One had only to reflect that compared to 70,000 labourers there were but a few hundred overseers. Could we imagine that number toiling under a harsh yoke without rebelling? Instead there was a sense of comradeship amongst the various gangs as well as healthy competition, evidence of which still exists in the form of early graffiti on the pyramid blocks. These range from the intriguing 'The crew, the White Crown of Khufu, is powerful' and 'The gang is vigorous' to the more practical 'For the Royal Tomb' and the inevitable 'This side up'! At last the many tribes of Upper and Lower Egypt were combined in a common cause, and it could be said that Imhotep had created the first organized society on Earth. It was a foundation upon which the later kings Snofru and Khufu were able to build a prosperous nation.

The rise and fall of the Old Kingdom prosperity can almost be paralleled by the size of the pyramids. Figure 9 shows to scale the pyramids of this period and it is easy to see how rapidly they increased in size and then correspondingly shrank. After Imhotep's innovation the next stage was to convert the step pyramid to a conventional pyramid shape. Of special significance in this development are the three known as the Pyramid at Meidûm, the Bent Pyramid and the Northern Red Pyramid.

The building of the Meidûm Pyramid saw the first disaster. Its architect (possibly Nefermaat or Ka-nefer) had first built a standard seven-stepped pyramid, probably commenced in the reign of King Huni. The pyramid was then raised to produce eight steps, and the architect then proceeded to fill in the angle of the steps with local stone, overlaying the whole

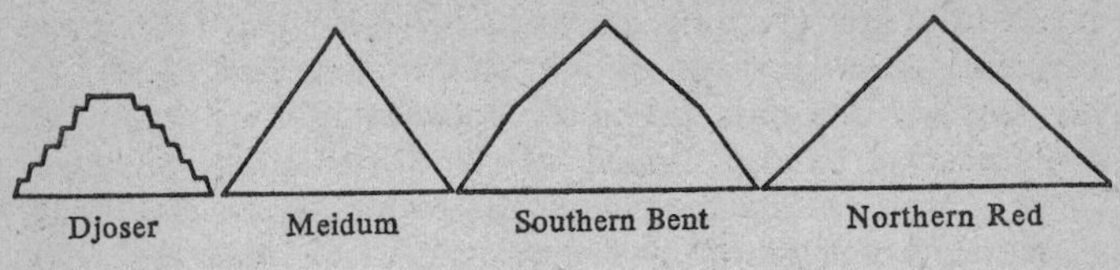

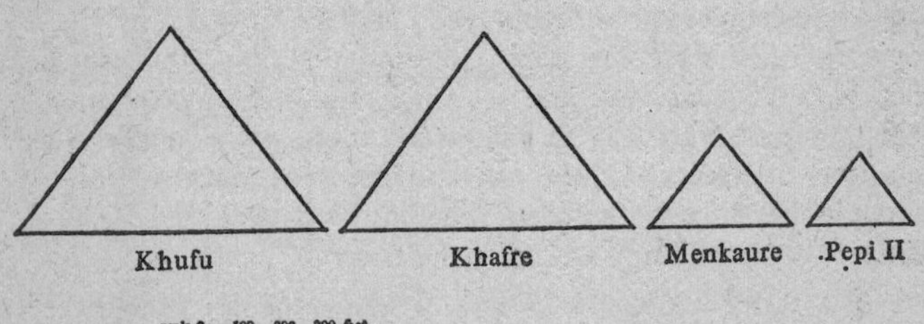

Figure 9. Chart showing comparative development of significant Pyramids.

structure with Tura limestone. The architect was still experimenting at this stage and was not aware of the various stresses and strains inherent in a pyramid shape. At one point, as Kurt Mendelssohn analyses, the structure became unstable and collapsed, leaving the unique shape seen today: a sheer, flat-topped tower, rising from a pile of rubble.[18]

It is likely that each new phase of design began before the previous stage had been completed, confirmation that the architect was unsure of his technique. Yet his failure opened the door to the giants.

Some time during the construction of the Meidûm Pyramid King Huni died. He was succeeded by Snofru, the greatest pyramid builder of them all. Snofru commenced the building of his pyramid at Dahshur, but unlike its predecessors it was a true pyramid in shape. Possibly it was Snofru who ordered the completion of the Meidûm Pyramid in the same manner. When disaster struck at Meidûm, the builders at Dahshur must have feared calamity for themselves. There was a rapid analysis of the situation and vizier Ka-nefer ordered that the angle of elevation of the Dahshur pyramid be reduced.

The packing and casing at the Meidûm Pyramid had been stacked to create an elevation of 52°, but they had been laid horizontally instead of at a safer upward inclination of 6°. As a result they had slipped through lateral pressures. Ka-nefer now reintroduced the inclined packing blocks, and at the same time reduced the angle of outer elevation from 52° to 43½°. (The reasons for these apparently arbitrary angles will be explained later.) Since the pyramid had been half completed, this sudden change in elevation gave it an odd appearance with the sides bending, hence its name as the Bent Pyramid.[19]

Snofru now began work on the next pyramid at Dahshur. Whilst this gives the impression Snofru was mass producing pyramids, it's more likely to assume he wanted to get it right. He only needed one tomb, but it had to be perfect. No collapsing or bent pyramids would suffice. With natural caution the new pyramid was built entirely at the 'safe' angle of 43½°. Its base measurement makes it the second largest pyramid, but because of its decreased elevation it is only the third highest. This, the first true pyramid to be completed, has been regularly plundered for its stone, so that nearly all its limestone casing has gone, unlike the Bent Pyramid, which is remarkably well preserved. The stone beneath is of a deeper hue than the Bent Pyramid, hence the later monument is known as the Red Pyramid.

The builders had learned much about pyramid design during Snofru's reign. They overcame the problem of instability by building regular internal buttress walls, and larger packing blocks slightly inclined. Thus when the time came to build Khufu's Pyramid, they were confident of tackling a giant, and even reverted to the steeper angle of elevation.

A word about King Snofru, possibly the greatest king of the Old Kingdom, but whose life is overshadowed by that of his successor, Khufu. Under Snofru Egypt saw its first major expansion as a nation. The king encouraged building of all kinds, not just pyramids. He established a number of settlements, strongholds within an enclosure about three hundred yards square containing a temple, a palace for the local administrator, and homes, Snofru increased the trade established by Kha-sekhemui with the people of Byblos, in modern-day

Lebanon. Their lush forests provided Snofru with the wood he needed for his many projects, including ship-building. The horse and wheeled cart were unknown in Old Kingdom Egypt, but with their huge fleet, Snofru's men could patrol the Nile and rapidly quash any uprisings. The fleet also allowed increased trade which boosted Egypt's economy.

Snofru was remembered by later generations as a beneficent king. Not so his son and successor Khufu. Herodotus tells us that he and the later king Khafre closed the temples and enslaved the peoples. He is even supposed to have prostituted his own daughter to raise funds for the Pyramid! As Herodotus was receiving the information two thousand years later we could view it simply as a distorted version of adverse propaganda issued by later pharaohs to blacken the name of the Great Pyramid king. Much the same is presumed to have happened when the first Tudor king of England, Henry VII, wrested the throne from Richard III. Today we remember him as a hunchback and murderer, but contemporary records show Richard III in a favourable light. Khufu could therefore be the victim of later prejudice, and what contemporary records do exist do not show him as a harsh ruler. However, subsequent events may have some bearing on Herodotus's account.

The heir apparent to the throne was Khufu's eldest son, and husband of the future Great Queen, Prince Ka'wab. Ka'wab never came to the throne, and possibly he and his full brothers were murdered. After Khufu's death another son by a secondary wife usurped the throne. His name was Djedefre, so we can conclude from the '-re' suffix that he was loyal to the priests of Heliopolis. Why should the priests condone a usurper?

Perhaps we can find an answer in Herodotus's story. Which temples did Khufu close? Since he built the most magnificent pyramid of them all it is hardly likely he would have banned the worship of Re. But he could have closed the temples to Ptah, who had a large following in Memphis, and he may have enslaved Ptah worshippers. Khufu was well aware of his strength with Old Kingdom Egypt now at the peak of its development. As Lord Acton noted, power corrupts, and this was supreme power, not only in the hands of Khufu, but also the Priests of Re. Ka'wab on the other hand, may not have approved of this situation, and a royal struggle ensued that resulted in the accession of Djedefre.

Whether this was the case or not, we do know that from this time forth pyramid building began to decline, and within a generation the religious clash would have decided their fate.

Djedefre was loyal to the memory of his father, but he abandoned the Giza site for his pyramid and commenced building five miles to the north at Abu Roash. We can imagine how this disrupted the organization of the plateau. Work on the second pyramid was probably already in hand, and under normal circumstances it would have been Djedefre's. His removal to Abu Roash indicates a complete break with establishment, although he cemented his position by marrying Ka'wab's widow, the Great Queen.

Many gangs of men were now redeployed to Abu Roash, along with the necessary building materials. Work at Giza came almost to a halt except for the final touches to Khufu's giant. However, Djedefre only ruled for seven years, and his complex was probably never finished. His successor, another half-brother, Khafre, resumed work at Giza and completed his own huge tomb, the Second Pyramid.

If Herodotus is correct, then Khafre's reign was as harsh as Khufu's, and religious unrest continued. When Menkaure came to the throne he wisely reopened the temples and reprieved the workers. Like Snofru, Menkaure is remembered as a kind and goodly monarch. Clearly he drastically reduced the work force, because his pyramid is only a fraction the size of its companions, and it was not completed during his reign. It was hurriedly finished by his son and successor Shepseskaf who then put a complete stop to pyramid building. For his tomb Shepseskaf returned to Saqqara and built a magnificent *mastaba* which somewhat resembled a flattened loaf with upright crusts. It measured about 330 feet long by 236 feet wide, and only 65 feet high, and was called by the Arabs the *Mastaba'at Fara'un* (literally 'the Pharaoh's seat'). It could not have signified a more complete break with pyramid tradition. Moreover, Ptah-shepses, one of his sons by a concubine, became High Priest of Ptah at Memphis.

Since the Great Queen Khentkaues also built a grand *mastaba* at Giza (between the pyramid causeways of Menkaure's and Khafre's), almost as a symbol of defiance, one would have thought the Pyramid Age was at an end, but such was not the case.

With the death of Shepseskaf a new king came to the throne, Userkaf, grandson of the usurper Djedefre and, more significantly, son of the Priest of Re. We must assume, with the lack of any firm evidence, that Khentkaues married Userkaf and passed on the royal inheritance. Whether Shepseskaf, or another, was the father of the next two kings, Sahure or Neferirkare, is not known. All we have is the fragment of a story recorded on papyrus. Djedefre, we are told, introduced Khufu to a wise old magician who revealed that the wife of a priest of Re was pregnant with three children who would one day rule Egypt with great beneficence. Was Khentkaues this lady of myth?

Userkaf, as the son of a High Priest of Re, reverted to the tradition of pyramid building, but on a far smaller scale. Instead the labour was poured into the construction of Sun Temples – the origin of the obelisks. Subsequent pyramids were minor efforts, few of which have survived the ravages of time and the elements. Figure 4 shows the locations of these later pyramids and their identities.

The need for mighty pyramids had now passed. It had been a sign of supremacy, but the ensuing struggles had enlightened pharaoh and priest alike. Imhotep's original plan for both building giant tombs and providing work for the idle had resulted in a united nation and now such major projects were no longer necessary. By creating lesser pyramids the labour was available for more important projects. It also drew less attention to the pyramids which were known to contain wealth and riches. Even during Khufu's reign pyramids were pillaged and when the tomb of his mother was defiled Khufu had her secretly reburied at the foot of his own edifice. Later dynasties sporadically revived the pyramid as a tomb, but with the constant plundering subsequent kings opted for secret rock tombs.

The last Egyptian king to build a pyramid was probably Amosis of the Eighteenth Dynasty in about 1570 B.C., but this served as a cenotaph, not a tomb. When Egypt was overrun by the Ethiopians in 721 B.C., their king, Piankhi, adopted the pyramid-form for his tomb, and these meagre imitations stayed with the Ethiopians after they were driven from Egypt by the Assyrians, and until the end of their kingdom at Meroe in the Sudan in A.D. 350, three thousand years after Imhotep erected the first pyramid.

Something never witnessed by later Egyptians was the pyramid funeral ceremony. Just how did the system work?

It must have been a tremendous experience for the Egyptian peoples, especially the workers. We can imagine the royal barges sailing down the Nile from Memphis bearing the body of the dead king. These barges were subsequently dismantled and buried with the king in boat pits around the pyramid base, as they served the king in after-life to sail across the heavens. Stopping at the steps to the valley temple the body is carried to a position on the flat roof. Here the ritual purification and embalming takes place. It was a ceremonial re-enactment. The actual purification would have been carried out by the Priests of Re soon after the king's death and embalming followed immediately. The body was washed, and then the stomach, lungs, intestines, liver and brains were removed, as they decayed rapidly. They were stored in preservative in containers called canopic jars which were buried with the king, but outside the sarcophagus. The bodies were wrapped in a preservative substance such as natron (a form of salt) which though effective, was slow. It might be many months before the king was ready for burial, but as no one knew when the king might die, this allowed time to complete the pyramid complex which, during a short reign like Djedefre's, was likely to be incomplete.

A third and very important ceremony was conducted at the valley temple. Called the 'Opening of the Mouth', it involved the priests (including a son of the dead king) applying water and incense to each of twenty-three statues of the king. Sacrifices were made, and various artifacts applied to the statues' lips. This ceremony is believed to have 'opened' the statue to future possession by the king's *ba*.

The body was then placed in a wooden coffin to protect its

purity and transported along the causeway to the mortuary temple. Here the procession passed from public gaze, through the temple, where daily offerings would be made, and into the pyramid to lie, so it was hoped, in eternal rest.

Such was not to be. No remains of any of the great pyramid kings have been found – with the possible exception of Djoser's foot. The greatest period of plunder was probably during the 'dark ages' following the end of the Sixth Dynasty when the country sank into anarchy under the rival commands of the local chieftains – the nomarchs. By the time Amenemhat I established the Twelfth Dynasty much of the knowledge of the Old Kingdom had been lost, and the ancient pyramids began to acquire their aura of mystery. Over thirteen hundred years later when the kings of Saïs ruled Egypt under the watchful eye of the Assyrians, Psamtik I and his successors began the restoration of the monuments and tombs of the Old Kingdom and resealed the pyramids. It was these rulers and their priests who venerated Menkaure, and whose descendants told Herodotus the history of Egypt. The truth remains that so much had been lost in the intervening centuries that the real story of the pyramids has become indistinguishable from legend. It was to be another two thousand years before any serious attempt was made to uncover the secrets of the First Wonder of the World.

THE REDISCOVERERS

Due to their sheer bulk and the excellence of their construction, the Pyramids at Giza have survived, despite their frequent use as convenient quarries for local building projects, and the assaults of conquerors. Knowledge of their purpose and origin dwindled until by the first century after Christ all that was known about ancient Egypt were the quasi-fabulous accounts by Herodotus, Diodorus, a handful of other Graeco-Roman writers, and the all-important transcribed history of the Egyptian High-Priest of Heliopolis, Manetho. He lived at about 300 B.C., and compiled a chronicle of the Egyptian kings from mythical times until Alexander the Great. It was

Manetho who devised the Thirty Dynasties, a division retained by modern Egyptologists. Unfortunately Manetho's original history does not survive, and we have to rely on contradictory and frequently confusing epitomes made in the third and fourth centuries A.D. by Julius Africanus and Eusebius, and in the ninth century by George Syncellus. It was not until the code of hieroglyphs was broken that the real story of the past could be unravelled.

The pyramids became objects of pure mystery. Some described them as the granaries of Joseph, others as refuges built to survive the Flood of Noah. These beliefs remained for centuries and are only slightly more sensible than others rife today. The truth was forgotten, and without contradiction the seventeenth-century historian and divine Thomas Fuller (1608-61) was able to write that 'the Pyramids themselves, doting with age, have forgotten the names of their founders.'[20]

At the time that Fuller wrote these words the first serious survey of the pyramids was being undertaken by the Oxford Professor of Astronomy, John Greaves (1602-52). Thanks to the patronage of William Laud, the Archbishop of Canterbury and former Chancellor of Oxford, Greaves was able to visit Egypt in 1638, and he published his findings in *Pyramidographia* in 1646.

Greaves was astonishingly perceptive, and has been called 'an Egyptologist ahead of his time'.[21] His inspired guesses and intelligent reasoning made his book the most thorough work of its kind for over a century. He avoided the traps of earlier theories, and presented boldly the facts as we know them – that the pyramids were tombs built for the early kings who believed in an after-life dependent on the preservation of the body.

It was to be fifty years before anything new was added to pyramid knowledge. Benôit de Maillet (1656-1738), the French Consul-General in Cairo was the first to suppose that the Great Pyramid 'well' was an escape shaft. In 1763, Nathaniel Davison explored the well but found no outlet. In 1817 a Genoese mariner, Giovanni Caviglia (1770-1845), discovered the connection between the well and the Descending Gallery. Earlier Davison had found the first of the relieving chambers of the King's Chamber. Gradually the Great Pyramid was revealing its secrets, but the reasons behind it were not known, nor a proof of identity.

The breakthrough was at hand, however. Until then, people like Greaves and Davison had worked without the benefit of understanding the ancient Egyptian language. The hieroglyphs of the past surrounded them, silent and secretive. Many attempts were made to interpret them, including one by Athanasius Kircher, but these were often misleading, and most hopefuls approached the hieroglyphs as a code rather than a dead language. To master them one needed a knowledge of many ancient languages, especially Coptic, still spoken by the native Egyptian Christian sect.

In 1799, during the French occupation of Egypt, the army found the now famous Rosetta Stone. It contained identical entries in the three languages of Ptolemaic Egypt—hieroglyphic, demotic and Greek. Scores of philologists pored over the texts and the dam was breached in 1822 by Jean-François Champollion (1790-1832). His findings were not totally accepted by the establishment until validated by the Prussian Karl Richard Lepsius (1810-84) who discovered a bi-lingual text known as the 'Canopus decree'.

Thereafter philologists and archaeologists worked both with and against each other to draw back the curtains of mystery from the pyramids, and the science of Egyptology was born. At first the archaeologists showed scant regard for the subjects of their enquiry, most of them being interested only in the commercial aspects of unearthing the greatest number of mummies for museums. One such showman was the 6′ 7″ herculean Italian explorer Giovanni Belzoni (1778-1823), the first man to discover the entrance to Khafre's Pyramid, although he was bitterly disappointed to find it already plundered. Almost certainly much of its value was lost to the dedicated researcher as riches were pilfered by opportunists in the name of science.

Even some of the experts could be accused of plunder for profit. Colonel Richard Howard-Vyse (1798-1853) treated his expedition as if it was a military campaign. Determined to discover whether further rooms were hidden in the Great Pyramid, in 1837 he used gunpowder to blast up through the roof of the King's Chamber. He thereby found the remaining relieving compartments and an inscription identifying the pyramid as that of Khufu. A triumph – but at what cost? He also exploded his way into the Third Pyramid, which having withstood the ravages of centuries and Khalif Malek's attempted destruction, now had to suffer another brutal assault. When Vyse finally made his way to the burial chamber he found an empty basalt sarcophagus. Further delving unearthed some old bones, and Vyse was convinced he had at last found the remains of an Old Kingdom Pharaoh. These remains are now in the British Museum where, decades after Vyse's death, dating by radio-carbon techniques revealed that the bones were less than two thousand years old and therefore clearly not Menkaure's. As for the sarcophagus, which probably was the pharaoh's, alas, that was lost in a storm at sea whilst being shipped to Britain, and today lies somewhere on the bed of the Mediterranean.

With Vyse in Egypt was John Shae Perring (1813-69) who methodically and painstakingly surveyed over thirty pyramids from Abu Roash to Hawwara, and his diagrams are still used for reference today.

When Lepsius came to Egypt he formulated the 'accretion theory' by which he claimed that the pyramids were built proportionately in size to the length of the king's reign. This agreed with the Giza pyramids, since it was known that Khufu and Khafre reigned for about the same length of time, and Menkaure somewhat less, but its neatness was quashed by Flinders Petrie when he established from the socket stones that the size of the pyramid was planned from the outset. Any remaining doubts were shattered when it was confirmed that King Pepi II ruled for at least ninety-five years, yet his pyramid was not even the size of Menkaure's, and he ruled for only eighteen years.

William Matthew Flinders Petrie (1853-1942) was without doubt the greatest Egyptologist connected with the pyramids. A grandson of the famous naval explorer Matthew Flinders, Petrie's interest in the pyramids arose from his father's involvement in the theories of Charles Piazzi Smyth whom, we shall see shortly, believed the Great Pyramid to be of divine origin. The elder Petrie intended to visit Egypt and undertake a detailed survey, and though he never went, young Flinders did. From 1880 onwards he revolutionized Egyptology. Shocked at the rough techniques in use he instigated his own painstaking, thorough and above all scientific investigations. Petrie's work salvaged most of our detailed knowledge of the pyramids, and whilst he might not always have drawn the right conclusions, he presented all the evidence for the other experts to speculate on. Petrie did not limit his work to the Pyramids, or to Egypt for that matter, as his autobiography *Seventy Years in Archaeology* (1932) reveals, but his greatest triumphs were in that field. At Meidûm in 1891 he found the earliest mummy yet discovered, dated to the Fifth Dynasty. Excavations at Nagada in 1896 and Abydos in 1900 established identities for tombs of the early dynastic and predynastic kings. Here Petrie was able to put flesh on the skeleton chronicle of Manetho. In support came more king-lists, such as the Turin Canon, a sacred papyrus of the Nineteenth Dynasty, and the Table of Abydos, inscribed on the walls of the Temple at Abydos during the reign of Seti I (1309-129. B.C.).

Although there have been many great archaeologists both before and since Petrie, especially the German Ludwig Borchadt (1863-1938), the American George Reisner (1867-1942) and of course Britain's Howard Carter (1873-1939), who trained under Petrie and who discovered the tomb of Tutankhamun, it was with Petrie that the rediscovery of the pyramids peaked. It would be a disservice however to ignore the Swiss archaeologist Gustave Jéquier who discovered the bulk of the Pyramid Texts, and the Belgian Jean-Philippe Lauer, whose sterling work on the Step Pyramid has enabled a near complete restoration of the original complex.

It would be foolish to think that all the problems of ancient Egypt, or even the pyramids, have been solved. Far from it. One of the great prizes is the tomb of Imhotep, which is presumed to be somewhere at Saqqara. Professor Walter B. Emery (1903-71) endeavoured to discover this treasure but with his death the research ceased. There is hope that one day the tomb of this genius will be unearthed, and who knows what revelations it might contain?

Then there is the intrigue of the Fourth and Fifth Dynasties.

Just what did happen between Khufu, Ka'wab and Djedefre, or between Shepseskaf, Khentkaues and Userkaf? Here are dramas being enacted beside the very construction of the pyramids, struggles for political and religious power, as fascinating as any modern history. Since Thomas Fuller wrote his defeatist words over three hundred years ago, the pyramids have remembered the names of their founders. How many more memories will be rescued from stone in the years ahead?

An interesting development in modern research came from the Japanese in 1978. Financed by a television company, Mr Sakuji Yoshimura planned his own pyramid at a site four miles south of Giza. Although the cutting and dressing of the stones was by hand, they were lifted into place by fork-lift trucks (definitely not the machines alluded to by Herodotus!). The Japanese pyramid weighed 25,353 tons and was 34 feet high, another miracle in miniature! However, the Egyptian authorities insisted that it be dismantled immediately after completion, 'because it might clash with the old ones'.[22] In order to save time and money the Japanese also used trucks to haul the blocks and dynamite to quarry them. Seven hundred blocks were used but only four hundred were limestone, the remainder were concrete. On the basis of the Japanese experiment it would have taken nearly 1200 years to build Khufu's Pyramid, which only goes to show that the ancient Egyptians knew best.

THE PYRAMIDS' OTHER SECRETS

Quite apart from the science of Egyptology, and certainly a pastime Egyptologists would rather remain hidden, is 'pyramidology' – literally, the study of pyramids. The archaeologists and the pyramidologists are in complete disagreement when it comes to the origin and purpose of the pyramids, especially the Great Pyramid, the focus of their studies.

To the pyramidologist, the Great Pyramid is not a tomb built for the Pharaoh Khufu. It is a time capsule – a repository of mathematical, astronomical and prophetical information. They believe it was built either by divine guidance, by visitors from space, or by survivors from Earth's last great civilization – be it Atlantis, Lemuria, Mu or wherever. It was not the end product of a natural development in pyramid construction. The Great Pyramid was built first, some estimates suggesting 30,000 years or more ago, and all other pyramids are poor copies. The announcement in June 1978 that a 470-foot high pyramid-shaped object had been discovered off the Florida coast within the notorious Bermuda Triangle certainly added fuel to their fire.

The earlier beliefs that the pyramids were granaries or refuges were fanciful enough, but at least one could see the logic behind that assumption by those who knew no better. But to suppose that they were a deliberate attempt to store prophetic information is another matter entirely. How did it originate?

The man who started the ball rolling was a retired London publisher and editor, John Taylor (1781-1864). He was, in addition, an accomplished amateur mathematician, and he was interested in the blossoming study of the pyramids, especially the work of Vyse and Perring. Taylor began to dabble with Perring's latest measurements of the Great Pyramid and stumbled on a few surprises.

The most famous was the 'pi' factor. Pi, as we all learned at school, is the ratio of the circumference of a circle to its diameter. It was first calculated by the ancient Greeks and set at the value of 3.142 by Archimedes in the third century B.C. It is known today by the Greek symbol π, assigned to it by the English mathematician William Oughtred in 1631. Computers have calculated pi to thousands of decimal places, but for convenience it is generally written as 3.14159. All this was certainly not known to the ancient Egyptians, hence Taylor was astonished to find that by dividing the base perimeter of the Great Pyramid by twice its perpendicular height he arrived at the pi ratio. It was later discovered (by Petrie) to apply equally to the King's Chamber where the ratio of its length to the perimeter is also pi. This spurred him to further discoveries, and he published his results as *The Great Pyramid: Why was it built, and who built it?* in 1859. Here he introduced the concept of the pyramid-inch, a unit destined to be of intense value to later pyramidologists. Using

Perring's statistics Taylor had observed a similarity between the base perimeter in inches (36,564) and the number of days in a year (precisely 365.242). By dividing the former by the latter and dividing the result by one hundred he arrived at the pyramid-inch, equal to 1.0011 imperial inches.

Taylor was faced with two seemingly irreconcilable problems: that the ancient Egyptians knew the value of pi, and used a measure equal to the British inch. How could this be?

For an answer Taylor turned to the beliefs of the American fanatic Richard Brothers (1757-1824). Brothers had died in a lunatic asylum, but before his incarceration had written *A Revealed Knowledge of the Prophecies and Times* (1794) in which he declared that the British were descended from the ten lost tribes of Israel. Taylor postulated that these same lost tribes stopped over in Egypt and, under the divine guidance of Jehovah, erected the Great Pyramid.

During his research, Taylor corresponded with the Astronomer Royal for Scotland, Charles Piazzi Smyth (1819-1900). Smyth was the protégé of the celebrated English astronomer Sir John Herschel (1792-1871), and the indirect association of these three was to have far-reaching results.

Herschel was also interested in Vyse and Perring's work, but from a more scientific angle. He set out to find whether the Great Pyramid could be dated astronomically, by finding what star would have been directly aligned with the polar entrance passage and when. He soon discovered that the star Alpha Draconis fitted the facts and was the pole star in 2800 B.C.

His interest was transmitted to Piazzi Smyth who worked with Herschel at the new observatory at Cape Colony in the 1830s. Smyth's enthusiasm was further fired by Taylor's discoveries, and upon his return to England, Smyth began his research in earnest. It initially fulfilled an unlikely purpose. Herschel was serving on a Commission investigating the merits of the British transition to the metric system, a policy he ardently opposed. The metre had been devised by a panel established by the French Revolutionary government in 1793 and headed by Joseph Legrange (1736-1810). The purpose was to find a measure related to the size of the Earth, and the metre was defined as one forty-millionth of the Earth's polar circumference. Smyth now strove to find similar geophysical support for the inch, and he succeeded. The pyramid-inch was equal to one five-hundred-millionth of the Earth's polar diameter, and since the pyramid was a divine construction the inch was clearly superior to the metre, spawned, as Smyth saw it, by a blood-thirsty revolution.

Whilst Herschel might not have agreed with Smyth's reasoning, it was nevertheless vindication for the inch, and due in part to Herschel's influence and eminence, the British conversion to the metric system was dropped. It is strange to think that today the arguments continue to rage for and against the system, and in the meantime we still talk of inches and yards because of the size of the Great Pyramid!

Charles Piazzi Smyth did not stop there. He published his findings in *Our Inheritance in the Great Pyramid* (1864), then, after spending the next winter in Egypt making an elaborate survey of the monument, he wrote *Life and Work at the Great Pyramid* (1867). He produced further evidence that the Pyramid could only have been the work of divine intelligence – such as the height of the pyramid multiplied by one thousand million corresponds to the distance of the Earth from the Sun, and that the weight of the Pyramid is one thousand billionth that of the Earth.

Over the years an enormous number of comparative statistics have been produced about the Great Pyramid, some of them irrefutable – such that the Pyramid is equidistant from the centre of the Earth and the North Pole; but it will be found that it is easy to concoct any statistics one wishes. For instance, it took me only a few minutes to find that the Pyramid's height multiplied by its perimeter, multiplied by five (the number of corners) and again by three (the holy unit of Osiris, Isis and Horus) equals the length of the River Nile (in feet), to within a 0.3% error, and I would maintain that the Nile was of far more importance to the Egyptians than the centre of the Earth. By a little ingenuity one could probably find any number of baffling statistics applicable to the Albert Hall, Mount Rushmore or any other famous monument.

There is also the fundamental problem of the measurements themselves. This was why Petrie set out in 1880 and his survey disproved Smyth's statistics. Surveyors disagree over the precise points from which to measure the original dimensions. The figures most frequently quoted today are those produced by the Egyptian ordnance in 1925, and these disprove both the pi ratio and the pyramid-inch. However, I shall leave it to the reader to experiment with these statistics as he wishes since there are numerous combinations and computations possible, providing sufficient intrigue to fill a rainy Sunday afternoon. The measurements you require are:

Height	481.4 feet
Base lengths	
north	755.43 feet
south	756.08 feet
east	755.08 feet
west	755.77 feet

A calculator and a set of trigonometrical tables are all you now need.

The proximity of the pi ratio is still sufficient to cause surprise, and it is interesting to see how one scientist resolved the mystery. Professor Kurt Mendelssohn worked on the hypothesis that the Egyptians regarded measurements in height and length separately and used different units. The royal cubit (about 20½ inches) was probably standard for height, but in measuring distances, especially over large areas, they might well have used a wooden drum with a diameter of one royal cubit. One complete circuit of the drum which he calls a 'rolled cubit', would naturally be 3.14159 times greater than the royal cubit. All the builders had to decide was the pyramid gradient. If they selected one of 4:1 – that is a height of four royal cubits to a radius of one rolled cubit – the dimensions of the Great Pyramid and its angle of elevation follow automatically. This theory is further supported by considering a 3:1 gradient. This produces an elevation of 43½°, the 'safe' angle of the Red Pyramid.

Had pyramidology ceased with Smyth perhaps matters would have been resolved. After all, he did inspire Petrie to his great work. However his book also fed that river of thought that declared the Pyramid to be a storehouse of prophecy. Using Smyth's measurements and the pyramid-inch, a contemporary fellow Scot, Robert Menzies, declared that the inner system of Pyramid passages and chambers was a time chart of the past and future. For all his theories and radical biblical crusading, at least Smyth was a sincere and dedicated scholar. But with Menzies we drift into the realms of fantasy. To suppose that any beings in the Earth's past, terrestrial or otherwise, could construct a massive monument to delineate future history was too much to swallow.

David Davidson, a structural engineer from Leeds, set out to disprove Menzies's theories, and ended up consolidating them. He produced a small library of books on the subject ranging from *The Judgement of the Nations in the Great Pyramid Prophecy* (1910) to the wartime *The Path to Peace in Our Time Outlined From the Great Pyramid* (1943), with the real encyclopedia in *The Great Pyramid – Its Divine Message* (1932), produced after twenty-five years of intense study.

Diagramatically Davidson extended the Ascending Gallery back to a point where it meets a downward extension of the pyramid's northern face. This junction marked the dawn of the race of Man in 4000 B.C. Thereafter, calibrated in pyramid-inches, Davidson calculated which dates fell at various changes within the pyramid system. For instance, the centre of the Descending Gallery at the point where the Ascending Gallery begins corresponds with 1486 B.C., which Davidson interpreted as the date of the Israelite Exodus. A point just before the top of the Ascending Gallery corresponding with the lower level of the passage to the Queen's Chamber represents 4 B.C., the accepted date for the birth of Christ, whilst the point where the roof of the Ascending Gallery towers into the Grand Gallery is A.D. 30, the date of Christ's crucifixion. The low passage from the Grand Gallery to the King's antechamber parallels the years of the First World War, but the second low passage leading to the King's Chamber does not correspond with the Second World War (remember Davidson charted this in 1932). When Davidson came to the end of the King's Chamber he ran out of room, so predicted the end of the world for August 20th 1953. Later pyramidologists renamed this the dawn of the Age of Enlightenment, and by taking further distances within the King's Chamber, reprieved the world until 2001.

The pyramidologists are sincere in their beliefs, and until every mystery of the Great Pyramid has been resolved perhaps we should not ridicule them too much. Their cause has now been backed by the discovery of 'pyramid power'. Various experimenters have found that by suspending items like used razor-blades within a pyramid shape (preferably imitation-Khufu), the dulled edge of the blade is rehoned, and can be re-used most effectively. Fresh fruit can be stored within a pyramid indefinitely, and the shape has been claimed to cure arthritis. It was a natural extension of this discovery to point out that the ancient Egyptians must have known of this property and that it would preserve the mummies buried within. If this was so then we would expect all burial chambers to be in the same place, but only Khufu's is at the heart of the pyramid.

Nevertheless the discovery has propagated a variety of products, mostly storage containers. A retired Czech radio engineer, Karl Drbal, actually patented a pyramid razor restorer as long ago as 1959. I have no doubt that as decades pass more revelations will be found regarding some aspects of the pyramids; people have been making them for centuries and they will not stop now.

But I feel that trying to be clever with shapes and statistics belittles the magnificence of the Giza Pyramids. They are stupendous enough without fantasizing. Instead let's remember how Philon closed his record of the Great Pyramid.

> Let fortune smile while she believes that she can touch the very stars by spending extravagantly. For by works of this kind, either men rise to the level of gods, or the gods come down to man.

NOTES TO CHAPTER II

1. Since the High Dam was completed at Aswan the Lower Nile in Egypt no longer floods.
2. I. E. S. Edwards *The Pyramids of Egypt* (Penguin, 1976) pp. 141-2
3. *Natural History* XXXVI.16
4. *Natural History* XXXVI.17
5. Herodotus II.127
6. Herodotus II.124
7. ibid.
8. *Natural History* XXXVI.17
9. *The Annals of Masûdi*
10. *The Pyramids of Egypt* (Penguin, 1976) pp. 123-4
11. Recent interpretations may be found in Professor Edwards's chapter on the pyramids in *Ancient Egypt: Discovering Its Splendour* (National Geographic, 1978)
12. Herodotus II.124. In his *Natural History* (XXXVI.17(78)), Pliny records that it took 360,000 men twenty years, and that all three pyramids took 88 years 4 months.
13. Kurt Mendelssohn, *The Riddle of the Pyramids* (Thames & Hudson, 1974) p. 137.
14. To accommodate the length of the causeway needed for the giant pyramids others have speculated on a spiral causeway, which however poses additional problems in the method of completion for the casing stones. For a graphic interpretation of both methods I recommend *Pyramid* by David Macauley (Collins, 1974)
15. There is no way of telling in hindsight just when these graves were disturbed, but there is no reason to doubt that in some cases the desecration may have happened at the earliest opportunity. Whatever graves escaped certainly suffered in the Dark Ages of the First Intermediate Period five centuries later.
16. The Egyptians held the view that inheritance passed through the female line and the key to being ruler was to be the husband of the Great Queen (the daughter of the previous Great Queen), and not the son of the last king. This was why the potential heir married his sister or half-sister to ensure the succession.
17. *The Pyramids of Egypt* (Penguin, 1976) p. 290
18. This theory, for all its logicality, remains controversial, many

Egyptologists adhering to the theory originated by Perring that the Meidûm Pyramid was incomplete and that its shell had regularly been used by locals as a convenient quarry over the centuries, as have all the pyramids.

19. The original theory for the Bent Pyramid's unique shape was that the ruling king died before its completion and it was finished in a hurry by reducing the angle of elevation so as to lessen the number of blocks required. However the volume of stones is not radically reduced by this change, and morover many kings died before the completion of their tomb, but there is only one Bent Pyramid.
20. *The Holy and Prophane States* (London, 1642-48)
21. *Who Was Who in Egyptology* by W. R. Dawson and E. P. Uphill (Egyptian Exploration Society, 1972)
22. *The London Times* 8 March 1978. See also *Egypt Today* September 1978, p. 4

CHAPTER III

BABYLON THE GREAT

Here grow grasses which are perennially green, and trees whose leaves move in the breeze. The branches are made soft by constant moisture and so the leaves grow more densely. The roots, which are never removed, exude water continuously, and this circulates through the pores of the roots which are buried and pressed into the ground, keeping the trees naturally firm and thick. And so the cultivator, in his many ways, has created strength through nature; this certainly is a work of regal splendour giving much pleasure suspended above the heads of onlookers.

With these words Philon closed his dissertation on the Hanging Gardens of Babylon. A few marvels later he was back in the city hailing the Walls as another 'wonder of the world'. Babylon still existed in Philon's day but it was a mere shade of its former glory. Herodotus, who saw Babylon a little over a century after its zenith, remarked that 'in magnificence, there is no other city that approaches to it'.

By counting two of Babylon's wonders amongst his Seven Philon was only stressing the richness of the many outstanding features in the city. The Walls and Hanging Gardens aside Babylon could boast the world's only stone bridge, an impregnable Royal Palace, the world's first museum, the Temple of Marduk and of course the famous *ziggurat* known to all as the Tower of Babel. It would have been more logical for Philon to have conserved his precious Seven and listed the City of Babylon as a solitary Wonder. I doubt that any of his contemporaries would have disagreed.[1]

Yet how do we reconcile this splendour with the Christian belief that Babylon was the essence of evil, described symbolically in the Book of Revelation (17.5) as 'the mother of the harlots and the disgusting things of the earth'? Was the real Babylon a city to be abhorred rather than marvelled at? The answer to that question will be obvious by the end of the chapter.

THE CITY OF WONDERS

The City of Babylon stood on the banks of the River Euphrates some four hundred miles north-west of the Persian Gulf and over six hundred miles east of the Mediterranean. It was in the southern part of that region known as Mesopotamia, which means literally 'between the two rivers' – Tigris and Euphrates. The land was monotonously flat but extremely fertile and, not surprisingly, was one of the cradles of civilization. Evidence of settlements can be traced back to before 6000 B.C.

Our concern, however, is essentially with the city rebuilt after the fall of the Assyrian Empire in 612 B.C. by the Chaldaean kings Nabopolassar and his son Nebuchadnezzar II, better known from the biblical Book of Daniel as Nebuchadnezzar. Under their direction Babylon became a city unequalled, envied for both its beauty and its fortifications.

The reader might like to refer to Figure 10, a plan of Babylon in Nebuchadnezzar's day. The Babylonians gave names to everything, and it is helpful to acquaint oneself at the outset with their rather outlandish pronunciation.

Nebuchadnezzar's city covered an area of about one and two-thirds square miles. The original city, with an area of just under a square mile, stood on the east bank of the Euphrates and was enclosed by a wall nearly four miles long. A new city was built on the west bank and was also enclosed by a wall, about two and a quarter miles long. The wall was itself surrounded by the river. Within the wall was set eight gates named after the various gods of the Babylonian pantheon.

The city was a criss-cross of long, straight streets not unlike the grid pattern of modern American cities. In the centre was the sacred Esagila – the Temple of Marduk – and the towering ziggurat Etemenanki. Farther to the north, dominating both wall and river, was the Citadel housing not only

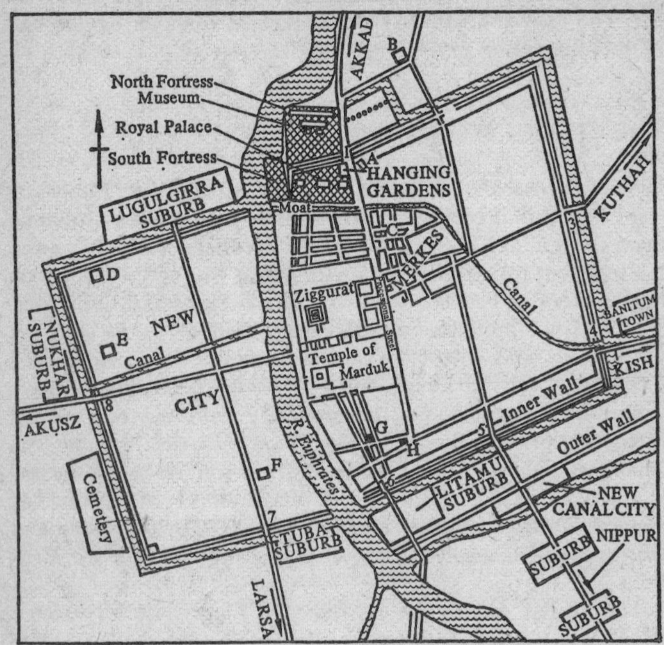

Key: GATES 1 Ishtar; 2 Sin; 3 Marduk; 4 Ninurta; 5 Enlil; 6 Urash; 7 Shamash; 8 Adad.
TEMPLES A Ninmah; B Akitu-house; C Ishtar of Akkad; D Belit Nina; E Adad; F Shamash; G Gula; H Ninurta.

Figure 10. The City of Babylon at the time of Nebuchadnezzar.

the soldiers' barracks, but also the museum, the principal Palace, and the Hanging Gardens.

The remainder of the city contained scores of temples and shrines – for Babylon was not only a commercial but a religious centre – and hundreds of houses and gardens. The houses were all based on the plan of a central courtyard surrounded by the living-quarters, kitchen and store rooms. Only one exit from the courtyard, via the keeper's lodge, led to the street. Herodotus tells us that the houses were mostly three or four storeys high.[2] This almost certainly related more to his day than Nebuchadnezzar's when most houses would have been single-storeyed except for those of the rich.

The population of Babylon has been estimated as high as a million, but this would have included the suburbs. The city itself probably contained about two hundred thousand.

Most of the houses and walls in the city were built from dried mud brick or timber. Stone was non-existent in Babylonia and had to be imported at great cost from the hills of the north. Consequently it was saved for only the most important of buildings. It is hard to imagine that mud could form a brick of sufficient strength to build a wall that could withstand its own weight, let alone the pressure of an army. The secret lay not only in the manufacture of the brick, but also in the method of construction.

The brick was made from clay mixed with finely chopped straw or other vegetable matter. This combination tripled the strength of the brick. The clay was then compressed into a four-sided wooden mould. The size varied, but most of the building bricks from Nebuchadnezzar's day were square-shaped, measuring a foot either side. The majority of bricks were left to dry in the sun, but others were fired in kilns and these proved to be more durable.

Clay bricks had one natural advantage. Whilst still wet they were easy to shape and manipulate, as well as write upon. Most bricks were stamped with the name of the ruling monarch, but many bore other inscriptions which provided future archaeologists with invaluable historical detail. In addition the Babylonians had learned how to glaze the bricks in bright colours, chiefly blue and yellow, and it was this that so enhanced the beauty of Babylon.

The majority of visitors to Babylon approached the city along the road from the north leading from the cities of Akkad, Asshur and, at one time, Nineveh. This road brought one ultimately to the famous Ishtar Gate, but, long before anyone reached Babylon itself, he would see ample evidence of Nebuchadnezzar's works. He was a great builder and renovator – one of the greatest of antiquity – and throughout the countryside were examples of new and restored canals, roads, suburban villas, and especially the many Walls of Babylonia. Nebuchadnezzar's father had usurped the throne and he was only too aware of his vulnerability. He began, and Nebuchadnezzar continued, a vast system of defences throughout the land, and although Philon's treatise alludes to only the City Walls as the World Wonder, in truth it was the many Walls of Babylonia that captured the imagination of the time.

The outermost of these great defences was the Median Wall built just north of the town of Sippar, seventy-five miles north-west of Babylon and marking the northern boundary of the old nation. It ran for forty miles linking the rivers Tigris and Euphrates and thereby, in the absence of any bridges, effectively isolated Babylon from its potential enemies in the north. The Greek historian Xenophon, who lived from 430-356 B.C., saw this wall still standing, and he estimated it to be one hundred feet high and twenty feet thick.[3] Although writers' estimates for the other walls are all highly dubious, Xenophon's is credible.

Babylon itself was surrounded by two walls: the city wall, known as Imgur-Enlil, and the suburban wall or Nimid-Enlil. The outer wall was the work of Nebuchadnezzar. 'I did what no other king had done,' he boasted in one of his inscriptions. 'That no assault should reach Imgur-Enlil, the wall of Babylon . . . I caused a mighty wall to be built on the east side of Babylon.'[4]

Nimid-Enlil was a little over five miles long and formed a triangular enclosure around the city and outlying fields to the east of the Euphrates, an area of over two and a half square miles. Babylon had suffered many attacks in its history. Its most recent siege, sixty years earlier, had ended when the city was reduced by famine. By encircling the fertile fields within a formidable barrier Nebuchadnezzar was ensuring that the city could survive any siege.

Ancient authorities disagreed on every dimension, but with so many walls to choose from perhaps that is not surprising. Whilst archaeologists have now established the width of the walls, their original height is open to conjecture. The most likely estimate is between fifty and seventy-five feet, although the regularly-spaced towers may have risen to a hundred feet.[5]

Outwardly the walls appeared just the same as the accepted impression of the walls of medieval castles, with crenellated towers and battlements.[6] The presence of a canal or moat only cements the comparison. Both the Inner and Outer Walls were double constructions. Imgur-Enlil was composed of an outer wall twelve feet thick with towers every sixty-seven feet. Behind was a mustering ground for troops and then came the inner wall twenty-one feet thick with towers every twenty yards. The inner defence was probably taller than the outer. Nimid-Enlil, as the main outer defence, would have reversed these dimensions.

Herodotus, who was surprisingly led to believe the walls were over three hundred feet high, gave the earliest accounts of how the walls were built.

> . . . As fast as they dug the moat the soil which they got from the cutting was made into bricks, and when a sufficient number were completed they baked the bricks in kilns. Then they set to building and began with bricking the borders of the moat after which they proceeded to construct the wall itself, using throughout for their cement hot bitumen, and interposing a layer of wattled reeds at every thirteenth course. On the top, along the edges of the wall, they constructed buildings of a single chamber facing one another, leaving between them room for a four-horse chariot to turn.[7]

The comparison of size with a four-horse chariot (or quadriga), was so vivid that it has been quoted, and distorted, by almost every subsequent authority, including Philon, who exaggerated it to allow for *four* such chariots to run abreast!

Herodotus concluded his account by saying that 'In the circuit of the wall are a hundred gates, all brass with brazen lintels and side-posts.'[8] Here he was almost certainly misled. Although it is not certain precisely how many gates were in the outer wall, it is obvious that to serve as the main defence it would contain a minimum of gates. Most likely these would have been positioned along the main roads to the north, east and south of Babylon, of which there were six. The city wall contained eight gates. As to their composition, Nebuchadnezzar himself records: 'Its broad gateways I set within it and fixed in them double doors of cedar wood overlaid with copper.'

The most famous of these inner gateways was the Ishtar Gate named after the Babylonian goddess of love and war. It consisted of a square central brick tower about seventy feet high under which passed a high vaulted passage with doors at either end. Two high towers buttressed the central tower along the line of the inner wall, and these were in turn flanked by two smaller towers in line with the outer wall. It is hard to imagine that such a formidable complex could be made from mere dried brick, but in constructing the Ishtar Gate and similar forts, the Babylonians made a major advance in engineering. They invented the expansion joint. A wall twenty feet thick was liable to crack if part of the subsoil was unstable. To avoid such disaster the architects left a narrow space between each layer of brick to allow each wall to shift as necessary. To ensure that the walls did not slant from the perpendicular a vertical fillet was joined to one wall and allowed to slide into a groove on the next wall. Time and again one will find in studying ancient architecture and customs that so-called twentieth-century innovations had their counterparts thousands of years ago; nothing is new. In this instance one can say that the Babylonians had invented a form of cavity walling.

The splendour of the Ishtar Gate however was not in the hidden mechanisms of its construction but in the magnificence of its exterior. The towers were all finished in blue-enamelled brick on which was superimposed an impressive display of bulls and dragons set in low relief and faced in multi-coloured glazed bricks. The dragon, or *sirrush*, is a bizarre mythological Babylonian creature, guardian of the Lord Marduk. Some authorities have compared it, somewhat irrelevantly, with the dinosaur, but the dragon is clearly a composite animal much like the sphinx or gryphon. The *sirrush* has a crested, serpentine head and neck with a single horn, the body, tail and forelegs of a cheetah, and the clawed hindlegs of a giant bird of prey. It has been suggested that the priests of Marduk kept lizards housed within the Temple and occasional glimpses of the flicking tongue and glaring eyes would have been sufficient to strike the fear of Marduk into any blasphemous upstart.

The other gates, whilst less impressive than Ishtar's, were no less impregnable. Clockwise from the Ishtar Gate, the others were named after Sin the Moon-god and son of Enlil; Marduk the chief Babylonian deity; Ninurta the god of war; Enlil the god of the earth and one-time king of the gods; Urash, a local deity of the town of Dilbat which route lay through his gate; Shamash, the sun-god and brother of Ishtar; and Adad, the god of storm and thunder.

Passing through the Ishtar Gate one came upon the grand Processional Way, so-called because it was the scene of the journey of Lord Marduk on the day of the New Year Festivals, one of the most important of the Babylonian ceremonies. The event ran for the first eleven days of Nisan (March 20-30). During its course it was essential that the king paid homage to the Lord Marduk. He pledged his allegiance to Babylon and received divine blessing for a further year as monarch. Later the king would 'take the hand of the god', and Marduk's giant, golden statue would be borne from his Temple along the Processional Way through the Ishtar Gate and out to the *Akitu*-house or New Year Temple.

To allow the passage of the Lord Marduk the Processional Way had to be of divine splendour and indeed it was; it ranked as a wonder in its own right. Over sixty feet wide, the Way was paved with large slabs of limestone set upon a foundation of brick covered with bitumen. It ran for a quarter of its length between high walls decorated in enamelled-brick relief with alternating yellow and white lions with manes of red and yellow respectively.

Babylon could claim that two of its wonders – the Ishtar Gate and the *ziggurat* – were linked by a third, the Processional Way. The distance from the Ishtar Gate to the *ziggurat* was just over half a mile and in that journey one also passed the Palace and the Hanging Gardens and the Temples of Ninmakh and Ishtar, all worthy of special attention.

The Palace and Hanging Gardens formed part of the vast Southern Citadel. A Northern Citadel was built as a further precaution at the apex of the Outer Wall, and here Nebuchadnezzar had a secondary palace, a form of suburban retreat. But his chief residence was the city palace 'because,' his inscription reveals, 'my heart did not wish the dwelling-place of my Majesty to be in another place . . .'. All the same, the palace of the earlier kings of Babylon was insufficient for the great Nebuchadnezzar. 'I sought at a distance room for myself,' he continues, and then he launches into a typically grandiloquent description of his works.

> I made . . . a lofty seat for my royal dwelling of asphalt and burnt brick, and joined it to the palace of my father. In a not unfavourable month, on a propitious day, I grounded the foundations firmly on the bosom of the underworld, and raised its summit high like mountains. I . . . selected fine cypresses to be laid lengthwise for its roofing. Door-leaves of *mismakanna*, cedar, cypress, and *usû*-wood and ivory inlaid with silver and gold and adorned with copper; bronze hinges and thresholds I fitted into its doorways, and caused its summits to be encompassed with a blue cornice.

The Palace was entered from the Processional Way through a giant gateway guarded by sculpted basalt lions. It led to an open court with gateways that led to further courts and the Throne Room. All were beautifully decorated with glazed bricks, predominantly blue and yellow, but enhanced by friezes of lions. The Throne Room measured about 170 feet by 60 feet, and it was here that the Book of Daniel records Belshazzar's feast and the forecast of doom in 'Mene, Mene, Tekel, Parsin', the writing on the wall. Surrounding the Throne Room and the courts, interlinked by passages and alleyways, were official residences, garrisons for the troops, store rooms, administrative offices and the king's own private rooms and harem.

To the north of the Palace was the Museum. For centuries conquering kings had held displays of their booty, and such exhibitions could be considered as early museums. In Nebuchadnezzar's case however it was the first recorded instance of a museum established for its historical and cultural importance. Nebuchadnezzar was intensely interested in antiquity, and during the course of rebuilding Babylon, he excavated temple sites and displayed treasures from the past. He also included items from elsewhere in the empire, one of the oldest being a statue of a king of Mari, a city-state several hundred miles upstream on the Euphrates dating from 2300 B.C. One of Nebuchadnezzar's successors, Nabuna'id, the last king of Babylonia, delighted in scholarly pursuits, and the museum undoubtedly thrived during his reign. It was called 'the Wonder Cabinet of Mankind' by Nebuchadnezzar and was open to the public.

In the north-west corner of the Palace, overlooking the Ishtar Gate and the Processional Way, were the Hanging Gardens. The term 'hanging' is a misnomer as it creates the impression that the gardens were magically suspended. A more correct expression would be 'terraced', since the gardens were raised in tiers in much the same way as the *ziggurats*.

Unaccountably Herodotus makes no mention of the Gardens. The most detailed and, surprisingly, the most accurate account was provided by that notoriously misleading historian Diodorus of Sicily.

> The Garden was 100 feet long by 100 feet wide and built up in tiers so that it resembled a theatre. Vaults had been constructed under the ascending terraces which carried the entire weight of the planted garden; the uppermost vault, which was 75 feet high, was the highest part of the garden, which at this point was on the same level as the city walls. The roofs of the vaults which supported the garden were constructed of stone beams some sixteen feet long, and over these were laid first a layer of reeds set in thick tar, then two courses of baked brick bonded by cement, and finally a covering of lead to prevent the moisture in the soil penetrating the roof. On top of this roof enough soil was heaped to allow the biggest trees to take root. The earth was levelled off and thickly planted with every kind of tree. And since the galleries projected one beyond the other, where they were sunlit, they contained many royal lodges.

> The highest gallery contained conduits from the water which was raised by pumps in great abundance from the river, though no one outside could see it being done.[9]

The passing reference to pumps was a simple way of evading detail which was unknown to the writer. Philon refers to them with even less conviction as 'certain mechanical devices'. Strabo talks of 'screws' built alongside a stairway 'through which the water was continually conducted up into the garden from the Euphrates by those appointed for this purpose.'[10]

It was not until Robert Koldewey excavated Babylon at the turn of the century that a possible answer was found to the mystery of irrigation. He unearthed a unique stone-vaulted building, and in its basement was a well which he described as differing 'from all other wells known either in Babylon or elsewhere in the ancient world.'[11] It consisted of a square central shaft with two sloping oblong shafts on either side. Koldewey reasoned that a form of chain pump had been devised whereby a chain looped through the two sloping shafts and drew water in leather buckets up from the well to the highest point where it was dispersed through the channels. The empty bucket then returned along the chain to the well. The central shaft allowed maintenance men access to the inner workings. The pump could have been powered by regular shifts of slaves working a windlass. The dimensions of the vault were 140 feet by 100 feet, sufficiently close to support Diodorus's account.

Koldewey, the discoverer of the Hanging Gardens, sketched his impression of them as shown in Figure 11. Somehow it gives the feeling of gardens cramped and confined, and upon considering the dimensions, it is clear that had this garden been placed at ground level it would have been most unimpressive. It was solely the fact that the gardens were raised that made them unique and thereby elevated them to the status of a World Wonder. The gardens provided an added bonus in the shaded galleries set beneath the waving greenery. Cooled by the constant flow of water they made a blissful retreat from the furnace of a Mesopotamian summer. In addition the vaults served as a storage place for perishable foods.

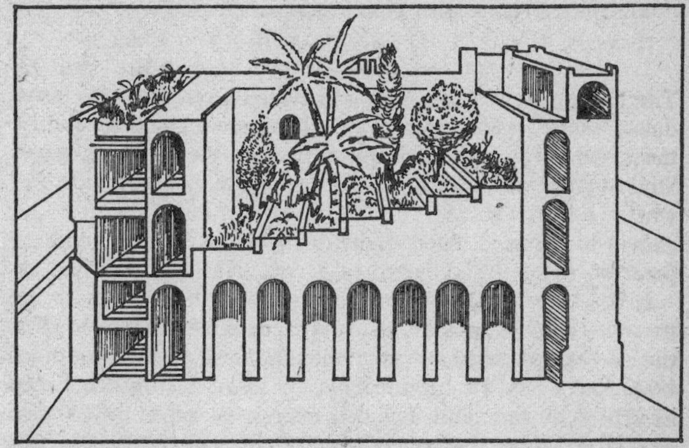

Figure 11. The Hanging Gardens of Babylon as reconstructed by Robert Koldewey.

The Garden architects realized that the standard building material of brick was useless for a construction to be saturated with water. The alternative was expensive stone, which makes one ask why Nebuchadnezzar should go to this extreme. He had many grandiose schemes but he was not reckless. He must have had a sound reason for requesting such a project instead of ordering a simple palace park. Do we know why?

The Greek writers of the time do not supply us with an answer, and their readers must have assumed it was pure self-indulgence. But then the Greeks did not even credit Nebuchadnezzar with the Gardens. Instead they showered praise upon Queen Semiramis whom they claim was the wife of King Ninus and co-founder of Assyria.[12] The real Semiramis lived over two hundred years before Nebuchadnezzar and had little in common with her counterpart in Greek myth.

Fortunately a very feasible explanation was supplied by a non-Greek, an explanation which is both charming and practical. The writer was Berossus, and he had the best credentials for accuracy. Although he wrote in Greek, and lived much of his life in Athens, he was a Babylonian by birth and had once served as a priest of Marduk. In his *History* written about 280 B.C., he says of Nebuchadnezzar:

> By planting what was called a 'pensile paradise', and replenishing it with all sorts of trees, he rendered the prospect of an exact resemblance of a mountainous country. This he did to please his queen because she had been raised in Media, and was fond of a mountainous situation.[18]

As will be seen later, Babylon owed its re-emergence to the strength of the kingdom of Media. Nabopolassar had arranged a tactful alliance between the two nations by marrying his son, Nebuchadnezzar, to Amytis, daughter of the Median king Kyaxares. Media was a mountainous plateau south of the Caspian Sea. Its height above sea level averaged between 3000 to 5000 feet, and included many peaks over 14,000 feet especially Mount Demavend which rises nearly 19,000 feet. Compare this to the uninterrupted flatness of Babylonia where the land rises only 125 feet from the mouth of the Euphrates to its northern border. It is easy to sympathize with Amytis therefore, pining for her mountain home. For Nebuchadnezzar it was more critical. He could not risk Kyaxares learning of his daughter's unhappiness, and so the Babylonian wisely appeased her whim.

Neat and satisfying though this explanation is, we should not overlook a contributory factor. Nebuchadnezzar was also following tradition, as the provision of gardens in capital cities was far from new. The Assyrian Sennacherib had established a great park around his royal palace at Nineveh. It contained all the plants and trees that grew in his Empire, and was later expanded to form a huge botanical gardens and a wild-life reserve. An earlier king, Ashur-nasir-pal, had also installed a wild-life park in his new city of Kalhu in 880 B.C., another example of twentieth-century innovations being but an echo of the past.

A park also existed in Babylon. Records show that Marduk-baladan, an earlier usurper of the throne and a possible forebear of Nebuchadnezzar, expressed an interest in botany and experimented with plants in the royal garden over a century before. Where Nebuchadnezzar varied from the norm was in

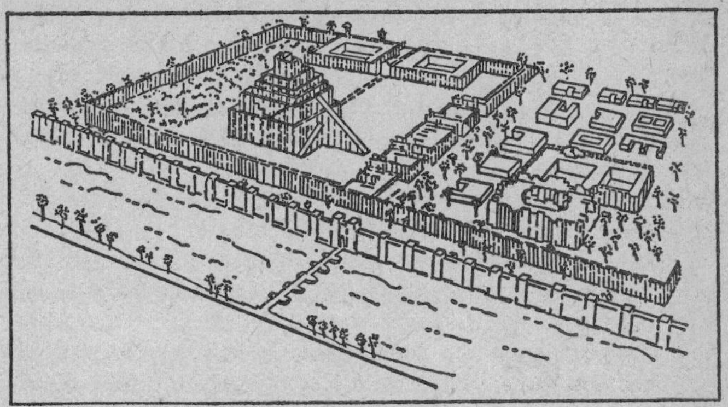

Figure 12. The 'Tower of Babel' (Etemenanki) and the Temple of Marduk (Esagila) as reconstructed by E. Unger.

setting his garden on the palace roof.

Dominating the Hanging Gardens, and for that matter all Babylon, was the *ziggurat* Etemenanki, which means 'the House of the Foundations of Heaven and Earth'. Because the surrounding land was so flat the top of the Tower would be visible from over twenty miles away.

Etemenanki was reached from the Processional Way through the Holy Gate, although there were further entrances from the Temple to the south. Unger's reconstruction (Fig. 12) gives one impression of the Tower and Temple complex, based on a model reconstruction in the Babylonian Museum. Herodotus who saw the *ziggurat*, described it thus:

> In the middle of the precinct there was a tower of solid masonry, a furlong in length and breadth, upon which was raised a second tower, and on that a third, and so on up to eight. The ascent to the top is on the outside by a path which winds round all the towers. When one is about half-way up one finds a resting place and seats where persons are wont to sit some time on their way to the summit. On the topmost tower there is a spacious temple, and inside the temple stands a couch of unusual size, richly adorned, with a golden table by its side. There is no statue of any

> kind set up in the place, nor is the chamber occupied of nights by anyone but a single native woman who as the priests of this god affirm, is chosen for himself by the deity out of all the women of the land. They also declare – but I for my part do not credit it – that the god comes down in person into this chamber, and sleeps upon the couch.[14]

Nowhere in his narrative does Herodotus refer to the Tower as circular; his dimensions infer a square plan. Yet all the best-known artistic impressions of this legendary Tower of Babel portray it as a form of giant helter-skelter.[15] Even the Bible stays mute on the point, Genesis 11.4 merely stating, '. . . let us build us a city and a tower whose top may reach unto heaven.'

In 1876 the Assyriologist George Smith discovered a Babylonian inscription written in 229 B.C. which detailed the dimensions of Etemenanki. The base measured 295 feet square. The bottom stage was 110 feet high and successive stages were between twenty and thirty feet leading to the topmost seventh stage (not eight as Herodotus states), which was fifty feet high and measured eighty by seventy feet. The total height was also 295 feet. The outward appearance was not unlike Djoser's Step Pyramid except that a stairway, thirty feet wide, led to the second terrace and further steps linked successive stages. The reason for the pyramid shape was entirely coincidental. The early temples were raised on a single platform so as to be visible to all in the city. Over the centuries the platform was elevated by additional stages – perhaps in the belief that it brought the temple nearer to the god, certainly that it was removed from the level of mere mortals. Steps were naturally added to allow easy access. Those who try to parallel the development in Egyptian and Babylonian civilizations will be following a blind alley by comparing pyramids and *ziggurats*.

Just how long Etemenanki had stood in Babylon is not known. Bible chronology places the division of mankind during the life of Peleg (Genesis 10.25) one hundred years after the Flood or about 2269 B.C. Curiously this is supported by an ancient Sumerian text which refers to the restoration of such a tower at Babylon during the reign of King Sharkali-sharri of Akkad from 2254-2230 B.C. No doubt it was restored and rebuilt many times over the centuries, but whatever was standing in 689 B.C. was totally devastated when the Assyrian king Sennacherib sacked Babylon. His grandson, Ashur-bani-pal, partially restored the complex, but the temple and tower seen by Herodotus had been the work of Nabopolassar and Nebuchadnezzar, and it was undoubtedly the most resplendent building in Babylon. So dedicated was Nabopolassar to the reconstruction of Etemenanki that he helped with the work.

> For my Lord Marduk I bowed my head, I took off my robe – the sign of my royal blood – and on my head I bore bricks and earth. As for Nebuchadnezzar my first-born son, the beloved of my heart, I made him bear the mortar, the offering of wine and oil, in company with my subjects.

The outer bricks of the Tower were glazed so that each stage shone a different hue, the topmost sanctuary being blue. Once again the number Seven intrudes upon our history and the connection between the Babylonian Seven Circles of Heaven and the seven stages of Etemenanki cannot be overlooked. Associated with the religious significance of the Tower was the astrological. The *ziggurats* made ideal observatories and the Chaldaeans, the originators of astronomy by way of astrology, read the skies to keep the king informed of the activities of the gods. It was presumably for this purpose that Etemenanki was aligned to the four cardinal points, just like the Great Pyramid of Khufu.

The temple of Marduk could not rival Etemenanki for size, but it could for splendour. It was known by the name Esagila – 'the House of the Raised Head' – and boasted a giant dome covered in gold. Within the Temple was the chapel of Marduk, 132 feet long by 66 feet wide, the walls and rafters all over laid with gold. At the end of the chapel stood the gold-plated statues of Marduk and his wife Zarpanit. Elsewhere in the Temple were other shrines to leading deities, especially Nabu, the son of Marduk. Nabu had his own impressive *ziggurat* at Babylon's sister town Borsippa, a few miles to the south, and its site has also been associated with the Tower of Babel.

The sanctuary about the Temple, enclosed within a crenellated wall six hundred yards long, was a city in miniature with quarters for the priests and servants of the temple, rooms for pilgrims, stables, workshops, offices and store rooms.

Esagila attracted pilgrims, be they princes or paupers, from all over the East; and Babylon catered for them in having literally hundreds of smaller shrines and temples dedicated to scores of gods. Babylon was a conglomeration of races, Kassites, Hurrians, Elamites, Chaldaeans, Assyrians, Egyptians and Jews, and there was provision for worship of all local deities. This was one reason, apart from the obvious hatred of the Babylonians for the destruction of Jerusalem, that the Jews, with their strict monotheistic outlook, painted Babylon black in their biblical writings. Another was the emphasis by the Babylonian religion upon sexual fertility. One such tradition was recorded by Herodotus.

> The Babylonians have one most shameful custom. Every woman born in the country must once in her life go and sit down in the precinct of Venus (Ishtar), and there consort with a stranger. Many of the wealthier sort, who are too proud to mix with the others, drive in covered carriages to the precinct, followed by a goodly train of attendants, and there take their station. But the larger number seat themselves within the holy enclosure with wreaths of string about their heads . . . A woman who has once taken her seat is not allowed to return home till one of the strangers throws a silver coin in her lap, and takes her with him beyond the holy ground . . . The woman goes with the first man who throws her money, and rejects no one. When she has gone with him, and so satisfied the goddess, she returns home . . . Such of the women who are tall and beautiful are soon released, but others who are ugly have to stay a long time before they can fulfil the law. Some have waited three or four years in the precinct.[16]

Such were the goings-on at the Temple of Ishtar of Akkad. Meanwhile, on certain evenings, another ceremony was taking place at the *ziggurat*. There a young virgin is led by the priests from the sanctum of the Temple to Etemenanki where, alone, she ascends the steps and enters the holy sanctuary of Marduk to await the visitation of the god. I, for one, cannot help but picture the priests drawing lots to see whose turn it would be that night!

This promiscuous nature of the Babylonians, which was closely related with their religious beliefs, would have disgusted the Jews and is the main reason why Babylon is portrayed as a city of evil in the Bible. All the same it also saved the city when it was taken by Alexander the Great. On his march across Persia Alexander had destroyed city after city, and the same fate might have befallen Babylon. But the Conqueror was welcomed with open arms, and the menfolk freely gave their wives and daughters to his soldiers. Babylon was reprieved.

To the west of Esagila and leading to Adad Street was the unique stone bridge over the Euphrates. Attributed by Herodotus to a certain Queen Nitokris (unknown in Babylonian history other than as the wife of the last king, Nabuna'id), and by others to the ever-capable Queen Semiramis, it was actually the work of Nabopolassar. Archaeology has since proved the bridge was not built entirely of stone. The piles were of burned-brick bonded with bitumen, and were capped in stone where the action of the river surface was the most erosive.[17] Nevertheless it was the first known bridge of such design. Hitherto rivers could only be crossed by boats, or at convenient fords, or by way of tree trunks or bridges of boats, none of them satisfactory for regular day-to-day traffic between the old and new quarters of Babylon.

To construct the bridge Nabopolassar had first to divert the Euphrates by taking advantage of a marshy basin to the north, as well as the new city moat. Then the seven piers were set in the river bed. Streamlined so as not to dam the river the piles were sixty-five feet long and thirty feet wide. Two piers adjoined the banks with five set in the river thirty feet apart with a gap of sixty feet by the west bank to allow the passage of ships. During the day planks were placed across the piers, but these were removed at night 'to prevent people passing from side to side to commit robberies' according to

Herodotus. A more likely reason was to prevent smuggling.

Along either side of the river bank ran another high wall with occasional gateways from the quay to the river. One single bridge was not enough to cater for the full traffic between the east and west cities, and small boats regularly crossed during the day.

Thus were the many wonders of Babylon, a city of which Nebuchadnezzar was justifiably proud. The prophet Daniel tells us how the king was walking upon the terraces of his palace, surveying the city and saying, '"Is this not Babylon the Great that I myself have built for the royal house with the strength of my might and for the dignity of my majesty?"'[18]

How bizarre then that only six centuries later the Greek Pausanias could state that he had not seen the walls of Babylon, nor knew anyone else who had; whilst the satirist Lucian was told that it was impossible to find the site of the city.[19] How was it that a city could become a World Wonder in less than a generation and yet vanish from the face of the Earth in only a few hundred years? What was the true story behind the Babylon of Nebuchadnezzar, and the man himself?

THE RISE AND FALL OF BABYLON

The Babylon we know from the Book of Daniel and from the Hanging Gardens only came into being after 612 B.C., the work of Nabopolassar and his son. But a settlement of sorts had existed at Babylon for some two thousand years, stabbing at history with spasmodic thrusts of importance. For much of its existence it had played a cat-and-dog war with Assyria and even more ancient nations, and a few of these early bouts are worth mentioning for the sake of background.

Figure 13 opposite is a map showing the three most important stages of Babylonian history together with many of the surrounding lands (not all contemporaneous). Babylon did not feature significantly in history until about 1900 B.C. Hitherto it had watched off-stage as the leading roles were

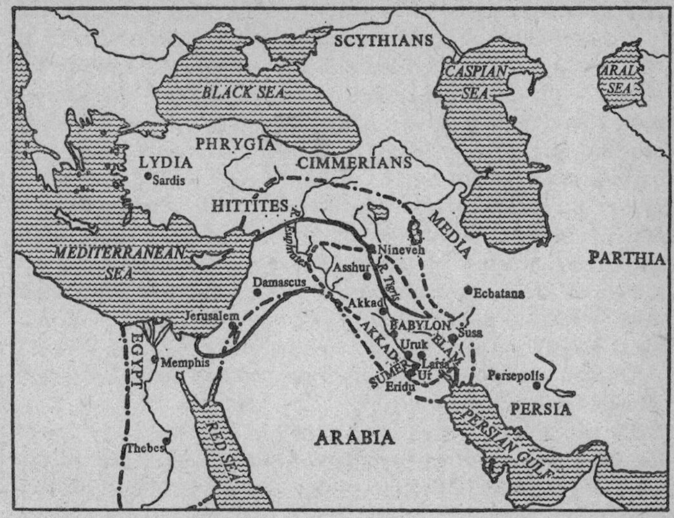

Figure 13. The Assyro-Babylonian Empires.

played by such city-states as Uruk, Lagash, Ur and Kish in the land of Sumer. The Sumerian King List, a chronology compiled from fifteen ancient documents, gives the names of rulers back to before the Flood. The most celebrated name in the list is that of Gilgamesh, king of Uruk after the Flood, and hero of the Sumerian fantasy epic. The Sumerian story of the Flood and that provided in Genesis bear such a similarity that it is clear they tell the same tale.

The Sumerian supremacy was destroyed in 2371 B.C. when the warrior king Sargon swarmed into Mesopotamia from Arabia. He was chief of the Amurru tribes (the biblical Amorites), and after killing the local rulers he established his own capital at Akkad and ruled viciously for over fifty years. He expanded his empire along the entire Euphrates valley. In later years the empire was called Babylonia with Akkad in the north and Sumer in the south. Akkad subsequently became Assyria.

Sargon's dynasty ruled for one hundred and forty years and finally crumbled under the invasion of the mysterious Guti tribe from the north. Thereafter the petty kingdoms were restored with a cultural revival at Ur under King Ur-Nammu (2113-2096) and his successors. It was probably at this time that the *Epic of Gilgamesh*, until now an oral tradition, was first recorded in clay.

Over the next few centuries Mesopotamia was again split into a number of small independent city-states, all vying for supremacy. In 1894 B.C. Sumu-abum established himself as king of Babylon. In his fourteen-year reign he fortified the town and began to dominate the surrounding lands. Naturally this created friction with the neighbouring city-states, a situation which climaxed during the reign of Babylon's first great king, Hammurabi.

Hammurabi succeeded his father Sin-muballit in 1792 B.C. The six city-states then battling for overall control of Mesopotamia gradually fell victim to one another until by 1761 B.C. Hammurabi was in absolute control of the Mesopotamian valley, and Babylon entered its first phase of supremacy.

History has treated Hammurabi kindly. He became known as the world's first lawgiver. Subsequently this has not proved true; Ur-nammu had instigated his own rigid set of laws over three hundred years earlier. But that was in the minor city-state of Ur, not the First Babylonian Empire. In truth Hammurabi was a savage conqueror who treated his enemies badly until the moment he was in sole control. Then, after 1761 B.C., he transformed. Perhaps it was a way of atonement, but he channelled his energies to more creative achievements. He became totally dedicated to running the affairs of state and took the minutest interest in his subjects.

He restored most of the cities he had destroyed. It is difficult to assess the size of Babylon in his day because the water table has risen to destroy almost all but the level of Nebuchadnezzar's city, but it seems likely the boundaries scarcely changed until Nabopolassar's reign.

To have lived in Babylonia at the time of Hammurabi would have made one a privileged citizen. Hammurabi's system of Judgement gave everyone a fair chance. In all there were some 280 laws, and they were set out on three large diorite slabs which formed one stele or pillar seven-and-a-half feet high. This stele, now in the Louvre, was rediscovered in the winter of 1901/2 at Susa, the ancient capital of Elam, where it had clearly been taken as booty by later conquerors. What was most remarkable about Hammurabi's laws was how much they resemble those recorded by Moses in the Book of Leviticus and, more especially, Deuteronomy. Moses lived only two hundred years after Hammurabi and clearly in that time the influence of the Babylonian laws had spread far and wide. Reference to a couple of examples will be sufficient to show the similarity:

Hammurabi: : 129. If a gentleman's wife has been caught lying with another male, they shall tie them up and throw them into the water.

Deuteronomy 22.22. In case a man is found lying down with a woman owned by another, both of them must then die together.

Hammurabi: : 195-6. If a man has destroyed the eye of a gentleman they shall destroy his eye. If he has broken a gentleman's bone, they shall break his bone.

Deuteronomy 19.21. . . . soul will be for soul, eye for eye, tooth for tooth, hand for hand, foot for foot.

Hammurabi's laws are interesting for their introduction of fines. If, for example, a man's ox gores a 'gentleman' and kills him, and is in the habit of goring, then the ox's owner must pay a fine of half a silver mina (about £13). We can see the significance of money in the eighteenth century B.C. and, for that matter, the value of a man's life, be he gentleman or slave.

Babylon flourished during Hammurabi's time; it rapidly became a cultural centre attracting sages and artists alike, thus acquiring a character it never completely lost. If we consider anyone compiling a list of Seven Wonders in 1750 B.C., his first two choices would almost certainly be the Pyramids and Babylon, just as they were fifteen hundred years later.

Unfortunately Babylon's supremacy was short-lived. The

constant rivalry for control of the fertile river valley would plague Babylon throughout its history. For the most part, its citizens let the battles rage about them, welcoming any invader who would allow them to continue about their business. This was an outlook that helped them survive for it would be over a thousand years before the prosperity of Hammurabi's reign was regained.

A generation after Hammurabi's death, Babylonia was divided, the southern portion claiming independence. At the same time Babylon was faced with attacks from tribes in the north and north-west and the importance of strong defences was even more apparent, Babylon's walls being fortified.

Babylon now became the prey of all aspiring nations – first the Hittites, then the Kassites, and finally the Assyrians under whose domination Babylon became a mere vassal state. There was a brief flicker of its former glory during the reign of Nebuchadnezzar I, but with his death in 1103 B.C., Assyria reasserted its dominance under Tiglath-Pileser I.

By now, six hundred years after Hammurabi, his laws had lost much of their significance. The Assyrians were a savage race with cruel punishments which they dealt out to both their enemies and their own people. In comparison the Babylonians were passive, more interested in trade and commerce than domination. That is not to say they could not fight, for the Assyrians frequently called upon them for assistance. One such example was upon the death of Shalmaneser III in 824 B.C. There followed an internal rebellion and the rightful heir, Shamsi-Adad V, requested the aid of the Babylonians to help secure the throne. Once safely installed Shamsi-Adad attacked and looted Babylon, an unnecessary action and one that illustrates the turbulent and barbaric nature of the Assyrians.

Ironic therefore is the indirect importance of Shamsi-Adad in this history. His queen was the enigmatic Sammu-ramat, immortalized by the Greeks as Semiramis. On the king's death his son, Adad-nirari III, was a minor, and for four years, 810-806 B.C., Semiramis ruled as regent.

The legend of Semiramis was recorded by Diodorus, the Sicilian renowned for entangling fact and myth. In this case he misquoted some of the myth as well.[20] Legend tells that Semiramis was the daughter of Oannes, the god of wisdom who was part-man, part-fish. Abandoned at birth she was fed by the doves of Ishtar until found by the shepherd Simmos who raised her. Her name became a byword for beauty, and she first married Menon, a general in the army of King Ninus. In these days Assyria was at war with the Bactrians. Semiramis joined her husband on the battlefield and noticed a weakness in the enemy's defences. She thereupon led her own battalion upon Bactria and the day was hers. Ninus instantly demanded Semiramis as his own and Menon, fearing the wrath of the king, hanged himself. After Ninus's death Semiramis desired to make herself as renowned as he, and she began mighty building projects including the Walls, canals, the bridge and the Hanging Gardens of Babylon.

Semiramis was revered and worshipped by the Assyrians, and considered an equal amongst their rulers, a rare privilege for a woman. After her death a memorial plaque, discovered in 1909, declared her 'King of the World, King of Assyria, King of the Four Quarters of the World'. By her own inscription she stated, 'in the midst of my politics and my wars I found time to satisfy the desires of my body'. Not surprisingly she later became associated and identified with the fertility goddess Ishtar and thereby the Astarte of Phoenician myth and the Aphrodite of the Greeks.

Reading between the lines we can imagine that in reality Semiramis continued the military campaigns of Shamsi-Adad (thus fulfilling her goddess of war attribute), but also instigated rebuilding works at Babylon to compensate for her husband's harsh retaliation. In her day the palace gardens may have been conceived, and with her amorous notoriety no doubt already legend, it is not surprising that later generations distorted the facts and linked the romantic pleasures of the Hanging Gardens with Semiramis.

Assyrian supremacy was cemented with the reign of Tiglath-Pileser III, who claimed descent from Semiramis. He overthrew the ruling family in 746 B.C., and was content to let the Babylonians manage their own affairs under a vassal king. Most Babylonians were content with this arrangement, but not so the Chaldaean aristocracy who regularly put forward claimants to the Babylonian throne. On several occasions Tiglath-Pileser and his successors sent armies to quell riots and matters came to a head in 689 B.C. when Sennacherib could suffer the Chaldaean rebels no longer. With a re-marshalled army he descended on Babylon which withstood a siege of nine months until disease and famine took their toll. Sennacherib now vented his wrath on the city.

> I threw down the city and its houses from the foundations to the summits; I ravaged them and allowed them to be consumed by fire. I knocked down and removed the outer and inner walls, and the temples and all the brick-built ziggurats and threw the rubble into the Arahtu canal. And after I had destroyed Babylon, smashed its gods and massacred its population, I tore up its soil and cast it into the Euphrates so that it was carried by the river down to the sea.

Could anything have been more final? What remained of the city was put under the control of Sennacherib's son Esar-Haddon, who subsequently acceded to the Assyrian throne in 681 B.C.

Under Esar-Haddon, Assyria reached its greatest expansion. It was he who led the army into Egypt and drove back the Ethiopian nomarchs – last of the pyramid builders – to their homeland. At his death the empire was divided between two of his sons. Ashur-bani-pal acquired Assyria, and Shamash-shum-ukin got Babylon. Shamash-shum-ukin, as the elder son, was dissatisfied with this arrangement, and once more the Babylonians were in revolt. Ashur-bani-pal laid siege to the city and it again fell to famine, its inhabitants resorting to cannibalism to survive.

In 646 B.C., Ashur-bani-pal finally annihilated the Elamite nation, and for a while there was peace. The king was now in complete control of the largest empire on Earth, and he turned his back on warfare. As we have seen before with Djoser in Egypt and Hammurabi of the First Babylonian Empire, once a nation reaches its peak, the time comes to cease hostilities and turn to more creative activities. Ashur-bani-pal's conversion was nothing short of miraculous. Totally out of character for a savage Assyrian he became a scholar and bibliophile. He founded the first library in the world at Nineveh and sent his scribes and savants throughout the Empire to collect ancient texts and have them translated into Assyrian. It was in this way that the *Epic of Gilgamesh* was saved for posterity. In all, the Royal Library contained over thirty thousand texts. The greatest miracle of all was that when Nineveh was destroyed the library, buried under the debris, remained intact, the clay texts baked hard by the conflagration that turned all else to dust. There, lost and forgotten, the library remained for two-and-a-half thousand years until it was unearthed by Austin Layard in the 1850s. Nearly all the texts were salvaged providing an unrivalled glimpse into the past.

Ashur-bani-pal was the last great king of Assyria. Already, before his death in 626 B.C., there was dissension amongst his Empire, dissatisfaction with a warrior-king turned 'bookworm'. After his death the nation was split between his successors. Another Chaldaean rebel, Nabopolassar, seized the opportunity and declared himself king of Southern Babylonia. He formed an alliance with King Kyaxares of Media, the emergent nation to the north-west of Assyria. Jointly they began to worry the Assyrians on two fronts. The Medes were further bolstered by the Scythians, and in 612 B.C. a combined army of all three forces conquered Nineveh and destroyed the city. Nabopolassar could be satisfied with his revenge for the sacking of Babylon seventy-seven years earlier in which his ancestors almost certainly suffered.

So complete was the devastation of the city that when Herodotus visited Babylonia only a century and a half later he had little idea where it had stood. It had come to pass as the Book of Zephaniah had recorded:

> And He will stretch out His hand . . . and destroy Assyria; and will make Nineveh a desolation, and dry like a wilderness.[21]

Considering the chequered fortunes of Babylon, it follows that Nabopolassar and Nebuchadnezzar would ensure the city was now strongly defended. Over the last eleven centuries it had suffered numerous sieges and almost total destruction from the Assyrians. If the Medes and Scythians decided to turn their attention to Babylon as they had to Nineveh, it might suffer again. How wise then was the construction of a dual system of formidable walls, the marriage alliance between Nebuchadnezzar and the Median Princess, and the provision of the Hanging Gardens to keep her contented. Clearly the grandiose rebuilding of Babylon was no regal whim, but sound political and military strategy.

Nebuchadnezzar ruled for forty-three years and his reign marked the appearance of the Neo-Babylonian Empire and Babylon's Golden Age. Before he could rest peacefully in his city he had to ensure that all of Babylonia's enemies had been routed. The remnants of the Assyrian army had sought refuge with the Egyptians. Attempts to regain lands had failed and the Assyrians withdrew to Carchemish on the Upper Euphrates. In 605 B.C. a vast Egyptian contingent under Pharaoh Necho marched to Carchemish, defeating the army of King Josiah of Judah at Megiddo en route. Nebuchadnezzar, then crown prince, met the combined forces at Carchemish in one of the world's decisive battles. Heavy losses were sustained on both sides, but at length the Egyptians fled and were pursued by Nebuchadnezzar through Syria to the very borders of Egypt. He would almost certainly have invaded the country had not he received news of his father's death at that moment, and he returned to Babylon.

The new king of Judah, Jehoiakim, was a vassal to Egypt, but Nebuchadnezzar prevailed upon him to change his loyalties. Jehoiakim briefly capitulated, but then rebelled. In 597 B.C. Nebuchadnezzar laid siege to Jerusalem during which the king died. His son, Jehoiachin, along with the royal household, officials, craftsmen and soldiers were taken into exile. (Jehoiachin was treated fairly, and over thirty years later was raised to a position of favour by Nebuchadnezzar's successor, Amel-Marduk.)

Nebuchadnezzar placed Zedekiah on the throne of Judah. In 587 B.C., the new Egyptian king Apries invaded Palestine and Zedekiah, fearing he might suffer the same fate as his father, Josiah, changed allegiance and welcomed the Egyptians.

Nebuchadnezzar promptly sent a great force to take Jerusalem. The Egyptians made good their retreat leaving the Jews to face the might of Babylon. They held out for eighteen months but finally surrendered. Zedekiah and his army fled, but were captured and taken before Nebuchadnezzar at Riblah. There Zedekiah's children were killed before their father's eyes, and then the king was blinded and taken in fetters to Babylon where he soon died. This brutal action by Nebuchadnezzar served its purpose in that no other subservient nation rebelled, but it does show that a savage streak lurked in the Chaldaeans much as it had in the Assyrians.

Little wonder then that the Jews were so embittered as they were taken into exile to Babylon, and one can sympathize with them. Trapped between the powers of Babylon and Egypt they had the misfortune to choose the wrong side twice. Pawns in a power struggle beyond their control they could only view it as judgement from Jehovah as prophesied by Jeremiah (34.22), '. . . and the cities of Judah I shall make a desolate waste without an inhabitant.' It should be no surprise then that no Bible book written by a Jewish exile records the wonders of Babylon, but concentrates on its corruption. In reality the exiled Jews were not enslaved and many of them prospered in the city. Nevertheless Nebuchadnezzar was a conqueror, and they could never forgive him. At the other extreme the Babylonians adored him. For the first time in living memory Babylon was at peace, secure and prosperous. It was the biggest and the richest city in the world and its businessmen and traders grew rich in turn. As a token of their appreciation they erected a golden statue of Nebuchadnezzar on the plain of Dura, south of the city, and night and day people came to pay homage. The story, as told by Daniel, is well known.[22] Three Jews, renamed Shadrach, Meshach and Abednego, refused to bow to the statue and were thrown into the Fiery Furnace where the spirit of Jehovah saved them. The Furnace was probably a brick-kiln, but I leave it to the reader to decide how much of the story is based on truth.

Nebuchadnezzar sustained a few further military campaigns against Egypt and Tyre, but the rest of his reign was devoted to enjoying his mighty city. Little is known of this part of his life although Daniel tells us that he experienced seven years' insanity, '. . . and vegetation he began to eat, just like bulls, and with the dew of the heavens his own body got to be wet, until his very hair grew long just like eagles' feathers and his nails like birds' claws',[28] an image grotesquely captured in a picture by William Blake.

Nebuchadnezzar died in 562 B.C., probably in his seventies. Barely two decades later the mighty, impregnable Babylon, second Wonder of the World, would fall without a struggle. Nebuchadnezzar's immediate successors were short-lived and in 555 B.C. the ageing but learned diplomat, Nabuna'id (or Nabonidus) was made king. As a link to the royal line he married Nebuchadnezzar's daughter, Nitokris.

The days of Nabonidus were numbered however. Suddenly Babylon suffered a financial slump occasioned by the high cost of the military campaigns and building projects. Prices soared, and citizens found food was too expensive. In an attempt to curb costs Nabonidus set out to open new trade routes, and he waged a ten-year campaign in Arabia, leaving his son Belshazzar as regent of Babylon.

During these years the power of the neighbouring king Kurush (better known as Cyrus) of Anshan waxed. By a circuitous route Nabonidus and Cyrus were related. Nabonidus was the son-in-law of Nebuchadnezzar who was the brother-in-law of Astyages, king of Media. Through his daughter, Astyages was the grandfather of Cyrus.

Nabonidus sensibly formed an alliance with Cyrus and so did not immediately concern himself with that king's activities. In the meantime Cyrus conquered Media in 549 B.C., and two years later captured Sardis, the capital of the Lydian empire ruled by Kroisos (or Croesus), renowned for his wealth.

By 546 B.C., Cyrus controlled an empire stretching from Anatolia to the Indus with only Babylonia not under his domination. At last Nabonidus realized his precarious position and he returned to Babylon to muster his defences. Had the Babylonians wished to save their city they could have withstood any seige. Perhaps they were over-confident in the wondrous walls, but, as we have seen before, the citizens were none too concerned who ruled them provided they were left alone. They would have rallied behind Nebuchadnezzar, but not Nabonidus. Not only had poverty increased in Babylon, but Nabonidus had attempted to promote the worship of the moon-god Sin, in place of Marduk, and this had led to much discontent. Cyrus took advantage of this mood, sending forth rumours of magnanimity and religious tolerance which were evidenced by his kindly treatment of the captured King Kroisos.[24]

And so, when the final attack came, Babylon fell without a struggle; Cyrus was welcomed.

Herodotus tells us the cunning way in which Cyrus finally took the city. The Persian knew Babylon's walls would withstand any force he could hurl against it, and a siege would last for years. But every chain has its weak links, and in this instance it was the very lifeblood of Babylon, the River Euphrates, which flowed unhindered through the city. After positioning soldiers at the gates that barred the entrance and exit points of the river, Cyrus withdrew several miles upstream. Here the remainder of his army built a channel to divert the river into a marshy basin – adopting the same tactics Nabopolassar had to build the bridge. As soon as the level of the Euphrates had dropped sufficiently, his soldiers could wade right into Babylon. They entered the city by the way of the river gates which the inhabitants had not even sealed, so sure were they of Babylon's strength. Apparently much of the population were unaware the city had fallen until it was a *fait accompli*.

Cyrus was true to his word. He ordered that Babylon be spared with no looting or destruction. He released all the captives in exile in Babylon, including the Jews, allowing them to return home. The first two chapters of the Book of Ezra detail and enumerate all the Jews who returned, some 50,000. Life was allowed to continue as normal, and Cyrus took a special interest in local, traditional affairs.

Once again Babylon had overcome potential disaster. In the final analysis it was not the conqueror who brought about the downfall of Babylon, but the Babylonians themselves.

In the years following the death of Cyrus, two Chaldaeans usurped the Babylonian throne, both claiming to be sons of

Nabonidus. The new Great King of Persia, Daryavush, or Darius, soon settled the rebellion. The first usurper, Nidintu-Bel, was killed in battle in Babylon. The second, Arakha, an Armenian, was crucified along with three thousand followers. Darius then partially dismantled the mighty walls and removed the gates.

The Babylonians did not learn. Another rebellion followed on the death of Darius, and that was more than enough for his successor, Xerxes. He had been Viceroy of Babylon for twelve years and knew the city and its customs, especially the New Year Festival. In 482 B.C. he sent an army against Babylon; the walls were demolished, the Hanging Gardens destroyed, the temples plundered, the shrines desecrated, and the statue of Marduk carried away. Babylon became a city without a soul.

The impact of this sacrilege is hard to appreciate by twentieth-century standards, and one has to remember that life in Babylon revolved about its religion, and above all the worship of Marduk. His association with the king was symbolic of Babylon's independence, and now that the statue – the earthly symbol of the god – had been pillaged, Babylon's pride was shattered, its spine broken.

Life still continued in Babylon, but not as normal. The walls were rebuilt, though on a much smaller scale. Babylon retained its importance as a religious centre because of its multifarious shrines, but its significance as an astrological centre grew.[25] Hopes were raised in 331 B.C. when Alexander the Great destroyed the Persian Empire and took Babylon. He too was welcomed with open arms. He left orders for the city to be rebuilt to its former glory, and work began on clearing the site of Esagila.[26] In 324 B.C., Alexander returned to Babylon, now as undisputed Master of the World. Babylon was to become the Eastern capital of his Empire. It might well have been at this time, as hypothesized in Chapter I, that Alexander suggested some form of publicity to proclaim the might and extent of his Empire, propaganda that was to evolve into the notion of the Seven Wonders of the World.

Alas, Alexander's schemes, and the Babylonians' dreams were dashed. Alexander, after one of his regular drinking bouts, caught fever and died, in Babylon, in June of 323 B.C.

The final curtain had been drawn on Babylon's history. All that remained was the epilogue. Following Alexander's death, as later chapters will reveal, his Empire became a battlefield as generals, friends and relatives fought for control. Babylon finally fell under the aegis of the Macedonian Seleukos Nikator. For a while he considered making Babylon his capital, but instead built a new city forty miles to the north, on the Tigris. It was called, not surprisingly, Seleucia. The government was moved there, and the businessmen and traders inevitably followed.

Babylon remained a backwater, the home of astrologers and sages. The wise men of Matthew's gospel probably came from the city or its vicinity. It maintained its importance as a centre of the Marduk cult only for as long as aspiring war-lords continued to adopt the New Year Festival as a pretext to elevate themselves to the rank of king. With the spread of Christianity even this significance passed. In time, even the Euphrates deserted it, the river meandering on to a more westerly path.

By the time of St Jerome (*c* A.D. 331-420), who visited the area in about 375, the walls had been partially rebuilt on a vastly inferior scale by a succession of petty rulers and the area within, once converted as a Royal Game Park by the Persian kings, had been abandoned. Jerome recorded that Babylon was a wilderness inhabited by all manner of wild animals.

How chillingly his words echo those written by the prophet Isaiah nearly a thousand years earlier.

> And I will cut off from Babylon name and remnant and progeny and posterity . . . And I will make her a possession of porcupines and reedy pools of water and I will sweep her with the broom of annihilation.[27]

Babylon the Great had fallen.

THE REDISCOVERY OF A LOST WORLD

By the Middle Ages the reality of Babylon was lost behind a welter of religious myth. Babylon was reduced to a heap of shapeless mounds, its very location suspect. Yet it retained its lure for travellers. The mystique of the Tower of Babel, the Hanging Gardens and the Fiery Furnace captured the imagination. Local tribesmen readily showed visitors the remains of Babylon or the Tower of Babel by pointing at any heap of rubble. Most travellers were satisfied because no one could disprove what they had seen. Just as with Egypt and its hieroglyphs, the secret of Babylon was locked in the mystery of the ancient cuneiform script. Examples were plentiful and travellers brought copies back to Europe, but nobody understood them.

The first to delve scientifically into the area was a Dane, Karsten Niebuhr (1733-1815), sent by King Frederik V to explore Mesopotamia in 1760. His party was struck by disease, and he was the only survivor, but the expedition was worthwhile. Niebuhr maintained he had identified the locations of the two major cities. Nineveh was near the modern village of Mosul on the Tigris, whilst Babylon was in the vicinity of Hillah, on the Euphrates.

The problem with identifying anything with certainty was knowing where to look. In the absence of local stone, the Arabs had regularly plundered the ancient sites where the baked clay bricks were a ready substitute. Thus the materials that had once constituted Babylon had been swallowed by many small villages. Nevertheless the French astronomer, Joseph de Beauchamp, who continued Niebuhr's investigations in 1771, aroused much interest when he reported he had discovered rooms and statues beneath mounds at Hillah and another village known as El Kasr, 'the Castle'. Simple European curiosity now burgeoned into a serious study, and the science of Assyriology was born. The biggest hurdle was to crack the code of the cuneiform script.

The man who first successfully chipped away at this barrier was a German classical scholar, Georg Friedrich Grotefend (1775-1853). He approached the matter as if he was breaking a code rather than translating a language, and with the good fortune of inspired guesswork he solved a simple Persian inscription bearing the names of Xerxes, Darius and Hystaspes. Grotefend presented his findings in 1802, but the academic world was not impressed. Grotefend's technique had been too scattershot to be reliable, and it was already appreciated that the best credentials for understanding cuneiform was a knowledge of Oriental, not classical languages, and in particular Old Persian (or Avestan), and Sanskrit.

Throughout the early decades of the nineteenth century scholars all over Europe sweated over ancient bi- and trilingual texts looking for that elusive key. Prominent amongst them were the German Jules Oppert (1825-1905), the Irishman Dr Edward Hincks (1792-1866), and most important of all Sir Henry Rawlinson (1810-95), dubbed 'the Father of Assyriology'.

Rawlinson was an English army officer who led a full and very active life. His brother, George Rawlinson (1812-1902), was the translator of the definitive edition of *The History of Herodotus* in 1858, from which I have frequently quoted in this volume. In 1835 Henry Rawlinson made his way to the rock-face at Behistun, a pass in the Kurdistan mountains on the route which once linked Babylon and the Median capital Ecbatana. Here, carved some three hundred feet up on the sheer face was an inscription by King Darius celebrating his succession to the throne. It was set in ten columns of cuneiform and written in three languages – Old Persian, Elamite and Babylonian – a giant Rosetta Stone.

At first Rawlinson studied the monument through his telescope, but then to ensure his transcription was correct he boldly tackled the mountain. He succeeded in reaching a ledge a few feet below the Old Persian text, but was unable to approach the Elamite inscription from that position. After nearly killing himself trying to jump from one ledge to another across a sheer drop, he succeeded in securing a rope to the rock, and swinging across the cliff face.

After such a hazardous undertaking it was only just that Rawlinson should prove to be the first to break the silence of the ancient language, and he published his initial findings in 1846.

Rawlinson's breakthrough came at a most exciting time in archaeology. The British excavator Austin Henry Layard (1817-94), excavating at a site he later proved to be Nineveh, had uncovered thousands of clay tablets. Rawlinson in Baghdad, and later George Smith (1840-76) at the British Museum, set about translating them and discovered that Layard had stumbled upon the Royal Library of Ashur-banipal. The door to the past was open.

Excavations blossomed at Nineveh, Nimrud, Khorsabad and elsewhere, but little was done to explore Babylon. A few sporadic expeditions were arranged, one by the French under Fulgence Fresnel (d. 1855) in 1852, and one by the British Museum under the control of Hormuzd Rassam (1826-1910) during the 1870s. Rassam was a most fascinating character. He was born at Mosul, near Nineveh, and claimed descent from the ancient Chaldaeans. He had assisted Layard on his excavations at Nimrud in 1845-47, and with Layard's prompting studied at Oxford. He later embarked upon a diplomatic career which included an incident with the king of Abyssinia whereupon Rassam spent four years in the king's dungeons. From 1876 to 1882 he again supervised various Mesopotamian excavations, and for a while believed he had discovered the site of the Hanging Gardens when he uncovered some pipes still containing water at the mound of Babil. This mound is now known to be the location of Nebuchadnezzar's country palace. Rassam published his own findings in *Asshur and the Land of Nimrud* in 1897, and he died at Hove at the age of 84. He thus lived long enough to witness the real unveiling of Babylon.

The honour of discovering the City of Wonders fell to a German professor of architecture, Robert Koldewey (1855-1925). Koldewey had first become acquainted with archaeology when he accompanied a colleague on an expedition to the acropolis at Assos, in Turkey, in 1882, where his expertise in architecture was invaluable. He soon developed an intense interest for the subject and when, in 1897, the German Oriental Society agreed to finance an expedition to Babil, Koldewey was placed in charge.

Work began on 26 March 1899, with over two hundred men under Koldewey's direction. However the methodical and systematic approach to the work attracted little attention from the public in contrast to the sensationalism which surrounded such headliners as Carter's discovery of the tomb of Tutankhamun, or even George Smith's quest for the missing tablets of the *Gilgamesh Epic.* Nevertheless, the excavations at Babylon were to continue for eighteen years, the first major and exhaustive study at a single site.

The real breakthrough came in the spring of 1902 when, after much diligent and meticulous work, Koldewey announced the discovery of the Ishtar Gate and the Processional Way. It was a moment of glory, for the discovery of such lost beauty is rare. But more; suddenly Babylon stepped from the shadows of myth to take its rightful place in the story of civilization.

Koldewey's work at Babylon continued until 1917 when the advancing British troops reached the Euphrates and excavations ceased. In that time he had uncovered about half of Nebuchadnezzar's city, and proved that all the old wonders of legend had actually existed. A replica of the Ishtar Gate was reconstructed at the Berlin Museum, the pride of its exhibits.

Tragically work was not resumed at Babylon after the war and the site was neglected. The locals once again took advantage of the readily available bricks, now carefully exposed, and Babylon was plundered for more building projects. Over the decades it began to resume the anonymity of the past. A few expeditions have studied minor aspects of the city, such as one under the control of H. J. Schmidt in 1966 to excavate the foundations of Etemenanki, but nothing on the scale of Koldewey's work.

Perhaps, with so much to discover elsewhere, archaeologists feel that Koldewey's admirable efforts have revealed enough of the treasures of Babylon, and enthusiasm has waned. If so then once again Babylon has become a city without a soul, and in time will return to the clay from whence it came.

NOTES TO CHAPTER III

1. Rather than quote them all, I would refer the reader to numerous Greek and Roman texts that glow with admiration for Babylon, especially Diodorus II.7-11; Strabo XVI.1.5; Q. Curtius *History of Alexander* V.1 and Herodotus I.179-82
2. Herodotus I.180
3. Xenophon *Anabasis* II.4
4. The ancient inscriptions quoted in this chapter are taken, for the most part, from *Babylon* by A. Champdor (Elek, 1958) and *Ancient Near Eastern Texts* by J. B. Pritchard (Princeton, 1955)
5. The problem is in knowing which cubit measurement the writers used. The standard Greek cubit was 17½ inches, but there was a long, or royal cubit, of 20½ inches, and in some cases the cubit came to be almost any length between these two. There was also a Macedonian cubit roughly equal to 12 inches. Even so the ancient writers could not agree on the height of the walls. Herodotus (I.178) says 200 royal cubits, Diodorus (II.7) reports Ktesia's figure of 50 fathoms, but himself prefers 50 cubits, a figure in accord with Strabo (16.1.5), Q. Curtius (V.1) and Philon.
6. The crenellated battlement arose from the increased use of archers in city defence. The archer was able to shelter behind the merlons, or raised sections, and then rest his bow and aim through the crenels, or lower sections.
7. Herodotus I.179
8. ibid.
9. Diodorus II.10. See also Q. Curtius *History of Alexander* (V.1)
10. Strabo XVI.1.5
11. *The Excavations at Babylon* R. Koldewey (Macmillan, 1914)
12. For once Diodorus does not fall into this trap, attributing the Gardens to 'a later Syrian king to please one of his concubines' (II.10)
13. Berossus *History* G. Syncellus *Chron.* 220. From *The Ancient Fragments* by I. P. Cory (London, 1876)
14. Herodotus I.181-2
15. The most famous painting of the Tower of Babel was by the Dutch painter Pieter Brueghel the Elder in 1563, supposedly based on the Colosseum. Other examples will be found in the work of Lucas van Valkenborgh (1530-97), H. von Cleve, Etienne Delaure (d. 1583), Philippe Galle (1537-1612), Hans Holbein (1497-1543), Matthieu Merian (1593-1650), and more recently Gustave Doré (1833-83)

16. Herodotus I.199
17. See also Q. Curtius *History of Alexander* (V.1)
18. *Daniel* 4.30
19. Lucian dabbles in some prophecy of his own in his dialogue *Charon, or the Inspectors* where he says: 'As for Nineveh, ferryman, it is already gone and there is not a trace of it left now; you couldn't even say where it was. But there you have Babylon, the city of the beautiful towers and the great wall, which will itself soon have to be searched for like Nineveh.'
20. Diodorus II.6
21. *Zephaniah* 2.13
22. *Daniel* 3.1-30
23. *Daniel* 4.33
24. The story goes that after Sardis was captured Kroisos was condemned to die on a pyre. As the fire was lit Kroisos called upon the name of Solon, the Greek lawgiver and philosopher who years earlier is purported to have told Kroisos that no man could claim to have led a happy life until he had met a happy death. Cyrus, hearing these words repented, but the fire was too strong. Kroisos offered up a prayer to Apollo who sent a shower of rain and extinguished the pyre. Thereafter Kroisos lived in Cyrus's court as a close friend and tutor of his children. One interpretation of this tale is that Kroisos chose to die by fire and was offering himself in a prayer to Apollo when a chance shower extinguished the fire. Kroisos accepted this as a rejection by Apollo whilst Cyrus, who as a Zoroastrian would never have normally burned his enemies, treated him as would befit a noble. Records show that a grandson of Kroisos lived to a great old age in the court of the later Persian kings.
25. The Chaldaean religion was Sabaism, or the worship of the stars and planets. The priests therefore devoted their time to studying the heavenly bodies and interpreting their movements. Even after Babylon faded as a political centre, the Chaldaean priest-scientists remained and their knowledge was much sought by neighbouring kings.
26. Arrian tells us (Penguin ed. p. 377f) that the workmen took their time over clearing the site of the Temple because the Chaldaeans were making much better use of the Temple funds than putting it to reconstructing the Tower. However, upon returning to Babylon Alexander, still grieving the death of Hephaestion, his closest friend, diverted the workmen into demolishing part of the walls to build an enormous funeral pyre or tomb (see Diodorus XVII.115)
27. Isaiah 14.22-23

CHAPTER IV

THE GOD OF THE GAMES: THE STATUE OF ZEUS AT OLYMPIA

As Kronos is Zeus's father in heaven, so Phidias is his father in Elis. Blessed is Phidias who, alone, has seen the king of the world and has re-created his awesome presence for all to see. If it belittles Zeus to call him the son of Phidias, might we still not consider his mother to be Art by which means Phidias created (Zeus's) likeness. We honour the other Wonders of the World with our admiration, but this is the only one that we venerate.

In his roundabout way Philon's copyist was stating an accepted opinion of the Greek world: that when one thought of Zeus, king of the gods, one envisaged the Statue by Phidias, which for over eight hundred years made Olympia the Mecca of the Greeks. Even the gruff Stoic philosopher Epiktetos, who lived from A.D. 55-135, conceded that it was a tragedy if one died without having seen the Statue of Zeus by Phidias.

The Statue was directly associated with the Olympian Games, the most important religious festival held in Greece, and one cannot be considered without the other. Once every four years tens of thousands of spectators flocked to the state of Elis; in the course of time there could scarcely have been anyone in the Greek world who had not seen, or heard about, the Statue; its fame was legendary.

After the rather alien histories of the Egyptians and Babylonians we are now in more familiar territory. Until the ancient languages were deciphered the antiquity and mythology of those two lands were unknown to us, but the tales and legends of ancient Greece are part of our literary heritage. Most of us will recall the exploits of such famous heroes as Herakles (or Hercules to the Romans), Theseus, Achilles, Jason and the Argonauts, Odysseus or Perseus. Similarly such historic episodes as the Battle of Marathon or the conquests of Alexander the Great spring immediately to mind; or art ranging from the Parthenon to the Venus de Milo; and mathematicians with names like Pythagoras and Euclid. Our debt to the ancient Greeks by way of cultural and scientific heritage is incalculable. And of course it is thanks to them that we have the Olympic Games.

OLYMPIA AND THE GAMES

Olympia was not a town but a sanctuary, sacred to Zeus, situated in the north-west corner of the Peloponnesos, that huge, leaf-shaped peninsula that hangs south of mainland Greece connected only by the slender thread of the Isthmus of Corinth. It stood in the land of Pisatis, itself dominated by the state of Elis, and the history of Olympia is pitted with hostilities between the two.

The site has changed little over the years, and its beauty is breathtaking. The sanctuary lay in a lush green plain sheltered by evergreen oaks, poplars, pines and olive trees. To the south ran the Alpheios, the longest river in southern Greece, and a favourite of Zeus. The River Kladeos waters the plain to the west, whilst the north is overshadowed by Mount Kronos, only 405 feet high, but conspicuous against the generally flat surroundings.

Figure 14 shows the location of Olympia in relation to the other important cities and countries of southern Greece. Although it might appear isolated, it was easily accessible from both mainland Greece, along the north coastal road of the Peloponnesos, and by sea, by way of the port of Pheia at the mouth of the Alpheios.

The first recorded Olympian Games were in 776 B.C., though as we shall see they had originated centuries earlier. Before its destruction the nearest town had been Pisa, less than a

Figure 14. The Peloponnesos in 432 B.C.

mile to the west, but at the time we visit the Games, in 432 B.C., they were administered from Elis, thirty-six miles to the north-west. The reason we are arriving in 432 B.C. is because this marked the first Games to be held after the completion of the Statue by Phidias, a most historic occasion.

The Games were held in late August/early September. Several months earlier heralds were despatched from Elis announcing the date of the forthcoming Games and proclaiming the sacred truce. This truce was a crucial part of the Olympic Code. It lasted, initially, for one month (later three), and not only acted as a guarantee for the safety of all travellers but also brought about a suspension of wars and hostilities. The competitors had to swear that they had dedicated themselves to training for ten months before the Games. The last month had to be spent in the special gymnasia at Elis. Then, conducted by the judges, and accompanied by trainers and relatives, the contestants would make the two-day journey from Elis to Olympia.

There they would find the plain around the sanctuary ablaze with colour, alive with fairs, bazaars and tradesmen. The Olympian Games were an Event in every sense of the word and all who could, took advantage of the crowds of tourists who flocked from every corner of the Greek-speaking world. Here too one would find painters and musicians, philosophers and poets. Herodotus enthralled the crowds with readings from his *History* which he had completed by the time of the 58th Olympiad in 444 B.C. He might well be present at the festival of 432 B.C., since he was a close friend of Phidias, and we might well see him standing in the rear portico of the Temple of Zeus recounting the mysteries of the Egyptians or the victories of the Greeks to a spellbound audience.

The sanctuary at Olympia grew over the years with buildings spreading out from the central *altis*, or sacred grove. In the time of Phidias the buildings were clustered predominantly within the *altis* as shown in Figure 15 overleaf. The *altis* was surrounded by a low stone wall intended as a boundary rather than a defence. Entrances to the grove were placed at various points along the western wall.

The most prominent building outside the walls, between the *altis* and the River Kladeos, was the workshop where Phidias and his assistants had made the famous Statue. Its dimensions were the same as the inner sanctum of the Temple of Zeus to assist Phidias in his planning and design: 106 feet long, 48 feet wide, with high, solid walls. A well was sunk within the studio to supply water to a large, bronze cauldron set beside two forges which were in the centre. When working Phidias spent most of his time in the workshop, so there was provision for eating and resting. It was the discovery of a clay mug with the inscription 'I am Phidias's' which identified this site as the Workshop to archaeologists in the 1950s.

South of the boundary was the *Bouleuterion* or Council House from whence the festival was administered. It took the shape of two apsidal buildings (oblong with the western wall curved), between which was the altar of Zeus, 'god of oaths'. Here the inaugural ceremony of the Games was con-

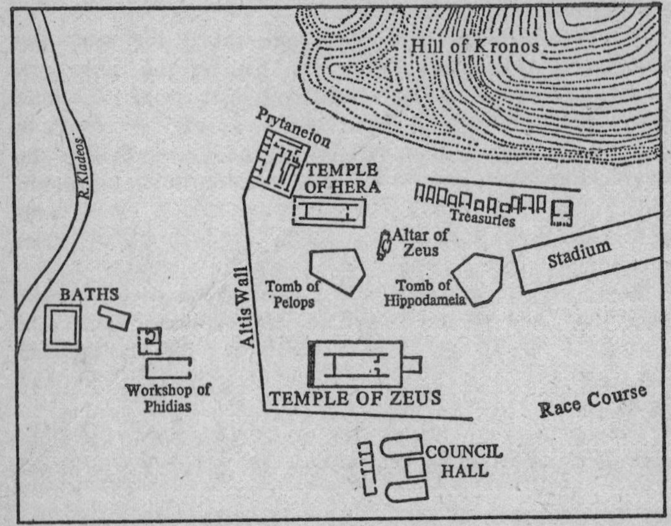

Figure 15. The Sanctuary of Olympia in 432 B.C.

ducted with the contestants swearing that they would perform honourably and the judges swearing that their verdicts would be honest and unbiased.

The *altis* proper measured 650 feet by 575 feet, and near the south wall was one of the most important buildings in Greece, the Temple of Zeus. The Temple had been completed in time for the 55th Olympiad in 456 B.C., but it had to wait for six Olympiads before the Statue was installed. In the interim they had transferred a much lesser statue of Zeus from the older Temple of Hera, but this was damaged by an earthquake soon after the Temple's inauguration, and Phidias was probably summoned as a consequence.

The architect of the Temple was one Libon of Elis about whom, alas, we know nothing. The Temple is described, rather soberly, as a Doric peripteral hexastyle'. Since we shall be visiting several temples in the next few chapters it will help to know the correct architectural terminology, so I shall use the Temple of Zeus as an example. The reader might also like to refer to the plan and elevation of the Temple in Figure 16.

A 'Doric peripteral hexastyle' means that the Temple was built in the Doric style with an enclosed sanctuary surrounded by a covered colonnade ('peristyle') with an entrance porch of six columns ('hexastyle'). The Doric style refers to the plain, severe approach of the architects as opposed to the more decorative style known as Ionic and the flamboyant style called Corinthian. This was most evident in the decoration at the capitals of columns. In the Temple of Zeus these were simple and unadorned.

The Temple measured 230 feet long, 95 feet wide and 68 feet high. The entrance faced the east and was raised on a platform ('crepidoma') of three steps with a sloping ramp in

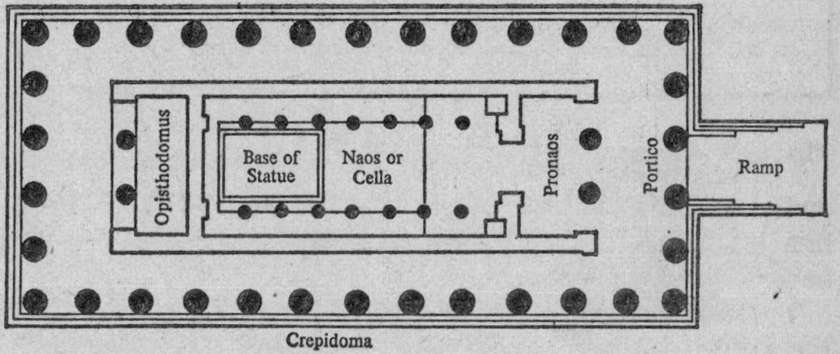

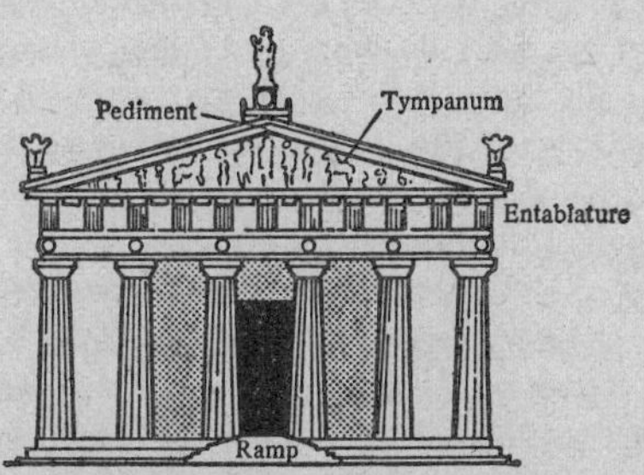

Figure 16. Plan and elevation of the Temple of Zeus.

the centre of the approach. The columns, of which there were six across the porch and thirteen along the sides, were fluted and tapering. The base diameter was 7¼ feet, and they were 34 feet high. Since there was no marble near Olympia, Libon made the columns from local stone and covered them with a coat of stucco to give the appearance of marble.

Above the columns ran the entablature which supported a ridged roof. The front and rear of the Temple therefore had a raised pediment, beneath which was the triangular tympanum. Above the apex of the pediment was set a golden shield dedicated to Zeus by the Spartans following their victory over the Athenians at Tanagra in 457 B.C. Two Olympiads after the inauguration of Phidias's Statue, the apex was further adorned by a statue of Nike, the goddess of victory. This was dedicated by the Messenians from the spoils of their victory over the Spartans at Sphakteria in 424 B.C., which only shows that despite a truce, Elis had no objections to benefiting from the outcome of hostilities, whoever the victor. The statue, which rises thirty feet above the pediment, shows the goddess hovering over an eagle, her drapery trailing behind her. Nothing is known about the sculptor, Paionios, other than that he came from the Thracian town of Mende, but his originality in portraying Nike shows that he was an artist willing to experiment and therefore possibly not very old.

The pediments at the east and west ends of the Temple were themselves adorned with sculptures, each representing a famous story from legend. The east pediment depicted the preparations for a chariot race between Pelops and Oinomaos. Oinomaos was a king of Elis who had been warned by an oracle that he would suffer at the hands of his son-in-law. He thereupon challenged the suitors of his daughter, Hippodameia, to a chariot race, convinced of his own victory because of his invincible horses. Oinomaos would give the suitor a start and then hasten in pursuit, spearing the unfortunate victim as he passed. Hippodameia must have been a rare beauty as there seemed no shortage of suitors. Then Pelops came upon the scene, himself an exile from Lydia. He bribed the king's charioteer to meddle with the chariot's linchpin and in the course of the race Oinomaos was thrown

above The Pyramids at Giza from the south (Egyptian Department of Antiquities, Cairo)

below The Pyramids of Djoser and Userkaf (Hamlyn Picture Library)

above The Pyramids as depicted by Heemskerck

right The ruins of the Ishtar Gate, Babylon (Radio Times Hulton Picture Library)

above Babylon as depicted by Kircher (British Library)

left Babylon from the Ishtar Gate (reconstruction by E. Unger)

above The Statue of Zeus depicted by Heemskerck

The Statue of the Ephesian Artemis (Turkish Embassy, London)

above top The Sanctuary at Olympia in Roman times (reconstruction by R. Bohn, Radio Times Hulton Picture Library)

The Temple of Artemis at Ephesos (Radio Times Hulton Picture Library)

The statue called 'Mausolos' (Trustees of the British Museum)

A suggested reconstruction of Colossus of Rhodes (Radio Ti Hulton Picture Library)

above top The Mausoleum depicted by Heemskerck

as-relief depicting the sun-god Helios (Rhodes Museum)

ove top The Colossus of Rhodes depicted by Heemskerck

above top The Pharos Lighthouse depicted by Heemskerck

left The Pharos Lighthouse based on the reconstruction by H. Thiersch (Radio Times Hulton Picture Library)

above Fort Cait Bey on the site of the Pharos Lighthouse (UAR State Information Service) from the chariot and killed. Pelops succeeded him as king and married Hippodameia. It was from Pelops that the Peloponnessos derived its name ('Isle of Pelops'). The *altis* at Olympia contained a grove sacred to Pelops between the temples of Zeus and Hera, and here sacrifices were made during the course of the Games.

The west pediment portrayed the battle of the Lapiths and Centaurs, a popular subject among the classical Greek sculptors as we shall see. The battle took place at the wedding feast of Pirithous, king of the Lapiths – a tribe in Thessaly. Through his father, Ixion, Pirithous was a half-brother of the Centaurs – the half-men, half-horses of legend – and they were invited to the wedding. The centaur Erution, overcome with wine, abducted the bride and a battle naturally ensued in which the Lapiths were victorious.

Passing beneath the east pediment we enter the peristyle, the gallery surrounding the sanctuary. Ahead is the entrance to the antechamber ('pronaos'), two pillars flanked by bronze gates. Within the pronaos was a statue of Iphitos, king of Elis and re-instigator of the Games, in 776 B.C. Here also, during the course of the Games, hung the olive wreaths awarded to the victors, and bronze shields carried in the race of the hoplites (armoured infantry). Around the top of the chamber's walls ran a frieze depicting six of the twelve labours of Herakles – the other six were in the rear porch ('opisthodomus'). Herakles had killed his own children and in penance he was sent to serve Eurystheus, king of Tiryns. He set him twelve, hopefully impossible, tasks, such as ridding the land of the nine-headed Hydra, a monster that grew two heads for every one cut off, and had one immortal head. By his strength and cunning Herakles accomplished all twelve tasks; in the case of the Hydra he burned each head and buried the immortal one. The presence of the frieze symbolized the constant need for athletes to prove themselves.

From the antechamber we pass into the inner sanctum, the 'cella' or 'naos', where one is immediately stunned by the overpowering presence of the Statue of Zeus. When Libon designed the Temple he had not intended it to contain the giant that filled the lower half of the nave. Two rows of seven columns divided the cella into a central nave and two side aisles. Fitting exactly between the last three columns was the Statue's pedestal, measuring 22 feet wide by 32 feet deep. From the pedestal to the top of the god's head was 40 feet, almost level with the roof of the temple. Phidias had sculpted the god enthroned which emphasized his size. Strabo commented, 'if Zeus arose and stood erect he would unroof the temple.'[1] The throne itself rose thirty feet to the top of the back. Consequently the first impression was one of tremendous, almost suffocating size.

Friedrich Adler, one of the leading archaeologists on the expedition of 1876, designed what many regard as the best reconstruction of the Statue, which can be seen opposite (Fig. 17). The Statue was completed in gold and ivory whereby it is called 'chryselephantine', a word concocted from the Greek *chrusos* for gold and *elephas* for ivory. It was a style originated by Phidias. Hitherto statues were predominantly bronze or marble, including those elsewhere in Olympia, but this would not produce the effect Phidias desired, to present a god full of vitality, a presence that radiated life. There was a practical as well as an artistic advantage to using these materials. A solid statue of such dimensions would have been too heavy to move into the Temple if sculpted outside, and too large to sculpt within the cella. Instead, working in his studio, Phidias produced a wooden frame upon which the outer casing was fitted piece by piece. Once satisfied with the result Phidias dismantled the Statue and re-erected it in the Temple. The sculptor was never sure of his own judgement. The satirist Lucian (A.D. 125-190) relates that Phidias would hide himself in his workshop and spy on visitors to see their reaction to the Statue. Pausanias also tells us that after the Statue was finally installed Phidias prayed to Zeus for a sign that the Statue was acceptable to the god whereupon the pavement about the Temple was struck by lightning.[2]

The unique aspect of the ivory prompted Philon to comment '. . . nature produced elephants so that Phidias might fashion their curved teeth.' The ivory was used for the flesh part—arms, feet, chest, face; the remainder – hair, sandals, drapery – were in gold. The iridescence of the Statue was complemented by the surroundings: the pedestal was of bluish-black limestone from Eleusis, whilst the throne was coated in

Figure 17. The Statue of Zeus as reconstructed by Friedrich Adler.

gold, ebony and ivory with every available space adorned with carvings. The spaces between the legs of the throne were filled by panels which screened the base of the central supporting stake from public gaze. The front panel was painted dark blue, whilst the side panels again portrayed scenes from legend such as selected labours of Herakles or scenes from the siege of Troy. All were the work of Panainos, the nephew of Phidias, a renowned painter of his day. Panainos assisted his uncle throughout the planning and execution of the Statue, and whilst it is impossible to assess his full contribution, he should not be entirely overlooked.

A spiral staircase by the entrance to the cella allowed access to a gallery from where one could inspect the god's head in more detail. Swathed in golden hair the head was crowned with an olive wreath, an innovation by Phidias. The victors of the Games were also crowned with a wreath of olive, with the accepted inference that the victors were in affinity with the god.

Instead of the traditional thunderbolt, Zeus clasped in his left hand a sceptre surmounted by an eagle, and his right hand supported a gold-and-ivory Nike, itself six feet high. With these innovations Phidias proved he was no slave to tradition. He is supposed to have based his Statue on the description of Zeus by Homer in Book V of the *Iliad*:

> The Son of Kronos spoke and nodded assent with his dark brows, and then the ambrosial locks flowed streaming from the Lord's immortal head, and he caused great Olympus to quake.

This caused Strabo to remark

> A noble description indeed, as appears not only from the 'brows' but from the other details in the passage, because the poet provokes our imagination to conceive the picture of a mighty personage and mighty power worthy of a Zeus . . .[3]

The effect was the same on all who beheld the Statue. I have already referred to Epiktetos who maintained that it was a tragedy to live and not see the Statue.[4] There was also the report of Aemilius Paulus (d. 160 B.C.), commander-in-chief of the Roman army and victor of the war against Macedonia. He toured Greece in 167 B.C., and was especially affected by the Statue, feeling that he had beheld the god in person.[5] Phidias had not just captured the likeness of the god, he had created it – indeed to many the Statue *was* Zeus.

No amount of estimating will place a value on the Zeus. It probably cost about nine hundred talents to build, which in today's terms runs into millions of pounds. This was the cost of an earlier chryselephantine statue by Phidias. But that outlay would have been returned many times over by the vast hordes who flocked to pay homage to Zeus all the year round and especially at the time of the Games. And its prestigious value to Elis was incalculable. Naturally such a precious investment had to be regularly maintained, the ivory constantly oiled, and this task became hereditary for the descendants of Phidias.

When the doors of the inner sanctum were open the Statue was clearly visible from the *altis*, and almost certainly from the stadium. In the century after the Statue was completed a new stadium was built farther away from the *altis* and separated from the sanctuary by a long colonnade, but in Phidias's day the athletes could feel proud that they were competing under the very eyes of mighty Lord Zeus.

Before the Temple of Zeus was completed in 456 B.C., the only temple in the sanctuary was that dedicated to Hera, the wife of Zeus, and the patron goddess of motherhood. It was one of the oldest temples in Greece. An original, built from wood around 650 B.C., had been destroyed by fire, but as the Greeks perfected working in stone so it was replaced and the present temple completed in about 570 B.C. It was a prototype of the classical Greek style and differed little from the Temple of Zeus other than in size. It was 164 feet long and 62 feet wide, but little more than 25 feet high which gave it a long, stunted appearance. Within the cella had been two statues: a seated Hera accompanied by a standing Zeus. It was this latter statue that was removed to the Temple of Zeus upon its completion.

To the north-west of the Temple of Hera was the Prytaneum, another part of the festival administrative quarters. Here the sacred fire of Hestia, goddess of the hearth, burned day and night, and all altar fires were lit from her single flame. A similar practice is continued today with the Olympic flame originating at Olympia and taken by athletes to the host stadium. The Prytaneum was a large building, 108 feet square, with the altar of Hestia in the very centre. Here also were large banqueting halls where the victors were treated to a huge feast by the Eleans.

A number of other altars and shrines existed in the *altis*, and the most important was the altar to Zeus, south-east of the Temple of Hera, which had existed for centuries. It consisted of a conical structure 22 feet high supported by an oblong base, or *prothyis*, measuring 40 feet by 22.

The northern boundary of the *altis* at the foot of Mount Kronos was flanked by a long retaining wall protecting the Treasuries – twelve small temples in which various Dorian towns throughout the Greek world stored their valuables. The largest and oldest was the easternmost, built about 600 B.C. for the town of Gela in Sicily. The most recent was the Treasury of Sikyon at the western end which contained three special discuses used in the pentathlon.

The victors of the Games were allowed to erect statues of their own; victors of three events could have them fashioned in their own likeness. The first statues had appeared in 544 B.C. and were of wood, but later they were of stone, bronze or marble depending on the wealth of the athlete. Not all victors could afford this honour, but there were still about three thousand statues of all kinds in this *altis*, in later years.

In Phidias's day the stadium extended into the *altis*, unlike the later stadium excavated and preserved today. It was, naturally, one stade (or stadion) in length, or a fraction over 202 yards, whilst its width was about 80 feet. On either side were artificially raised embankments which could support the thousands of spectators. The hippodrome, or race course, ran parallel several yards to the south. Unlike the stadium which was oblong, the hippodrome sported the more traditional arena-shape, with straight sides and turning circles at either end. The overall length was 666 yeards and the width 245 yards, with a circuit of about 1600 yards.

In their final form the Olympian Games consisted of eighteen events, and it differed only slightly in the time of Phidias. Only men, and later boys, of Greek descent were eligible to enter (though this was later widened to include Romans); married women were banned from competing or even spectating on penalty of death – though there is no record that any execution took place.

The most prestigious event, and also the oldest, was the foot-race over one stade. In later years when the historian Timaeus of Sicily (345-250 B.C.) established the sequence of Olympiads from the first in 776 B.C., it became the tradition to link the winner of the stade-race with the Olympiad.

This is evident in many histories such as that by Diodorus of Sicily who details his chronology for the year 304 B.C. thus:

> When that year had passed, Pherekles became archon in Athens and in Rome Publius Sempronius and Publius Sulpicius received the consulship; and in Elis the Olympian Games were celebrated for the one hundred and nineteenth time, at which celebration Andromenes of Corinth won the foot-race.[6]

There were also two longer foot-races – the *diaulos* of two stades (404 yards) and the *dolichos* of twenty-four stades ($2\frac{3}{4}$ miles), the pentathlon (discus, long-jump, javelin, stade-race and wrestling), boxing, the pankration (combination boxing and wresting with no holds barred, on occasions competitors were killed), a race in armour, and similar events for boys. Distinct from the athletics events were the horse and chariot races held in the hippodrome. Rulers and nobles could enter employing their own charioteers or riders. The prize went to the horse owner, and in this instance women were eligible to enter their teams.

The time-table of the Games began with the inaugural ceremony at the *Bouleuterion*, with the declaration of oaths by competitors and judges, followed in the afternoon by the contests for boys. The second day saw the horse and chariot races whilst the pentathlon took place in the stadium. The day closed with a ritual ceremony in memory of Pelops.

The important sacrifice to Zeus heralded the start of day three. A hecatomb, or a hundred oxen, were slaughtered and their legs consumed as offering upon the altar fire. (The bodies were retained at the Prytaneum and cooked for the ritual banquet that evening.) Many private citizens also made individual sacrifices at lesser altars about the sanctuary. The afternoon was reserved for the foot-races starting with the long *dolichos*, and then the heats and finals of the stade and double-stade races.

The fourth day saw the boxing and wrestling events including the dangerous pankration. In the event that a competitor was killed, the deceased was declared victor and the opponent disqualified, the ultimate humiliation. This happened in the case of Kleomedes of Astypalaea in 492 B.C. He unintentionally killed his opponent Ikkus of Epidauros and was forthwith disqualified. Kleomedes was greatly distressed and returned to his home town where he was ostracized. Embittered, in a fit of frenzy he pulled down the supporting pillar in the schoolroom trapping some sixty boys. Kleomedes escaped and hid in the Temple of Athene. His pursuers tried to find him but he was never seen again. Thereafter he was honoured as a hero.

The day closed with the race of the hoplites. Originally run in full armour it later devolved into a straight race of two stades with the athlete encumbered by a heavy shield. The Games were concluded on the fifth day with the prize-giving ceremonies and a final banquet.

The Olympian Games were not the only competitive festivals held in Greece. There were the Isthmian Games at Corinth and the Nemean Games at Nemea in Argolis, both held biennially, and the Pythian Games at Delphi, held in the third year of each Olympiad. But the Olympian Games were the oldest and most prestigious, and Olympian victors were honoured as heroes and received a variety of privileges. In Sparta they were allowed to fight beside the king in battle, whilst in Athens they were awarded a prize of five hundred drachmas.

Perhaps the most significant victory in the Games was in 356 B.C., when King Philip II of Macedonia's team won the horse race. At the same time as Philip received this news he learned that his General, Parmenion, had defeated the Illyrians, and that his wife Olympias had given birth to a son. A sage told him that a son born under such circumstances would prove invincible, and so Alexander the Great entered the world.

Why were the Olympian Games so prestigious? How did they originate, and how could a small, agricultural state like Elis afford to stage them and raise the capital needed for the Temple and the Statue of Zeus? To resolve these questions and others, we have to follow two stories, the origin and growth of the Olympian festival and the war between the Greeks and the Persians.

THE SPIRIT OF GREECE

Legends abound accounting for the origin of the Olympian Games and Herakles, as the prototype super-hero, naturally has his share of the honours. Diodorus of Sicily tells us that following the success of the quest by Jason and the Argonauts for the Golden Fleece, Herakles declared that the men should

> . . . choose the most excellent place in Greece, there to instigate games and a festival for the whole race, and should dedicate the Games to the greatest of the gods, the Olympian Zeus.[7]

Another legend, recorded by Pausanias, tells us however that Herakles arrived in Elis with his four brothers and challenged them to a race, the winner to be crowned with a wreath of olive.

Then there is the legend of Pelops and King Oinomaos, already recounted, that originated the chariot race. Are all these just legends or is there some core of truth, just as Heinrich Schliemann (1822-87) proved when he excavated the ruins of Troy and Mycenae in the 1870s?

The real origin of the Games lies in the worship of Zeus and Hera which in time resulted in our Third World Wonder, the Statue of Zeus.

The Greeks were not a single race but a disharmonious cluster of different tribes who had individually invaded the peninsula over a long period in the second millennium B.C. The last great influx was the arrival of the Dorians from the dark lands of the north around 1100 B.C. This resulted in a resettling of the various races, and prompted the Ionians to migrate to the coast of Asia Minor where they established colonies like Ephesos and Miletos. This upheaval created friction between the many Greek states sustained over the ensuing centuries by constant petty wars with the consequence that until they were dominated by the Macedonians the Greeks were too disunited to establish an Empire. The two divisions that concern our history are those between Elis and

Pisatis, and Attica and Lakonia. Attica, with its centre at Athens, was Ionian, whilst Lakonia, dominated by Sparta, was Dorian. Elis was Aetolian, but Pisatis was controlled by the ancient Achaeans, or Arcadians.

Such an intermingling of races naturally brought about a clash of religious beliefs with strong elements of an older religion being absorbed with further attributions by successive creeds.

The earliest inhabitants of Greece were basically agrarian, and their religion consisted of a simple worship of the earth, which miraculously revived all life each spring, and of the seed that fertilized it. The earth-goddess, originally called Ge, was later identified as Hera (which means 'year'), and the seed, which the early immigrants had called Zeus, was further identified by the epithet Pelops, which means 'one who produces an abundance of fruits'.

At this early stage festivals were held every year in the autumn in the hope of satisfying the gods so that they would be fruitful in the following spring. This fertility rite took the form of two races: one for girls in favour of Hera, and one for men, representing Zeus. The victors were married, the sacred marriage bed being made from entwined branches of the olive tree. The girl subsequently became the Priestess of the earth-goddess, later identified with Demeter, the corn-goddess, sister of Hera. The girls' foot-race continued into the classical era and was held in conjunction with the Olympian Games. The Priestess was the only married woman allowed to witness the festival.

This simple fertility race had greater significance to the later Greeks. It was interpreted in two ways. Firstly, being held in autumn, the festival honoured the death of the earth and its seed, and called for their resurrection. This evolved into the games held at the funerals of heroes. In the *Iliad* Homer recounts the games held in honour of Patroklos, the close friend of Achilles. These included a chariot race, boxing and wrestling, a duel, shot put, archery, javelin and the foot-race (won by Odysseus). Although Homer was telling of events that took place in the twelfth century B.C., it is reasonable to assume that he was merely embellishing tradition with details from his own day, about 800 B.C.

However, at the time the *Iliad* was finally written down the Olympian festival had yet to be revived, and it is conceivable that the popularity of Homer's national epic contributed significantly to that revival.

The other interpretation of the fertility race was that of a suitor's race: a young man proving his worthiness of a bride. There are many examples of this in legend, not least the Pelops race already recounted.

Whatever the original purpose of these games, it is clear that by the eighth century B.C., they were popular amongst the Greeks. I have already mentioned their link with Zeus as part of the original fertility race, but the connection of Zeus, and thereby the Games, with Olympia is less apparent. It was probably as straightforward as the invading Dorians, for whom Zeus was the principal deity, usurping the sanctuary and replacing the earth-goddess worship with one of their own creation. A further link may be that Olympia had, at one time in its history, been struck by lightning. Such places were declared holy in Greece and dedicated to Zeus, the god of the thunderbolt. The name Olympia would have followed by association with Olympus, the cloud-shrouded mountain in Thessaly, traditionally the home of the gods.

In the years leading to 776 B.C. it is believed that the celebration of the Zeus-Hera fertility games had dwindled, and possibly ceased completely in about 860 B.C. The ensuing decades saw Greece ravaged by famine and pestilence, and King Iphitos of Elis sought guidance from the Oracle of Apollo at Delphi. The priests advised the restoration of the Olympian Games, and this Iphitos did.

The first Games, held in 776 B.C., consisted solely of the one stade foot-race. The winner was Koroebos of Elis who was subsequently elevated to hero status with tales about his exploits against the demon Poene. Initially the entrants were from Elis and Pisatis, fighting out their old rivalry in competitive spirit, but in later years, as the fame of the Games spread, other states flocked to join. In the fourteenth Olympiad in 724 B.C. the double-stade race was introduced, followed at the next festival with the *dolichos*. The eighteenth Olympiad in 708 B.C. included the pentathlon and wrestling, and new events were added spasmodically thereafter.

But King Iphitos achieved more than the resurrection of the Olympian Games. He maintained they should be conducted with a purely competitive spirit between friendly nations and that all hostilities should cease for the duration of the Games. In addition all visitors to the Games should receive safe conduct. He concluded a treaty with King Kleosthenes of Pisa and the great Spartan lawgiver Lycurgus, and the terms were carved upon a sacred discus installed in the Temple of Hera. The treaty was later accepted by all the states of Greece. In turn Elis promised to stay neutral in any future wars.

The neutrality of Elis became legend and it frequently attracted refugees from other states. No one could bear arms in Elis and even troops crossing the land had to surrender their weapons. This gave Elis an almost unnatural feeling of security; its cities had no protective walls, and its peoples led a peaceful, bucolic life.

The agrarian society of Elis may outwardly have seemed Utopian, but it had one possession that was rapidly becoming the envy of Greece, and a very profitable one at that – the Olympian Games. The very festival which grew to symbolize the spirit of peace and competition also resulted in the unrest that constantly plagued Elis until the Roman conquest.

The contention arose with the rivalry between Elis and Pisatis. Elis administered the Games, but Olympia was in Pisatis, and the Pisatans wanted a share of the profit. An opportunity arose in 668 B.C. when King Pheidon of Argos, seeking to overthrow the Spartan domination of the Peloponnesos, assisted the Pisatans against Elis. At this time Sparta, the only ally of Elis, was at war with Messenia and the Arcadian tribes, and without support Elis could not retaliate. The Pisatans consequently presided over the 28th and 29th Olympiads. With the death of Pheidon, the Spartans were able to defeat Argos, and Elis regained the Games. Hostilities were not at an end, however. As a last-ditch resistance the Arcadians allied with the Pisatans and in 644 B.C. seized Olympia and celebrated the 34th Olympiad. A combined Spartan-Elean force crushed the Arcadians, and reduced the Pisatans to vassals of Elis. Nevertheless a compromise was reached and the Pisatans were allowed to administer the Games. It was during this period that there was a revival in the worship of Hera and Pelops. The Temple of Hera was built, and boys' events instigated, all of which betray the influence of the more ancient Achaean culture.

In 572 B.C. however the Eleans regained complete control of the Games, and this situation continued for the next century. In 479 B.C. the Eleans sent a contingent to assist the Greek confederate army against the Persians at the Battle of Plataea, the first time they had broken their neutrality. Much to their chagrin, their troops arrived too late to join in the victory. Due partly to this shame, Elis underwent a radical change in government. A new city-state was established and the city of Elis was built. In 472 B.C. the subservient states of Pisatis and Triphylia rebelled and this time the Eleans totally quashed the revolutionaries. The town of Pisa was destroyed without trace. Now the Eleans had complete control of the valley of the Alpheios, including the rich port of Pheia.

The Eleans now reorganized the rules governing the truce and eligibility for the Games, and rearranged the schedule. They elevated the Games from a straightforward competition to a national festival administered on a commercial basis. The financial rewards from the Games were considerable. There were the thousands of spectators who needed feeding and accommodating, the competitors and trainers, the horses who needed quality grazing. Elis controlled some of the finest grazing land in Greece, and this would be booked well in advance by the highest bidders. The Olympian Games were a goldmine, and it was from these profits that the Eleans could afford to build the Temple of Zeus and subsequently the mighty Statue.

But it was not just the financial wherewithal that produced the Third Wonder of the World. It was only the fifth century B.C. that could have produced the circumstances for such a statue, and it was only Phidias who could have accomplished it.

Phidias was born in Athens in about 490 B.C., the son of a man called Kharmides of whom we know nothing. He grew up during a critical period of Greek history when, almost alone, Athens faced the might of the Persian Empire. This episode is worth recounting briefly for its bearing on later events.

In 500 B.C., Athens infuriated the Persian Great King Darius by assisting the Ionian cities in Asia Minor to revolt against Persia. Persian ambassadors sent to Greece were humiliated, and thereafter Persia and Greece were at war.

The first conflict took place at Marathon in 490 B.C., where, unaided, 10,000 Athenians and Plataeans faced, and defeated, 100,000 Persians – a victory that sent Greek morale soaring to Olympian heights. For the next decade Persia was occupied with an Egyptian revolt, but hostilities resumed in 481 B.C. under a new Great King, Xerxes. Commanding an army a quarter of a million strong, bolstered by a fleet of twelve hundred men-of-war, Xerxes made his way through Thrace and Macedonia to the Greek border. Despite a valiant stand at Thermopylae by the Spartan king Leonidas where just 10,000 Greeks held the Persian army at bay for two days, Xerxes came at last to Athens, the last stronghold before the Peloponnesos.

There was more than just the fate of the city at stake, there was a principle. Athens was a democracy where all citizens were eligible to elect members of the governing Senate. Much of the rest of Greece, symbolized by Sparta, was controlled by oligarchies dominated by the *ephori* (magistrates). The majority of the people, the helots, were without rights.

All eyes of southern Greece turned to Athens to see how the future would be decided. The Greek army was massing at Corinth where a wall was being constructed across the Isthmus, but for it to be successful the Persian fleet had first to be destroyed.

The archon Themistokles convinced the Athenians to abandon the city and seek refuge in the south which they did, apart from a few diehards who barricaded themselves in the Acropolis and soon met their fate. The Persians marched into Athens and, in his moment of triumph, Xerxes ordered that the city be destroyed. All private dwellings and the sacred temples on the Acropolis were fired and razed to the ground.

The destruction of the city was watched by the Athenian fleet which lay in wait across the bay by the island of Salamis.

But revenge was nigh. The Persians were unused to sea warfare and the Greeks decimated the opposition at the Battle of Salamis on 20 October 480 B.C. Xerxes now retreated and returned to Persia leaving the army under the command of Mardonius. The decisive battle came the following spring at Plataea where, after a day of solid fighting, the Greeks lost 1300 men and the Persians were annihilated. The Greeks hammered home their victory by setting sail for Ionia and liberating the colonies.

The victor of Plataea had been the Spartan general Pausanias, but he later fell from grace leaving Athens the supreme Greek state. Aristides, the new man in power in Athens, now formed the Delian League, a confederation of Ionian cities united against the Persians. Every member state paid a tribute of ships or money to Athens and by 443 B.C., Athens was the richest city in Greece.

In that year Perikles, the leader of the democratic party, became the supreme controller of the city, and he set out to make Athens the envy of the world. It had never fully recovered in the generation since its destruction by Xerxes, so in 440 B.C., he instigated a programme to beautify the city, with finances voted from the Delian treasury. The man Perikles appointed as director of the rebuilding programme was his close friend Phidias.

As a boy Phidias would have witnessed the Persian destruction of Athens, perhaps of his own house. We can only surmise what effect that might have had on a ten-year-old, but it is not beyond the bounds of credibility to imagine that his interest in art, the creation of beauty from chaos, was born at that time. His first inclination was to be a painter, but he later studied sculpture under two of Athens's most prominent artists, Hegias and Ageladas.

One of his earliest commissions was of a group of Athenian legendary and historical heroes in bronze, as a gift by the Athenians to Apollo at Delphi; the cost was met from the spoils of Marathon. It was probably requested by the statesman Kimon, son of the Marathon hero Miltiades, and the central figure of the group. This helps date the work to about 464 B.C. when Kimon was in unrivalled power, and Phidias was about twenty-six.

He produced a number of other items at this time, experimenting with a variety of materials. His first chryselephantine statue was probably one of his patron goddess Athene Pallas, for the town of Pellene. Athene was the goddess of war and the divine protectress of Greece, and there was an increased demand for her statues during the Persian wars.

By about 457 B.C., Phidias became involved in the initial restoration of the Athenian temples. He also began to experiment with large statues of which the most impressive was a thirty-foot-high bronze Athene erected in the entrance temple, or Propylaea, of the Acropolis in 456 B.C. The statue was visible to those approaching Athens harbour from the south, with the sun glinting from the helmet crest and the point of her spear. At this stage the sculptor's work carried little ornamentation, because in later years the engraver Mys embossed Athene's shield with the scene of the battle between the Centaurs and the Lapiths.

In advance of the main Athenian restoration programme, work began on one of the most famous buildings of the Greek world, the Parthenon, a Temple to Athene erected on the south side of the Acropolis – the rocky heights in the centre of Athens that marked the site of the original town. The Temple dimensions were not dissimilar to the Temple of Zeus at Olympia which had already been completed at this stage. 228 feet long, 101 feet wide and 64 feet high, planning began in 450 B.C., and work started in 447 B.C. Phidias was in overall charge, but the two chief architects were Iktinos and Kallikrates, and a great many other sculptors worked on the pediments and associated statues. Phidias's own contribution was a forty-foot-high chryselephantine statue of Athene. The goddess was standing, draped in a long gown, and wearing a triple-crested helmet. Her left hand supported a shield and spear, her right the goddess Nike.

It is quite reasonable to assume that during the work on the Parthenon, which lasted from 447-432 B.C., Phidias would have visited Olympia to investigate the Temple there, the only other major Temple built at this time. After the initial design work the supervision of the Parthenon could be left in the hands of the two architects, leaving Phidias time to complete his massive statue. It was dedicated in 438 B.C., so, if Phidias began work concurrently with the Parthenon, it took him eight years.

It was at this stage that Phidias ran into trouble. His patron Perikles was overwhelmingly popular with the citizens of Athens, which made other politicians jealous. They regarded the squandering of money on Athens as a misappropriation of military funds, and were afraid that Perikles would become too powerful. Because of his popularity it was unwise to attack him personally, so his enemies began to weaken Perikles through his friends. It was inevitable that Phidias would be one to suffer. He was charged with stealing gold from the Parthenon Athene.

Perikles was ahead of his enemies. He had foreseen such an eventuality and had ensured that accountants kept a thorough check on the gold. There had been over two and a half thousand pounds' worth used on the statue, and it was all recorded in case any 'went missing' on the site. The gold was affixed to the statue as plates which could be easily removed, and when they were weighed it was found that all the gold was present. The charge was dropped, but Perikles advised Phidias to seek safety outside Athens.

Phidias therefore made his way to Elis, still noted as a sanctuary, and probably arrived in 437 B.C. It would seem too much of a coincidence to imagine that the Eleans immediately asked him to sculpt the Statue of Zeus for them, and it is more likely that he had received the request earlier, especially when news of his Athene Parthenos had spread through Greece. We do not know the circumstances with any certainty, and it is even feasible to conjecture that Phidias left Athens voluntarily after the dedication of the Athene with a firm commission from the Eleans.

Whatever the sequence of events it is almost certain that Phidias returned to Athens in 432 B.C. We know his family now lived in Elis, since his descendants cared for the Statue of Zeus,[8] and in all probability Phidias was merely visiting Athens to see the dedication of the Parthenon. He was promptly arrested and thrown into prison, charged with impiety in having sculpted his likeness and that of Perikles on the shield of the Statue of Athene. If this was the case then we have a rare self-portrait of a classical sculptor; Phidias portrayed himself as an old, bearded but bald man with a high forehead. Perikles was prepared to defend Phidias himself, as he had when his mistress, Aspasia, the woman closest to his heart, had also been charged with impiety and immorality. Alas Phidias died in prison, either of a disease, or more likely as a result of poison from Perikles's enemies.

The death of Phidias had far-reaching consequences. Embittered by the news Perikles sought a diversion, either to lessen his own grief or to direct public scrutiny away from himself; perhaps both. He issued a decree against the town of Megara, a former ally of Athens which had slaughtered an Athenian garrison in 446 B.C. At this time Athens was honouring a treaty with Sparta which included that city's allies, of which Megara was one. However Perikles's decree of 432 B.C. which banned Megarans from trading in Attic markets and ports, was felt by Sparta to violate the treaty. It was the spark that flared into the Peloponnesian War in the following year.

It was as if the death of Phidias had been a signal to mark the decline of Athens. The Peloponnesian War would drag on till 404 B.C. with the ultimate defeat of Athens. More immediately in 429 B.C., a plague erupted in the city which decimated a third of the population, including Perikles.

The war had its effect on the Olympian Games. The truce still held and hostilities were suspended during the festival, but in 420 B.C. Elis banned the Spartans from the Games on the grounds that they had occupied the border towns of Lepreum and Phyrkos during the truce. Fearing trouble, the Eleans ensured that Olympia was protected by several thousand allied troops.

The Spartans did not besiege Olympia but, despite the precautions a Spartan charioteer, Lichas, registered for the Games as a Theban, and won! At the prize-giving ceremony he was recognized, ordered to be publicly flogged and driven from the sanctuary. Agis II, king of Sparta, had a long memory. As a direct consequence of that humiliation, following the conclusion of the Peloponnesian War, he led his army into

Elis, subjugated the land and enslaved many of its people (402 B.C.).

Thereafter Elean neutrality ceased to be sacrosanct. In 365 B.C., Elis renounced its neutrality and declared war on the Arcadians, with whom they had been having border troubles. The Arcadians were victorious at first, and in 364 B.C., at the 104th Olympiad, they seized the sanctuary and proclaimed they would preside over the Games. The Eleans were enraged. Bolstered by Achaeans they descended on Olympia in the midst of the festival just as the wrestlers were contending in the pentathlon. A battle was fought in the very heart of the *altis* beneath the eyes of mighty Zeus, an unforgiveable sacrilege. The Arcadians won.

However it was expensive for Arcadia to maintain its army at Olympia, and so they plundered the Temple treasures. The Arcadian town of Mantinea declared this an outrage whereupon the other towns of Arcadia capitulated and withdrew from Olympia, restoring the treasures and relinquishing the Games to Elis.

The significance of these developments was that the religious importance of the Games had diminished until it had become little more than a ritual. Nations were now interested in them solely for their prestige and financial reward. Having renounced its neutrality Elis was no longer considered sacred. In 312 B.C. it was occupied during the Wars of the Diadokhoi (successors of Alexander the Great) and the sanctuary plundered. In 219 B.C., Philip V of Macedonia waged war on the Aetolians and occupied Olympia for two years.

Despite this, the Games continued, every four years, inviolable. New buildings were erected to cater for increased interest. Most of these appeared soon after the Arcadian war; a palaestra was provided for the training of young boys, and a gymnasium for the older youths. These were built to the north of Phidias's studio. To the south, Leonidas of Naxos built a large guesthouse, 262 feet by 243 feet, completed in 320 B.C., to cater for the increased influx of important guests.

In 146 B.C. Greece fell to the Romans. The conqueror, Lucius Mummius, plundered Corinth, and the worst was feared for Olympia. But the consul respected the sanctuary, erected a new statue to Zeus (called Jove or Jupiter by the

Romans) in the *altis*, and donated twenty-one gilded shields to the Temple. The Romans honoured the Games until 80 B.C. when their dictator, Lucius Sulla (138-78 B.C.), removed them to Rome to celebrate his victory over King Mithridates the Great of Pontus. He had already plundered the Treasuries to help finance the war, and there was a fear they might be transferred to Rome permanently, but Sulla's death resolved the problem.

Olympia also suffered at the hands of the Emperors Caligula and Nero in the first century A.D. Both ordered many of the statues to be brought to Rome, and in A.D. 40 Caligula demanded that the Statue of Zeus be removed. At the risk of his life, the governor Memnius Regulus told the emperor it could not be done. Nero had a Triumphal Arch built during his reign, and the 211th Olympiad was postponed for three years to coincide with his visit to Greece in A.D. 67. He instigated new contests for singers and lyre-players and naturally won all the contests he entered. After his suicide in A.D. 68, the Eleans expunged the Nero Olympiad from the records. Fortunately under Emperor Hadrian (A.D. 117-138) the Games had a resurgence with many new buildings decorating the *altis* including a most beautiful fountain financed by the wealthy Greek rhetorician Herodes Atticus (A.D. 101-177).

By now Phidias's Statue had surveyed the Games for nearly six hundred years. The artist's descendants had carefully maintained it, but in that time it had suffered. In about 175 B.C. a major earthquake damaged both Temple and Statue and the artist Damophon of Messene was selected to execute the repairs. Nevertheless after five centuries the Statue still caused pilgrims to gasp in awe. The great traveller Pausanias, who visited Olympia some time before A.D. 160, recorded:

> I know that the height and breadth of the Olympian Zeus have been measured and recorded, but I shall not praise those who made the measurements, for even their records fall far short of the impression made by a sight of the image.[9]

Dio Khrusostomos, who lived a generation earlier than Pausanias, remarked:

> A man heavy-laden, who had drained the cup of misfortune and sorrow, if he were to stand and gaze at this statue, would forget the heavy and weary weight of this unintelligible world.[10]

Long after the pagan worship of Zeus had become little more than an anachronistic ritual, pilgrims still came to see the Statue at Olympia as the quintessence of life, power, wisdom and strength, and to be humbled by its perfection.

Still the Games continued, even though the Roman world was starting to crumble. In A.D. 276, Greece was invaded by the Heruli, a tribe from southern Russia, and as a hasty barricade the Eleans demolished the outer buildings and used the material to build a defensive wall about the *altis.* In the end, however, it was not the barbarians who destroyed Olympia. The Games had been initiated in the name of religion, and it was religion that brought about their end. In A.D. 312, the Emperor Constantine the Great had been converted to Christianity, and this now spread throughout the Roman world. In 391, Emperor Theodosius I banned all pagan cults, and it has been traditionally assumed that the last Olympian festival was held in 393, the 293rd Olympiad, 1168 years after its official inception. However, another story reveals that although Zeus-worship ceased, the Games as a competitive festival continued. If they did then it was no longer under the 'dark brows and ambrosial locks' of Zeus. Following the ban on pagan worship, the Statue was removed to the Palace of Lausos in Constantinople.

It thereby survived the destruction of the Temple of Zeus in 426 when Emperor Theodosius II ordained that all pagan places of worship be burned. The Games may therefore have survived until 425, the 301st Olympiad, but with the desecration of the sanctuary they ceased.

The Statue of Zeus did not long outlive them. In 462 Constantinople was ravaged by fire, and the Palace of Lausos destroyed. The wooden frame of the Statue would have immediately flared and as the temperature rose the ivory would have curled and fallen, the gold melted. Shedding golden tears Phidias's Wonder passed from the world.

THE REBIRTH OF THE GAMES

In the years that followed the fall of the Roman Empire, Greece was subjected to raids by the Visigoths and Vandals, and later the Avars and Slavs. The Olympians, converted to Christianity, had rebuilt Phidias's workshop as a church, and in this form it was the only building to survive at the site. Then in 522 and 551 two earthquakes devastated the sanctuary. The courses of the rivers Kladeos and Alpheios changed and swept through the sanctuary, and soil washed down from Mount Kronos covered the site. Olympia vanished beneath thirteen feet of mud.

So it would remain for over a thousand years. The Greek writers, especially Pausanias, had left a wealth of information about the site, but to the scholars who visited the Peleponnesos, Olympia had vanished without trace.

When Fischer von Erlach published his impression of the Statue of Zeus in 1721 it was based entirely on the description of Pausanias. Scholars now began to show an interest in locating the original Temple, and the spark of enthusiasm was lit by a French Benedictine monk, Dom Bernard de Montfaucon (1655-1741). He was a pioneer academic on ancient manuscripts, and in a letter in 1723 he suggested that someone should excavate at Olympia. Nothing came of it at the time, but in 1766 the British antiquarian Dr Richard Chandler (1738-1810) toured Greece and in *Travels in Greece* (1776) indicated the location of the site.

In 1768 Johann von Winckelmann (1717-68), the founder of Scientific Archaeology, proposed a reconstruction of Olympia and obtained permission from the Turkish Sultan Mustapha III to excavate the site. Regrettably von Winckelmann was murdered in Trieste by a robber interested in some gold medals in the German's possession, and his plans came to nothing.

Nevertheless interest was aroused in Olympia, and in 1829 an opportunity arose to investigate further. In that year the Greeks rebelled against their Turkish overlords and King Charles X of France sent troops to assist the Greeks.

Emulating Napoleon Bonaparte, he also sent a team of scholars and scientists, including the architect Abel Blouet, the man who completed the Arc de Triomphe. For six weeks he excavated at Olympia and diligently cleared much of the outline of the Temple of Zeus, discovering the metope sculptures of the labours of Herakles.

The French did not take sufficient advantage of this situation, and the site was abandoned. In 1852 Professor Ernst Curtius (1814-96) of Berlin University published a treatise on Olympia and recommended the revival of Winckelmann's proposed reconstruction. Curtius had been tutor to the Crown Prince Frederik of Prussia and he interested the royal family in the project. Curtius's ambition was at last fulfilled in 1874 when the Germans secured a treaty with the Greeks which gave the Germans the sole rights to excavate at Olympia.

Excavations began in 1875 and continued until 1881. Curtius led the team which also included the architect Friedrich Adler (1827-1908) and the archaeologist Wilhelm Dörpfeld (1853-1940). Dörpfeld made his name as the successor of Heinrich Schliemann at Troy and Mycenae, but he constantly returned to Olympia often carrying out research on his own.

The Curtius-Adler expedition transformed Olympia. They excavated in their entirety the Temples of Zeus and Hera, and identified the sites of most other monuments. Of course there was no statue of Zeus to discover, but they identified the plinth within the temple where it had stood, and they unearthed several Elean coins dating from the time of the Emperor Hadrian which depicted the enthroned god.

The highlight of their excavations however was the discovery of the all but undamaged Statue of Hermes with the infant Dionysius in the Temple of Hera. It was discovered on 8 May 1877 in the exact position described by Pausanias. Sculpted from marble it depicts a nude Hermes (the messenger of the gods, called Mercury by the Romans) standing and supporting the baby Dionysius in his left arm. His right arm, to which the infant is reaching, is unfortunately lost, but he was probably tempting the child with a bunch of grapes. The artist was Praxiteles who lived nearly a century after

Phidias, with whom he ranks as the greatest of Greek sculptors. His statue of Aphrodite at Knidos was classed by many writers of antiquity as the most beautiful work of art in the world, though it could not rival Phidias's Zeus for majesty. The ability of Praxiteles can be attested by the remarks of a German critic when first shown a photograph of the statue. Praxiteles had sculpted some drapery hanging from Hermes's left arm to disguise the support needed for the statue, but it was so realistic that the critic asked why the cloth was left hanging there when the photograph was taken! Its importance is that it is the only surviving original Greek statue whose artist can be identified with certainty.

Public interest was now aroused in Olympia and in 1894 the French educator and sportsman, Baron Pierre de Coubertin, succeeded in establishing an Olympic Committee, and in 1896 the first of the revived Olympic Games was held, in Athens. We are now in the twenty-first Olympiad, and in that time the Games have been postponed three times because of the World Wars, yet in all its previous twelve hundred years of existence the Games were never cancelled once.

Excavations continue at Olympia, although the site has been almost exhausted. Work recommenced in 1936 when interest was rekindled in Germany with the staging of the 11th Olympiad in Berlin. Apart from a break between 1942 and 1952, the Director of Excavations since 1937 has been Emil Kunze (b. 1901), who was responsible for the rebuilding of the Olympic stadium, which was opened in 1961.

The most important discovery under Kunze was the identification of Phidias's workshop, and the dating of his presence at Olympia to the years up until 432 B.C. Until then it had long been an argument amongst scholars as to which statue Phidias executed first, the Athene *Parthenos* or the Zeus *Olympeos*. We now know that the Zeus, the Third Wonder of the World, was his final triumph.

NOTES ON CHAPTER IV

1. *Geographica* 8.3.30
2. Pausanias V.11.9
3. *Geographica* 8.3.30

4. *Dissertationes* I.6
5. Polybius XXX.15. See also Livy 45.28
6. Diodorus XX.91
7. Diodorus IV.53
8. Lucian *Ikaro-menippos*
9. Pausanias V.11.9
10. *Orations* XII

CHAPTER V

THE HOME OF THE HUNTRESS: THE TEMPLE OF ARTEMIS AT EPHESOS

The Unique Temple of Artemis at Ephesos is the abode of gods. Whoever has gazed upon it will believe that the heavenly world of the immortal gods has changed places with the earth. The Giants, or Aloidae, who undertook to conquer Olympus with mountains, have now built not a temple but a dwelling fit for gods.

Readers will recall that the epigram by Antipatros of Sidon quoted in the first chapter praised the Temple of Artemis by ranking it as superior amongst the Seven Wonders. Philon also classified it as 'unique', but why? In the Greek-speaking world there were hundreds of beautiful temples such as the Temple of Zeus at Olympia or the Parthenon, which were discussed in the last chapter. Yet the writers of old did not hesitate in singling out the Temple of Artemis at Ephesos, the only temple classified as a World Wonder. Why?

Simple questions seldom have clear-cut answers, and this is no exception. Two of the most significant factors must be its size – it was the largest completed temple in the Greek world – and its location. In Philon's day, Ephesos was the most important city in Asia Minor. But there is more to it than that. Regardless of the worship of Artemis herself, the temple had a long and important history. It was favoured by royalty: two great kings, Kroisos and Alexander, had both contributed to its construction, and the Persian king Xerxes spared it whilst he destroyed many others. It was also filled with many wonderful works of art much of which today we can, alas, only guess at. And there is one factor that certainly makes the Temple of Artemis unique: it was the only one of the Seven Wonders to be rebuilt.

THE TOWERING TEMPLE

Ephesos was one of the twelve Ionian Greek colonies established on the shores of Asia Minor (see Fig. 18). Built on the lower slopes of the hills Koressos and Pion near the mouth of the River Kaystros, it overlooked the Aegean Sea near the island of Samos. Priene was twenty miles to the south, and Miletos a little farther.

During the period of Athenian supremacy, the fifth century B.C., and for many centuries after, Ephesos was a thriving and prosperous port. A harbour was established at the estuary of the Kaystros and it formed the western terminus of a major trade route into Asia, along the Kaystros valley running adjacent to the Mermus and Maeander valleys, and thence to the famous Persian Royal Road which ran from Sardis to Susa. A visitor at any time between, say, 500 B.C. and A.D. 300, would have found the city alive with merchants, traders and pilgrims, be they Greek, Persian, or (later) Roman and even Christian. No one could claim to have seen Ephesos without visiting the Temple. It stood nearly a mile outside the main town on a road that skirted the north-west flank of Mount Pion and passed through a flat area of marshland.

It was here on a picturesque, if swampy, plain that the goddess Artemis welcomed her worshippers for nearly a thousand years. The odd fact about the Ephesian Artemis was that although she owed her name to the Ionian Greeks, she had virtually nothing in common with the Greek or Arcadian Artemis.

In Greek legend, Artemis was the daughter of Zeus and Leto (his cousin), and twin sister of Apollo. She was originally worshipped as an earth-goddess, caring for wild-life and childbirth, and in this guise was associated by the early

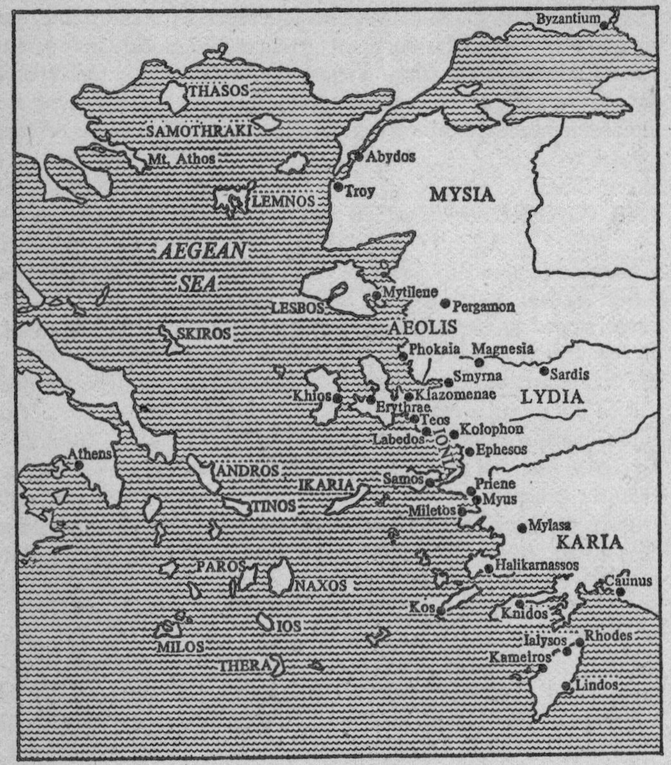

The Dorian Hexapolis comprised: Lindos, Ialysos, Kameiros, Halikarnassos, Kos and Knidos.

The Ionian League comprised: Miletos, Myus, Priene, Ephesos, Kolophon, Lebedos, Teos, Erythrae, Klazomenae, Phokaia, Samos and Khios. Smyrna (orginally Aeolian) was later admitted to the League.

Figure 18. The Greek Colonies in Asia Minor.

Romans with their divinity Diana. Subsequently Artemis was regarded as the goddess of the hunt, a virgin and thus the guardian of chastity. As a counterpart to Apollo, god of the Sun, Artemis was also worshipped as goddess of the Moon. Much of this developed after the Dorian invasion, hence the migrating Ionians still regarded Artemis as an earth-goddess. On arriving in Asia Minor they discovered the worship of a local fertility goddess, Kubele or Cybele, and associated with the Phoenician Astarte and the Babylonian Ishtar. To the Ionians of the tenth century B.C., she had the same attributes as their native Artemis and they unhesitatingly adapted the name.

The two goddesses, however, were subsequently visualized as opposites. The Arcadian Artemis was a lithe girl, fleet of foot, somewhat stern of expression, but every inch female. The Ephesian Artemis by contrast was rather grotesque. The lower half of her body was encased, rather like a mummy, and decorated with a variety of symbols and creatures, especially bears and bees which were sacred to her. The upper half appears to have been adorned with scores of breasts, but these have also been interpreted as eggs or even dates, both symbols of fertility. The head was crowned, behind which rose a halo or nimbus.

Unlike temples on mainland Greece, that at Ephesos faced the west, towards Europe and thus towards the road from the city along which pilgrims hastened. The Temple which is regarded as the fourth Wonder of the World was the last to be completed at Ephesos, commenced during the reign of Alexander the Great. It resembled its immediate predecessor in all but height, and in this respect it was the largest of all Greek temples.

Figure 19 is a plan of the later, Alexandrine temple. It stood on a platform with a base measurement of 239 by 436 feet, covering an area of 2.4 acres. A series of nine or ten steps raised the stylobate (the top of the platform) clear of the marshy surroundings. Climbing the steps one first paused on a flat promenade which bordered the peristyle, and one must ascend a further three or four steps before entering the impressive colonnade.

The temple was octastyle tripteral: the front was flanked by

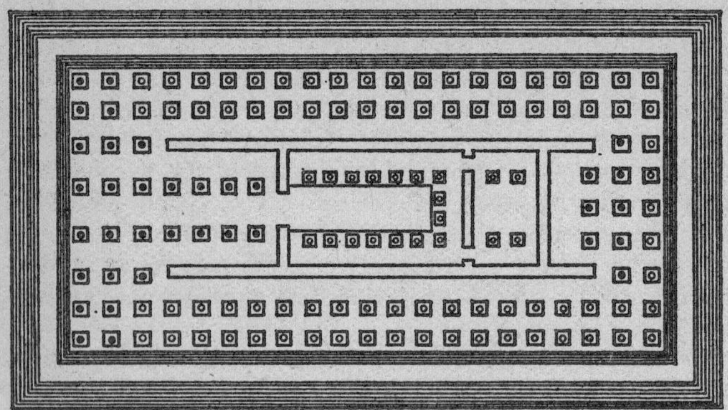

Denotes columns

Denotes sculptured columns

Figure 19. Plan of the Alexandrine Temple of Artemis at Ephesos. (Based on reconstructions by J. Fergusson, W.R. Lethaby and W.B.Dinsmoor)

three rows of eight columns. They were set about twenty feet apart, were six feet in diameter and fifty-eight feet high.[1] In all there were 117 columns,[2] and Pliny the Elder tells us that thirty-six were sculptured (*caelatae*).[3] As the remains of the temple are scant it is almost impossible to be certain where these *caelatae* columns stood, but Professor W. B. Dinsmoor has devised a possible layout as shown in Figure 19. He suggests that sixteen sculptured columns constituted the first two rows of the entrance, with a further twelve in the pronaos and the remainder in the opisthodomus. Recent research by the Austrian Anton Bammer has introduced the revolutionary theory that the columns were sculpted not only at the base but also just below the capital.

Above the columns rose a decorated entablature scarcely ten feet high and above that was the tympanum and pediment. Three large openings, like windows, were left in the tympanum to relieve the entablature of the weight of the pediment. These windows were probably concealed by sculpture.

The overall height of the temple to the ridge of the pediment was probably about 110 feet. The cella measured 48 by 21 feet, although there was a screened recess behind the giant statue of Artemis which stood on a plinth. Steps within the cella raised the inner sanctum above the stylobate. The dimensions of the earlier 'archaic' temple were very similar. It stood on a crepidoma of only two steps which reduced the total size of the base to 181 by 377 feet. The columns were also smaller, probably only about 41 feet high.

As so little remains of either temple it is difficult to assess what form the decorative friezes and sculptured columns took. Pliny tells us that one of the columns of the Alexandrine temple was the work of the very popular Skopas of Paros. It has puzzled scholars why Pliny should single out just one of the thirty-six for mention, since Praxiteles, another very popular artist who produced a number of statues for the altar, may well have sculpted columns himself, especially as the best-preserved surviving drum bears comparison with his style. The German philologist J. Sillig suggested that the correct translation of Pliny's text implies that Skopas assisted as architect as well as sculptor.[4]

The surviving column shows Hermes conducting Alkestis to the Underworld, being led by Thanatos (Death). It derived from the legend of King Admetos, whom the Fates allowed to live provided someone died in his place. At the point of his death his wife, Alkestis, offered herself, but she was saved by Herakles who was on his way to complete one of his twelve labours. He wrestled with and defeated Thanatos and delivered Alkestis back to the world of the living.

A sculptured column of the archaic temple also survived but merely portrays an unidentified figure, possibly Lydian, one of a number that surround the base.

Closely associated with the Temple is the legendary race of Amazons, the renowned female warriors who cut off their right breasts so as not to hinder the use of the bow. The Amazons, who were probably the beardless Scythian and Mongol nomads who settled in Anatolia from the Caucasus Mountains in the thirteenth century B.C., are supposed to have founded Ephesos. Within the sanctum were four statues of Amazons, far from breastless, and sculpted, according to

Pliny, by Phidias, Polykleitos of Argos, Kresilas of Kydonia, and Phradmon of Argos, all contemporaries. A story exists, reported by Pliny[5], that these four, present at Ephesos, voted amongst themselves on the merits of the statues with the result that Polykleitos was voted first, Phidias second and Kresilas third.

The significance of the Amazons can possibly give us a clue to the nature of some of the friezes or sculptures, as a number of their escapades feature strongly in Greek myth. The ninth of Herakles's twelve labours was to secure the girdle of Hippolyte, Queen of the Amazons. Herakles was at first well received, but the goddess Hera spread forth the rumour that Herakles was about to abduct Hippolyte at which point the Amazons seized their weapons. A battle followed in which Herakles killed the Queen and escaped with the girdle.

In another version Herakles was accompanied by Theseus who abducted the Queen's sister Antiope.[6] To avenge her, the Amazons invaded Attica but were defeated by Theseus. Antiope bore Theseus a son, Hippolytus, who became a famous hunter and charioteer, and favourite of Artemis. Banished because of alleged misconduct with his stepmother Hippolytus was killed when a sea-monster frightened his horses and he was thrown from his chariot.

In the Trojan War the Amazons sided with Troy and a famous battle took place between Achilles and the Amazon Queen Penthesilea. Achilles was victorious but he later grieved over the dying queen because of her valour and beauty.

All these incidents doubtless have a grain of truth in the battles between the early Greek settlers and the natives of Anatolia, and the legends that arose lent themselves admirably to the artists and sculptors of classical Greece.

The temple was also richly decorated with paintings, most notably those by Apelles, the greatest of all Greek painters. A friend of Alexander the Great, he painted a picture of the king wielding a thunderbolt on horseback. Apparently Alexander was not taken with the picture but his horse, Boukephalos, whinnied with delight at his own representation which prompted Apelles to remark that his horse was a better judge of paintings than Alexander. Apelles also painted a scene of the procession of the High Priest of the Temple along the road to the town and into the theatre. The Temple was administered by a sizeable staff of eunuch priests and virgin priestesses, plus a retinue of temple slaves. Every year in the month of Artemision (March-April) there was a festival in honour of the goddess which included a procession through the streets bearing statuettes of Artemis. At this time tens of thousands of people would flock to Ephesos from all over the Mediterranean.

The Temple was built predominantly in white marble, with doors and supports from cypress and cedar timbers, all decorated in gold and bright paints. Although we can only reconstruct the Temple by guesswork, it is not difficult to imagine that the pilgrim would be overcome by its beauty and grandeur, and no doubt felt that he was entering not just a simple place of worship but an Olympian Hall of the gods. But they would have appreciated that there was more to this Wonder than its beauty. Within its portals they would be humbled by the weight of historic significance. Here was the greatest Temple in the Greek world, but it was one that was rebuilt twice, both times at the request of conquering kings. But as they bowed to the goddess none would believe that in a few centuries Artemis would stand aside to another divine Mother, the Virgin Mary.

'GREAT IS ARTEMIS OF THE EPHESIANS'

A settlement existed at Ephesos long before the Greeks arrived. Under the name of Apashash it is mentioned in the *Annals* of the Hittite king Mursilis II (1345-1315 B.C.) when the god Teshup struck down the king of Apashash with a fireball. This was possibly a meteorite from which stone the statue of Cybele-Artemis was later sculpted.

Greece in the eleventh century B.C. was a land of legends. It was a time of upheaval with the Dorian invasion eclipsing the Mycenaean culture and scattering tribes throughout the Aegean. Heroes became super-heroes and myths rapidly surrounded their exploits. One of the last valiant stands was that of the Ionian king Kodros of Athens. Kodros learned from an oracle that if he lived, Attica would fall, so he vowed to sacrifice his life for his land. Disguised as a peasant he entered the enemy Dorian camp and started a fight with the first soldier he saw. He was promptly killed by another. The Dorian attack was repulsed and Athens saved. When the Athenians learned of the sacrifice they agreed that no one could succeed him as king. His son, Medon, was appointed the first of the hereditary archons, and Athens's long journey on the road to democracy and supremacy began.

In the meantime other sons of Kodros set sail to new lands. Neleos led his followers to the settlement of Miletos, seized the territory and slew all the native Karians. As a consequence it was maintained that the Milesians were the only pure-bred Ionians in Asia Minor. Another son, Androklos, brought his followers to the settlement of Ephesos, but here the invasion was peaceful and in time the Ionians and Karians blended into one community.

Here the Ionians discovered the worship of Kubele, at a shrine in the sacred grove of Ortygia. Now Ortygia was also the original name for the island of Delos, the legendary birthplace of Artemis, and it may have been this association that sparked the Ionians into identifying other attributes of Kubele with Artemis.

For several centuries the shrine consisted merely of a simple altar approached by steps of yellow limestone set within an open precinct. Then in the seventh century B.C. the Ionians found themselves facing a double menace, the Lydians and the Cimmerians.

The Lydians, distant cousins of the Karians, were a warlike race with their capital at Sardis, scarcely sixty miles inland from Ephesos. In 680 B.C., Gyges, a general in the service of the Lydian king Kandaules, usurped the throne and embarked upon a series of sieges against the Ionian cities. He took Kolophon, a dozen miles north-west of Ephesos, in 665 B.C., but then had to divert his forces back to Sardis where the capital was under attack from the Cimmerians.

The Cimmerians were nomads from the steppes of southern Russia driven south by the infiltration of the Scythian tribes. In 657 B.C. they captured Sardis, except for the citadel, and in their triumph they swooped along the Ionian coast. The original shrine to Artemis at Ephesos was destroyed. The

Ephesians promptly set about restoring and fortifying the shrine. It was raised upon a platform of green schist and surrounded by a low rectangular wall. It has been postulated that the origin of the Greek temple was an increase in the belief that the gods required a proper house for their earthly sojourns. Certainly the first great temples were built at about the same time, but it would seem more as a result of a protective defence than for any reason of domiciling the gods, which probably came as an afterthought in times of peace.

The first temple (or second sanctuary) did not last for long. Ardys, the son of Gyges, temporarily repulsed the Cimmerians and renewed his attacks upon Ionia, conquering Priene. In 627 B.C. the Cimmerians advanced again, sacking Magnesia, and destroying the temple at Ephesos. The war between the Cimmerians and Lydians continued until the reign of King Alyattes (605-560 B.C.). Having finally repulsed the nomads he now focused all his forces on the coastal Greek cities, especially Miletos. Sieges were maintained for years and though some cities fell others, like Miletos, continued to trade and prosper in defiance of the Lydians. Alyattes realized that without a fleet of his own he could never capture a seaport and so he relinquished his positions and made peace with the Ionians.

It was a wise and practical peace. The Ionians continued to expand their influence along the coast, the Milesians founding colonies as far north as the Black Sea, and prospered accordingly. The Lydians could now channel their defences to the eastern boundary of the empire where conflict was brewing with the burgeoning Median empire under King Kyaxares. The inevitable collision came on 28 May 585 B.C., on the banks of the River Halys, but the battle was never resolved. In the midst of the struggle the sun was eclipsed by the moon, and the opposing armies were so stricken by this omen that they ceased fighting and sought peace. We know from Herodotus that the philosopher Thales of Miletos had predicted the eclipse and the date has now been computed scientifically. Its significance is that it is the earliest precise date accurately assigned to a specific historical event.

The result of the peace between the Lydians and Medes was the marriage of Alyattes's daughter Aryenis to Kyaxares's heir Astyages. The reader may remember from the chapter on Babylon that Kyaxares's daughter Amytis was married to Nebuchadnezzar, so that there now existed a formidable triple alliance between the Lydians, Medes and Babylonians controlling the Middle East from the Euphrates valley to the Ionian coast.

With this enviable security it was inevitable that the Lydians would again try to wrest control of the important seaports from the Ionians. The offensive was revived by Alyattes's successor Kroisos who came to the throne in 560 B.C. He promptly marched on Ephesos where the siege took a bizarre turn.

By now the Ephesians had rebuilt the Temple to Artemis. It consisted simply of the cella and an entrance porch – the pronaos. The walls of mud-brick were surmounted by small, overhanging eaves, but as these were little protection against the weather, a row of columns of cypress wood was placed along each flank and across the front of the pronaos.

The Ephesians appealed to the religious nature of Kroisos. Unlike his predecessors he was an admirer of Greece and worshipped Artemis and Apollo. Sardis was the centre for Kubele worship, and the Ephesians hoped Kroisos would spare the Temple. They stretched ropes between the Temple and the town, securing the walls and the pronaos columns. It was not intended as a physical defence; the Ephesians were declaring that if the city fell so would the Temple.

It worked. Kroisos respected the stratagem and granted the Ephesians their liberty in return for their homage to him. The Ephesians, then ruled by a tyrant called Pindaros, readily agreed. Pindaros was exiled and Ephesos submitted to Kroisos.

Kroisos's wealth has become proverbial, but he was no hoarder. He walked in fear of the gods and regularly made massive tributes to the temples of Apollo and Artemis, even as far afield as Delphi.[7] At Sardis, the centre for Cybele worship, Kroisos was having a magnificent temple constructed, and now he offered huge subsidies towards the reconstruction of a similar Temple to Artemis-Cybele at Ephesos to replace the one that Pindaros had allowed to fall into disrepair.

There could have been no more munificent conqueror than Kroisos, and thanks to his riches the fourth Wonder of the

World began to take shape. The master architect was a Cretan, Khersiphron from Knossos, but he did not work alone. He almost certainly used as his model for the Artemiseum the Temple of Hera, then nearing completion on the island of Samos. This was the first temple in the dipteral style, with the sanctum surrounded by two rows of columns. Herodotus called it 'the largest of all temples known to us' and regarded it as one of the greatest works in all Greece.[8]

The dimensions of the Hera temple were 174 by 314 feet, only slightly dwarfed by the Artemiseum when it was completed. The size of the temple meant it stretched into the marshland surrounding the sanctuary of Hera, and the architects had to divert a stream and strengthen the foundations.

When Khersiphron came to look at the site of the Temple of Artemis, he discovered much the same situation. The land around the sanctuary was a swamp watered by springs feeding the Kaystros, a site chosen to lessen the likelihood of damage by earthquake, but a most unsatisfactory base for a mighty temple. To help him therefore, Khersiphron called upon the Samian family of architects headed by Rhoekos.

Rhoekos was the designer of the Heraeum, and he was credited as being the first to cast statues in bronze and iron. He is also credited with having produced the giant statue of Artemis from the meteorite that fell nearly eight hundred years earlier, and as this meteorite was likely to contain a high percentage of iron, Rhoekos is a favourable candidate.

He had two sons, Theodoros and Telekles. Telekles also had a son named Theodoros, and this son and his uncle are frequently confused. It is now generally accepted that the elder Theodoros was the architect whilst the younger was a sculptor of statuary.

At Ephesos, Theodoros the Elder (*c* 600-540 B.C.) adopted the same technique as he had at Samos, and packed the ground with many layers of charcoal interspersed with fleeces of wool. Upon this foundation Khersiphron now laid his platform, a solid block of masonry covered by a marble pavement. Khersiphron's technique here is somewhat questionable as there were no adequate foundations allowed in the platform for the walls or columns.

Khersiphron had designed the Temple as octastyle, but because of the dimensions this resulted in long spans between the columns. They averaged about twenty feet, but the central span between the fourth and fifth columns was twenty-eight feet. Since the architraves were of marble the operation of raising just one lintel to rest atop this entranceway was a feat in itself. But Khersiphron was equal to the task, as was his son Metagenes, who helped with the construction. They piled a mountain of sandbags between the columns until it was slightly higher than the capitals. Then, by a rope hoist and sling they raised the architrave until it rested atop the bags. The bottom layer of sandbags was then ripped, and as the sand spilled out, so the lintel slowly settled on to the columns, allowing ample time for minute manoeuvres to align the lintel accurately.

Nevertheless this operation was exhausting, and it is not surprising that the lintels to the inner columns were of wood, whilst the rear of the temple had nine columns, thus reducing the span. Quite apart from the raising of the lintels was the problem of both their transportation and that of the drums which made up the columns from the marble quarries eight miles distant.

Khersiphron was responsible for the drums and, after they had been roughly shaped, he turned a drum on its side and built around it a wooden frame linked to the drum by a central pivot. The frame was then harnessed to a team of oxen and hauled along like a road-roller. Once on the site the column flutes could be sculptured. Metagenes, who was concerned with the lintels, could not roll them in the same manner, so he fitted wide wheels to their sides and transported them that way. We know of the resourcefulness of these early architects because both Theodoros and Khersiphron wrote books about their achievements. Regrettably neither survives, but the Roman engineer Vitruvius quoted much of the relevant detail.

Work on the Temple was slow. The Heraeum on Samos had never been satisfactorily completed, and it might have seemed the same fate would befall the Artemiseum. Columns bearing an inscription to Kroisos have been found, so it is probable that the temple was substantially completed during his reign, which ended abruptly in 546 B.C. Work on the cornices and other roof appurtenances were left unfinished. The sanctum was not roofed over, and a drain existed to remove any floodwater. This was once interpreted as belonging to a sacred pool which may well have existed as a disguise for the overflow.

Pliny tells us that the temple took 120 years to complete, though there is no reason to assume work was continuous for that period. We have no idea of the ages of Khersiphron or his son, but it would be unreasonable to presume they lived beyond 500 B.C., as work probably commenced on the Temple soon after Ephesos submitted to Kroisos, possibly about 555 B.C. It is possible Pliny's text has been wrongly copied (it would not be the only example), or that he was referring to the Alexandrine temple (of which more in a moment), but there are ways of reconciling this figure as we shall see.

What probably happened is that some of the more grandiose aspects of the building were abandoned in 546 B.C. when the security of the Lydian Empire dissolved, and the temple was hurriedly completed. The fall of Kroisos is almost as legendary as his wealth. In 546 B.C. he determined to quash the expanding nation of Persia under Cyrus, and the two armies met in a bloody but indecisive battle near the River Halys. Presuming the battle over, Kroisos returned to Sardis only to find the Persians in hot pursuit. On his way home he had disbanded his army, unaware of the impending peril, so that he was defeated by the sheer weight of numbers. After a brief siege, Sardis fell.

All this happened on the very doorstep of Ionia and the Greeks, who had regarded Kroisos as a friend, were shaken. For the next two years Ionia was besieged by the Persians, and one by one the cities capitulated. Finally only Samos retained its independence since its tyrannical ruler, Polykrates, commanded a powerful fleet. His greed was his downfall, however. In 522 B.C. he was lured to the mainland with promises of great treasures, but was captured at Sardis and crucified.

The Persian Empire, which had started to crumble upon the death of Cyrus in 529 B.C., was now re-formed with even greater strength under Darius in 521. He organized it into twenty-four provinces, or *satrapies*, each under its own governor, or *satrap*. Artaphernes, Darius's own brother, was *satrap* of Ionia.

The Ionian revolt of 500 B.C. and the subsequent Persian invasion of Greece has already been related in the previous chapter. When Xerxes returned ignominiously after the Battle of Salamis in 480 B.C., he wreaked his revenge on the cities in Ionia. However in the following year a confederate Greek fleet landed at Mykale, near Miletos, and an army attacked and devastated the Persians. The Ionian cities promptly declared their independence.

It was not the end of the Persian Wars, which continued sporadically for a further thirty years. Ionia was the inevitable battleground and there was clearly little time or finance for major construction projects. In 448 B.C., however, the Athenian negotiator Kallias was sent to the court of the Great King Artaxerxes Makokheir ('the long-handed') at Susa. Although no formal agreement was concluded a working peace was arranged with the Ionians maintaining their independence.

If we assume Pliny's 120 years began in 555 B.C., it brings us to the year 435 B.C., thirteen years after the peace treaty. In those thirteen years, which we know saw the heyday of Athens, the Ionian cities prospered as never before with trade thriving between the Greeks and Persians. Now was a period when the Ephesians could let their thoughts return to the Temple so inadequately completed with the fall of Kroisos. It probably required some maintenance as well as improvement, and additional embellishments were made to the roof and gables. We do not know for sure the architect who concluded this work though it was possibly Paeonius of Ephesos, assisted by a temple slave, Demetrios. Paeonius is usually assigned a later date because he is associated with Daphnis of Miletos in the rebuilding of the Temple of Apollo at Didyma, another giant, in about 313 B.C. However Strabo infers that work began on this temple soon after its destruction by Darius in 494 B.C., and it was so large that work was incomplete even in the days of the Roman Emperor Caligula in A.D. 40. It is quite feasible therefore that Paeonius lived in about 440 B.C., and because of his work on completing the

Artemiseum he was commissioned to design the new Temple of Apollo which work later passed to Daphnis.

Herodotus, who hailed from Halikarnassos, a Dorian colony a hundred miles south of Ephesos, probably knew of the Temple from his youth and certainly visited it at this time. With customary restraint, he refers to it as 'a building worthy of note', but this in the same breath as 'the pyramids likewise surpass description'.[9] So in the historian's eyes the archaic Temple of Artemis was certainly classifiable as a World Wonder, and would no doubt have been so honoured had it survived the Alexandrian era.

But it did not. On the night of 13-14 October 356 B.C., a youth called Herostratos burned it down. His reason was solely to perpetuate his name, which signifies the importance of the Temple since he chose it above all others. And of course it worked. The Ephesians passed a decree condemning the youth to oblivion and heavily punishing anyone who dared even whisper his name. However, the historian Theopompos of Khios, then writing his *Histories* recorded the name for posterity. Hence the seventeenth-century writer Sir Thomas Browne quipped: 'Herostratos lives that burnt the Temple of Diana, he is almost lost that built it.'

What really perpetuated the name of this vandal was not his desire for immortality but an astonishing, if manufactured, coincidence. The poet Hegesias of Magnesia, who lived perhaps sixty or so years after the incident, was compiling his biography of Alexander the Great, now lost. Wishing to attach significance to the birth of the king he maintained that Alexander was born on the same night that Herostratos destroyed the Temple and that Artemis was unable to save it as she was on more urgent business in Macedonia.[10] Although Hegesias was ridiculed by his colleagues, this coincidence became famous and by this strange quirk Herostratos achieved his desire.

In 336 B.C., Philip II was murdered and Alexander, scarcely twenty, was proclaimed king. In the century since the peace with Persia, the Persians had nevertheless involved themselves in Greek affairs and Artaxerxes II conducted a six-year war with Sparta from 399-394 B.C. After the Battle of Khaeronea in 338 B.C., when the Macedonians routed the Greeks, the

Greeks agreed to renew the war with Persia, with Philip II as commander. After his assassination the command went to Alexander, and in May 334 B.C., the army began the long march into history.

During the Spartan-Persian War, Ephesos had formed the headquarters for the Spartan king Agesilaos II, and after the War the Spartan diplomat Antalkidas negotiated a treaty which placed several Ionian cities back under Persian control. This included Ephesos, and in 387 B.C., Antalkidas handed the city over to the Persophile and tyrant Syrphax.

Syrphax's tyrant successors were still in control in 333 B.C. when Alexander's army marched on Ephesos. The Persians sought sanctuary in the ruins of the Temple, but for once this tradition was ignored. The tyrants were dragged from the Temple and stoned to death. Alexander liberated Ephesos but advised the citizens not to take further revenge upon the Persians. That was his glory. He stayed in Ephesos for several months planning his campaign, and he offered sacrifices to the goddess in the midst of the Temple ruins. Alexander expressed his wish to help finance a new Temple, to which the Ephesian nobles tactfully replied: 'It is not fitting for a god to build a temple to a god.'

Nevertheless the money was forthcoming, as well as the assistance of Alexander's architect, Deinokrates, who helped not only with the new Temple but in replanning the city.

As we have seen the Temple was built on the same plan as its predecessor, only higher. There was the matter of overcoming the problem of flooding, water having seeped into the building over the centuries. The elaborate system of drains had not sufficed, and the resolution was to raise the platform from the original two steps to ten.

One of the most impressive features of the new temple were the thirty-six specially commissioned sculptured columns. Various rulers contributed towards their cost, just as Kroisos had two centuries earlier.

Although Deinokrates probably designed the new Temple, it is unlikely that he was the supervising architect as Alexander required him for more urgent duties in Egypt. I have already mentioned that a possible translation of Pliny's text implies that Skopas performed this duty. In addition a clue is provided by the introduction of square bases for the columns. This concept had originated with the Temple of Apollo at Priene completed in 334 B.C., and was the work of Pytheos. It is quite possible for Skopas and Pytheos to have been involved as both had recently worked on another World Wonder, the Mausoleum at Halikarnassos.

Pliny's statement regarding the 120-year period for completing the Temple is sometimes attributed to the Alexandrine one, which would mean it was not finished until 213 B.C. However, we have seen that such a time scale is well suited to the archaic temple. At that time temple building on such a scale was in its infancy and the fall of the secure Lydian Empire would have severely crippled resources. It is true that Alexander's Empire fractured after his death in 323 B.C., and it is unlikely that the Temple was complete at that stage – for all the anecdote about Apelles's painting. In the fight for power that followed the Conqueror's death, Ionia finally fell to Lysimakhos, and in about 290 B.C., he ordered a complete rebuilding of Ephesos.

The Kaystros brought with it large quantities of silt down from the mountains and the deposits were blocking the harbour. A new one was built, plus a five-mile wall about the city. The city centre was a large public forum, or agora, a market place in the middle of which was a small artificial lake. Between the agora and Mount Pion a new theatre was constructed, and just to the north a new stadium and gymnasium.

The Temple remained a mile beyond the city walls, near the old town. Lysimakhos called the new town Arsinoeia, after his wife Arsinoe, the daughter of Ptolemy Soter, but the name reverted to Ephesos after his death in 281 B.C. He transferred the populations of old Ephesos, Kolophon and Lebedos to the new town and made it the leading port in Asia Minor. It is inconceivable to imagine that during this period of rebuilding the Temple was not completed to everyone's satisfaction.

The Ephesians surely felt the favour of Artemis was upon them in return for the glorious Temple. Over the next few centuries they had the fortune always to choose the right side in the various wars that raged about the Aegean. Even their errors worked in their favour. In the war between Antiokhos III of Syria and the Romans, Ephesos sided with the Syrian who was defeated in 190 B.C. The Romans took Ephesos and handed it to the Roman ally, Eumenes II, king of Pergamon, a great scholar and builder. His successor, Attalos II, enlarged the harbour and docks, and as a consequence the importance of Ephesos soared. In 133 B.C. it passed back to the Romans who made it the capital of the province of Asia.

The only black spot in its history at this point came in 88 B.C., when Mithridates the Great, king of Pontus, usurped the province of Asia and entered Ephesos. Discontent over heavy Roman taxes was rife in the city and Mithridates aroused the Ephesian tempers. The Roman residents of the city, believed to number about 80,000, were all massacred. However, when the Ephesians realized the tide was turning in favour of Rome, they sided against Mithridates and were thus spared the wrath of Sulla. When he landed in Ephesos to reorganize the administration his only punishment was to levy even greater taxes than before.

Mithridates accomplished one other matter of consequence. The Temple had for centuries served as both a bank and a sanctuary. No one dared violate the Temple, which effectively meant it was the safest place to keep valuables. At the same time criminals could find sanctuary within the Temple, and in an area around it, consequently it was the only place where both criminals and treasures were safe together! The orbit of the sanctuary had been set by Alexander at about one stade (202 yards). Mithridates extended this sanctuary by firing an arrow from the temple to a point a little beyond one stade. When Mark Antony and Cleopatra visited the city in 33 B.C., he decided to extend the sanctuary even farther and brought it to within the limits of the city, an absurd situation as it allowed criminals free licence within the town. In 6 B.C., the Emperor Augustus reduced the boundary to its former distance, and this would provide the archaeologist J. T. Wood with a valuable clue in his search for the Temple centuries afterwards.

Such was the importance of Ephesos as we enter the Christian Era. The town was the most important in Asia, and its Temple the most magnificent and the centre of the cult of Artemis/Diana.

Paul had stopped at Ephesos in the course of his Second Missionary journey and the Jews had pleaded for him to return, which he did in the winter of A.D. 52-53. He stayed for nearly three years preaching 'so that all those inhabiting the district of Asia heard the word of the Lord' (Acts 19.10). Opposition began to grow against him from the priests because of his miraculous powers. He was noted for the exorcisms he had performed in the name of Christ, and as a consequence the priests started to invoke the name of Christ in their exorcisms. A rumour rapidly spread that at one such exorcism the evil spirit had said, 'I know Jesus and I am acquainted with Paul; but who are *you*?' and the man possessed had attacked the exorcists. The physician Luke continues the story:

> This became known to all, both the Jews and the Greeks that dwelt in Ephesos; and a fear fell upon them all, and the name of the Lord Jesus went on being magnified. And many of those who had become believers would come and confess and report their practices openly. Indeed quite a number of those who practised magical arts brought their books together and burned them up before everybody. And they calculated together the prices of them and found them worth fifty thousand pieces of silver. (Acts 19. 17-19)

Paul's preaching was converting hundreds of people away from the worship of Artemis, and this troubled the silversmiths of the town. They had a very profitable trade in making replicas of the shrine of Artemis for pilgrims, and there was fear that their income would be greatly reduced by Paul's rival religion. One silversmith, a Greek called Demetrios, stirred the passions of his fellow craftsmen:

> 'Men, you well know that from this business we have our prosperity. Also, you behold and hear how not only in Ephesos but in nearly all Asia this Paul has persuaded a considerable crowd and turned them to another opinion, say-

> ing that the ones that are made by hands are not gods. Moreover, the danger exists not only that this occupation of ours will come into disrepute but also that the temple of the great goddess Artemis will be esteemed as nothing and even her magnificence which the whole of Asia and the inhabited earth worships is about to be brought down to nothing.' Hearing this and becoming full of anger, the men began crying out, saying: 'Great is Artemis of the Ephesians!' (Acts 19.25-28)

A riot followed and crowds captured Paul's companions Gaius and Aristarkhos, dragged them into the theatre and for two hours shouted, 'Great is Artemis of the Ephesians!'

> When, finally, the city recorder had quieted the crowd, he said: 'Men of Ephesos, who really is there of mankind that does not know that the city of the Ephesians is the temple keeper of the great Artemis and of the image that fell from heaven? Therefore, since these things are indisputable it is becoming of you to keep calm and not act rashly.' (Acts 19.35-36)

Eventually the crowd was dispersed and soon after Paul left Ephesos. But the seed was sown. Five years later Paul, then imprisoned in Rome, despatched Tychikos with a letter of encouragement for the growing Christian community in Ephesos. It soon became one of the most powerful Christian congregations, and subsequently one of the Seven Churches of Christendom. The apostle John spent the last years of his life (from A.D. 98) at Ephesos, and wrote his Gospel there. Tradition maintains that John had visited Ephesos earlier and had taken with him Mary, the mother of Jesus. Similarly Luke is supposed to have died and been buried there. The Bible is quiet on the final days of these and others, and there may well be some truth in the tradition. Certainly by the third century A.D. these beliefs were a strong foundation for the growing Church.

The growth of Christianity was not the only faith sapping the strength of Artemis. The cult of Emperor-worship had grown throughout the Roman world and during the reign of the tyrant Domitian (A.D. 81-96) the Ephesians raised a temple in his honour to the south-west of the theatre. They also raised one to Hadrian (117-138). Shortly afterwards one was built by Egyptian immigrants to their god Serapis, and possibly another for Isis. What had once been the sole domain of Artemis was now being shattered.

During the reign of the Emperor Decius (249-251) the Christians were persecuted with great severity, Decius passing a decree promoting the worship of Apollo, Artemis and Athene. At Ephesos seven Christian youths fled the persecutors and hid in a cave where they were walled in. Nearly two hundred years later the cave was discovered by a shepherd, and as he opened it, so the youths awoke. The Ephesians flocked to the cave where they were told the miracle had been worked to renew their faith in the resurrection. This is the legend of the Seven Sleepers of Ephesos. The Emperor Theodosius II heard the news and hurried to the city, but the youths had died. He declared that they should be buried in their cave and a church founded on the spot.

In the interim period the Temple of Artemis had suffered at the hands of the Goths who plundered it in 262, and although it was temporarily restored it was no longer venerated with such enthusiasm as in the days of Paul. In 290 the Christians began to build a church within the Temple sanctum but an earthquake damaged it and the idea was abandoned. But the cult of the Great Mother survived. Instead of Artemis, a Church to the Virgin Mary was raised by the Christians soon after A.D. 300, in an abandoned Roman corn exchange to the north of the harbour.

As for the ruins of the Temple of Artemis, this was readily used in building the Church of St John which overlooked the temple site from the north. The marble went for the walls, and the beautiful statues were smashed for use as mortar. The Christians must have taken great relish in destroying the Temple, the greatest single symbol of pagan worship. They were thorough, for the Temple was devastated, and what remained was soon reclaimed by the marshes. Paul had triumphed.

THE MISSING WONDER

The importance of Ephesos remained but now it had become established as a Christian centre, rather than for the worship of Artemis. It became a centre for meeting of the Ecumenical Council, the third meeting in A.D. 431 being of import because it was then that the members agreed to accept the statement that Jesus was the Son of God. The city continued to flourish, especially during the reign of Emperor Justinian (527-565), when many major building works were completed. However, the continual deposits of silt by the Kaystros made the harbour costly and unmanageable, and the city was eventually abandoned for a new one located near the original site, and now called Ayasoluk. The name was changed by the Turks

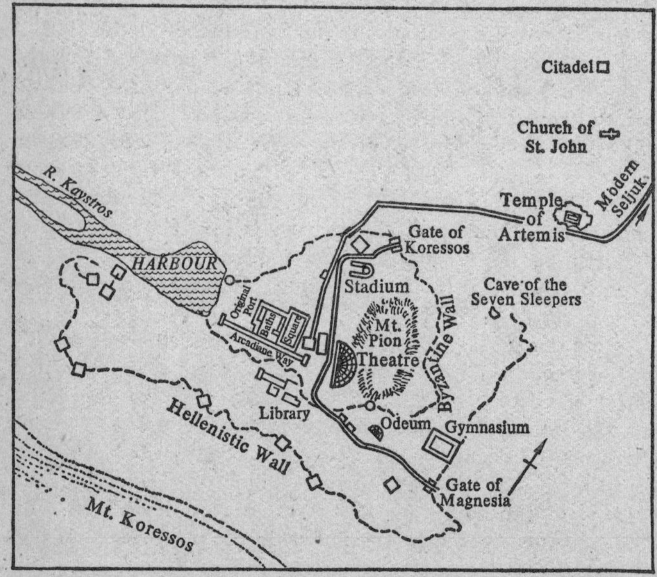

Figure 20. Partial Plan of Ephesos.

in 1914 to Selçuk, and in recent years it has seen some redevelopment.

When Richard Chandler of the Dilettanti Society visited Selçuk in 1764 he puzzled as to how 'a World Wonder could vanish like a phantom without leaving a trace behind'.

This was the scene that faced the English archaeologist J. T. Wood (1821-90) when, under the auspices of the British Museum, he went in search of the Temple of Artemis. Ancient Ephesos was not hard to find since scanty remains of the walls had survived, but whilst Wood was captivated by the beauty of the natural surroundings, the Temple eluded him. All he had as guidelines were vague and ambiguous clues by the ancient Greek writers like Pliny and Strabo which only told him it was situated in a marshy plain within a mile of the city. By Wood's time the silting of the river (now called the Cayster) had extended the marshy plain several miles seaward, and Wood was first misled into searching to the west of the city.

After a year Wood discovered nothing and suspected that the Museum Trustees would not renew his grant. In anticipation of further funds, and in the hope of a more substantial clue to the Temple's location, he set to excavating the whole of the ancient city of Ephesos, starting at the theatre where Paul had faced the hostile crowds.

The money was forthcoming, but for a further five years Wood hunted in vain for the Temple. Each year he had to produce something worthwhile to coax the Museum trustees into providing further finances. In addition he was beset by a number of physical dangers. He fell from his horse and broke his collarbone, and in another year he was attacked and knifed by a Turkish fanatic. At last his determination and hard work were rewarded, but let him tell it in his own words:

> In March 1864 Mr Newton came to Ephesos. At that time it had occurred to me that the best way to find the Temple would be to find one or two of the ancient gates of the city, outside which I might perhaps find a well-worn road which might lead to the Temple. As the position of the gates could not be determined without extensive excava-

tions it was decided that Mr Newton should recommend the Trustees of the British Museum to grant me £100 for the exploration of the Odeum.[11]

The Odeum provided clues which led to the discovery of the Magnesian Gate where Wood made a further advance.

I eventually found a marble paved road, thirty-five feet wide, turning northward around Mt Coressus[12] with four distinct chariot-ruts deeply cut in it . . .

As I decided now to follow the road leading round Mt Coressus, I devoted all my energy to tracing its course up to the precincts of the temple; and I was duly authorized to devote the rest of my grant to its discovery, with a warning that I should have no more if I did not with it find the temple. At a short distance from the Magnesian Gate I found the remains of the portico built by a rich Roman named Damianus in the second century A.D. This portico, vaguely mentioned by Philostratos in his *Lives of the Sophists*, was intended to shelter people going from the city to the Temple and it ran alongside the road . . .

At the distance of 2600 feet from the Magnesian Gate were found remains of what I presume must have been the tomb of Androklos. Pausanias describes this tomb and the temple of Jupiter as being on the road from the Magnesian Gate to the temple. 600 feet beyond the tomb of Androklos I found the road I had been searching for leading off at right angles towards Ayasoluk. This road was forty-five feet wide, ten feet wider than the road I had been following, and it had handsome sarcophagi on each side. At the time I found this road I had nearly come to the end of my grant, and the barley had grown to its full height, about eight feet. I had no means of compensating the landowners if I cut down the barley but, tracing the direction of the road by taking advantage of one or two boundaries which crossed it at right angles I saw that it pointed to a modern boundary marked by some old olive trees and bushes which had long before attracted my attention. I now determined to put on a dozen men at this point and make a more extensive excavation. This resulted in the discovery of a thick wall of rough masonry. Extending the excavation I struck upon the angle of the wall and at about eight feet below the surface laid bare two inscriptions on the south side which were repeated on the west side. These inscriptions showed that I had discovered the peribolus wall of the temple described by Tacitus, which was built by Augustus to restrict the temenos or sacred precinct which had approached the city and facilitated the escape of the wrongdoer.

This important discovery was made on 2 May 1869. The search for the temple had commenced on 2 May 1863, and consulting my diaries I found that during this long period I had worked on my enterprise for twenty months. The day on which this wall with the inscriptions was found terminated the long period – six years – of great anxiety and misgiving, and of almost hopeless endeavour; and the discovery now made compensated for all.[13]

With the news of the discovery, the British Museum renewed Wood's grant and he recommenced his work in September.

At a distance of some hundred yards from the angle first found I struck upon a building which proved to be 700 feet long, running from west to east, in which I found at the depth of two feet, a beautiful Roman mosaic pavement of a Triton who is represented carrying in one hand a dish of fruit, in the other a pedum, or crooked stick, with which he obtained the fruit. A dolphin carries his trident in his mouth; a large dragonfly threatens to attack the fruit, but the Triton is guarding it with a watchful eye. Two small fish, which I suppose might even now be found in the Cayster, complete the group. The whole is surrounded by a guilloche border.[14]

Wood had discovered the Roman pavement that surrounded the base of the Temple, and his detailed description gives a good idea of how impressive the site must have been. Wood had triumphed. He continued his excavations until

1874 and in that time he uncovered all that remained of the Alexandrine temple, including the noted sculptured drum.

> The position in which this was found proved that it was part of one of the sculptured columns of the west front, which was, like the other columns, 6 feet ½ inch in diameter. It had fallen upon its side and the side which lay uppermost was to a great extent chopped away . . . It took fifteen men fifteen days to raise it up to the surface and I put it at once into a temporary wooden case to protect it from injury.[15]

I make no apology for quoting from Wood's work at great length since he transmits much of the excitement of his discovery into his writing, unlike many of the dry reports written by some archaeologists. One last comment. Early in 1870 Wood was visited by Heinrich Schliemann.

> Looking around he exclaimed in excited tones, 'So this is the veritable pavement of the Temple of Diana? Let me shake hands with you, Mr Wood, you have immortalized yourself.'[16]

Schliemann then confided in Wood his lifelong desire to find Troy, and in the following year he began his series of excavations which would immortalize his name.

Wood also found evidence of the pavement of the archaic temple, but dug no further. He returned to the site nine years later in 1883, but with little result. When A. S. Murray of the British Museum visited it in 1896 he reported that it was in a deplorable, overgrown state. It was left to David George Hogarth to further the excavations in 1904. Hogarth (1862-1927) was also financed by the British Museum and he determined to excavate to the lowest levels. Because of the marshy surroundings he had constantly to pump water out from the foundations, and considering the conditions, it is a wonder that anything had survived the two and a half thousand years from the time of the earliest shrine. Yet in his nine months at Ephesos, Hogarth found thousands of small golden statuettes and votive offerings. He traced the succession of shrines and excavated the archaic temple.

One would imagine that the site had been exhausted by then, but not so. Since 1898 the Austrian Archaeological Society has financed a number of excavations at Ephesos which have proved very fruitful. During the 1960s Dr Fritz Eichler unearthed two huge Roman apartment blocks six storeys high. They constituted a ground floor of shops and the upper storeys for flats and offices, no different to the tens of thousands of similar apartments throughout the modern world.

In the years since 1965, Anton Bammer has made an exhaustive study of the Artemiseum site, constantly hampered by the flood waters, but his determination resulted in the discovery of the altar of the Alexandrine temple.

A stir was caused in 1957 when Dr Franz Miltner unearthed two statues of the goddess Artemis. Hitherto Roman copies of the Ephesian Artemis had been found at several sites, but these were the first found at Ephesos. Neither was the meteorite-statue carved by Rhoekos, which still eludes hunters, but they were magnificent examples nonetheless. Both came to light on the site of the Prytaneion, or Town Hall. One was twice life size and has been dated to about A.D. 90. It stood in the courtyard to the Hall. The other, life-sized, and dated to about thirty years later, possibly stood within the main Hall. The Prytaneion was pulled down during the third century by a Christian woman named Scholastikia for her own building projects, but these statues were hidden beneath the floors of one of the side rooms. Since this must have happened shortly after the Temple itself had been plundered by the Goths, this hall may have been the last redoubt for Artemis worshippers, and they reverently wished to protect her image from the Christians. Somewhere in the heart of Christian Ephesos, the flame of wondrous Artemis still flickered.

NOTES ON CHAPTER V

1. In *Natural History* XXXVI.21 Pliny says the height of the columns is sixty feet (*LX pedum*), but these would be Ionic feet, equivalent to 11.5625 inches.
2. Pliny's report (op. cit.) states 127 columns, but archaeological evidence has proved otherwise and we can only conclude a copyist's error. However, there are ten columns within the cella, and though these are little more than decorative pillars, Pliny may not have thought it necessary to distinguish them.
3. *N.H.* XXXVI.21
4. The original text reads '. . . *columnae CXXVII a singulis regibus factae LX pedum altitudine, ex iis XXXVI caelatae, una a Scopa. operi praefuit Chersiphron architectus* . . .'
5. *Natural History* XXXIV. 75 (ibid. XXXIV. 53)
6. The wedding feast at the end of Shakespeare's *Midsummer Night's Dream* is to celebrate the marriage of Theseus and Hippolyte.
7. Herodotus I.50-52 lists some of these offerings.
8. Herodotus III.60. His other two great works were a tunnel and a mole, also on Samos, thus demonstrating the expertise of the Samian engineers.
9. Herodotus II.148
10. In all probability Alexander was born a month or more earlier if we have to reconcile the story of Philip II's Olympic victory with the same date.
11. *Modern Discoveries on the Site of Ancient Ephesus* by J. T. Wood (Religious Tract Society, 1890) p. 29
12. Wood confused the two hills. This was actually Mount Pion.
13. Wood (op. cit.) pp. 37-40
14. ibid. p. 42
15. ibid. pp. 48-9
16. ibid. p. 44

CHAPTER VI

DIGNITY IN DEATH: THE MAUSOLEUM AT HALIKARNASSOS

The contemporaries and rivals of Skopas were Bryaxis, Timotheos and Leokhares whom we must discuss along with him because together with him they worked on the carvings of the Mausoleum. This is the tomb that was built by Artemisia for her husband Mausolos, the viceroy of Caria, who died in the second year of the 107*th Olympiad. These artists were chiefly responsible for making the structure one of the seven wonders of the world.*
(Pliny *Natural History* 36.4.30)

The Mausoleum is at once the most obscure and intriguing of the Seven Wonders: intriguing because it was unique as a tomb, and obscure because although a number of ancient writers mention it Pliny is the only one who gives us a thorough – if ambiguous – description, as Philon's entry has regrettably vanished in the course of time. I would be the last to cast aspersions on Pliny's accuracy. The man was a dedicated investigator and met his death by too close an inspection of the eruption of Vesuvius, where he was overcome and suffocated by the fumes. The problem is that Pliny's *Historia Naturalis* was a best-seller in its day and copyists were hard put to keep up with demand. Errors were bound to creep in, a snag with many of the ancient texts, leaving us with a description of the tomb that can be only partly trusted. Consequently archaeologists have become increasingly fascinated by this ancient novelty with the result that there have probably been more varied artistic re-creations of the Mausoleum than any other building of antiquity.

THE CITY AND THE TOMB

Before looking at the Mausoleum and trying to resolve Pliny's report, let us see just where this vast tomb stood.

Halikarnassos was the new capital of the Persian satrapy of Karia, a land in the south-west corner of Asia Minor (see Figure 18 on page 156). The city was founded by the Dorians on one of the many long promontories that thrust themselves out into the south Aegean waters. It overlooks the island of Kos, whilst farther south is the peninsula of Knidos.

Some time after 377 B.C., Mausolos began a campaign of building and expanding Halikarnassos by uniting six of the surrounding localities to form one city-state. Today the site is almost totally covered by the town of Bodrum, and what excavations have been carried out have failed to identify all the known sites in the original city. We therefore have to rely for our knowledge of Halikarnassos on the writings of another Roman, the architect and engineer Marcus Vitruvius, who lived some time around 30 B.C.

> The place (Halikarnassos) has a curvature like that of the seats in a theatre. On the lowest tier, along the harbour, was built the forum. About half-way up the curving slope, at the point where the curved cross-aisle is in a theatre, a broad, wide street was laid out, in the middle of which was built the Mausoleum, a work so remarkable that it is classed among the seven wonders of the world. At the top of the hill, in the centre, is the fane of Mars, containing a colossal acrolithic statue by the famous hand of Leokhares. Others think it is by Timotheos. At the extreme right of the summit is the fane of Venus and Mercury, close to the spring of Salmacis . . . On the extreme left is the royal palace which King Mausolos built there in accordance with a plan all his own. To the right it commands a view of the market-place, the harbour and the entire line of fortifications, while just below it to the left there is a concealed harbour hidden under the walls in such a way that nobody could see or know what was going on in it. Only the king himself could, in case of need, give orders from his own

palace to the oarsmen and soldiers, without the knowledge of anyone else.[1]

Figure 21 is a hypothetical partial reconstruction of Halikarnassos. The Mausoleum, set half-way up the hill, was in a very prominent position and was visible for many miles across the sea, and it is possible that its fame first spread be-

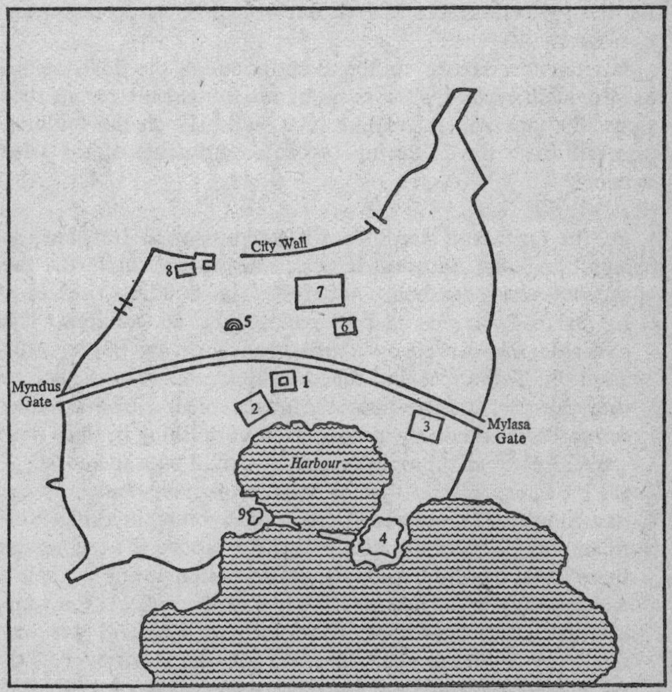

Figure 21. Suggested plan of Halikarnassos

1 Mausoleum
2 Agora (Market Square)
3 Royal Palace
4 Knight's Castle of St. Peter
5 Theatre
6 Temple of Demeter
7 Gymnasium
8 Temple of Ares (?)
9 Salmakis

cause of its aid as a naval landmark. It was almost certainly part of the original plan of the city, the location doubtless chosen by Mausolos himself, as would be expected by a king with his tomb. Otherwise such a conspicuous position would have been the site of a temple. If this was so then it clashes with the tale perpetuated by Pliny and others that Artemisia built the tomb in memory of her husband in much the same way as the Indian Emperor Shah Jahan built the famous Taj Mahal at Agra in 1630 as a testimony to his love for his dead wife Mumtaz Mahal. But I shall return to this question later.

Let us now return to the description of the Mausoleum as provided by Pliny, the basis of all subsequent reconstructions. Perhaps you might like to try and sketch the building yourself from the following before seeing some of the later versions.

> On the north and south sides it extends for 63 feet, but the length of the façades is less, the total length of the façades and sides being 440 feet. The building rises to a height of 25 cubits and is enclosed by 36 columns. The east side was carved by Skopas, the north by Bryaxis, the south by Timotheos and the west by Leokhares; and before they completed their task, the queen died. However, they refused to abandon their work without finishing it, since they were already of the opinion that it would be a memorial to their own glory and that of their profession; and even today they are considered to rival each other in skill. With them was associated a fifth artist. For above the colonnade there is a pyramid as high again as the lower structure and tapering in 24 stages to the top of its peak. At the summit there is a four-horse chariot of marble, and this was made by Pytheos. The addition of this chariot rounds off the whole work and brings it to a height of 140 feet.[2]

How did you do? It is not that straightforward, even though on first reading it seems as though all the facts are given. This was the problem that faced artists like Marten van Heemskerck and Fischer von Erlach, and their impressions fit the above description as accurately as more recent interpretations.

The first dilemma arises from the dimensions. If the two longer sides are both 63 feet then the total perimeter could not amount to 440 feet. At the start Pliny says the building is 25 cubits high (about 37 feet), but at the end he gives the total height as 140 feet. All we know for certain is that there is a building surrounded by a colonnade above which is a pyramid surmounted by a quadriga. Can we reconcile the other facts?

It was not until 1856 that Sir Charles Newton discovered the site of the Mausoleum and was able to measure the base. Since then further investigations have added substance to Pliny's description and give an opportunity to resolve his apparent contradictions.

The base of the Mausoleum measured 127 by 108 feet, giving a total perimeter of 470 feet. This is close to Pliny's 440 feet from which we must deduce that he had access to accurate figures and that we must interpret his report in a devious way in order to extract the hidden facts.

We have a clue in the 'building' 25 cubits high and 'enclosed by 36 columns'. This means that the columns must also have been 25 cubits high. He then says the pyramid is as 'high again as the lower structure'. Since the only lower structure mentioned is the building and colonnade the pyramid must also be 25 cubits, making fifty cubits in all, or about 75 feet. If the overall height is 140 feet there must be a further stage apart from the quadriga, and since the columns would be insufficient to support the remainder of the building we must deduce that this stage formed the base or podium of the tomb.

With this in mind the architects working on the problem of the Mausoleum's design perceived that the building was in four stages: a podium base, a colonnade surrounding a 'building' which probably corresponds with the cella of a temple, a pyramid roof, and a quadriga. Knowing the Greeks' desire for symmetry, and adapting Pliny's statistics, some surmised that the podium, colonnade and pyramid were all 42 feet high, leaving 14 feet for the quadriga, a proportion of 3:3:3:1.

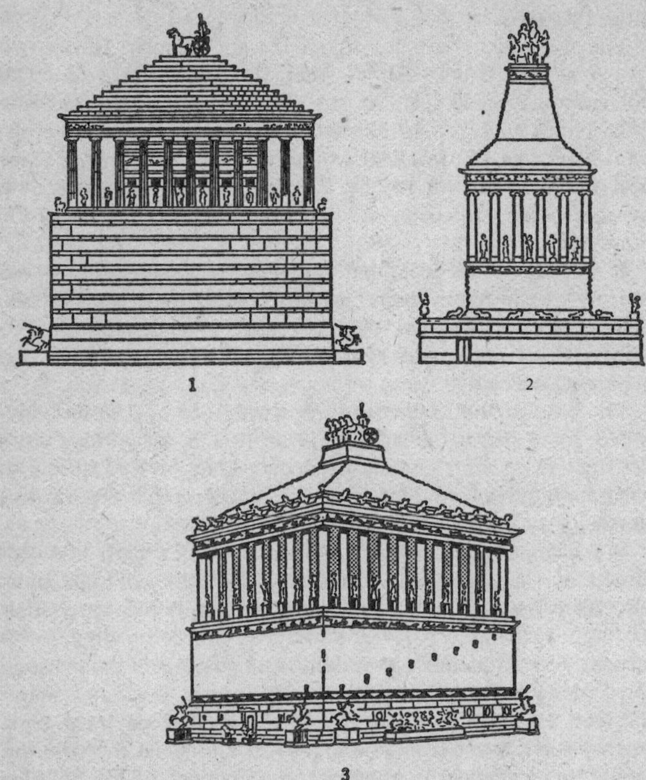

Figure 22. Suggested reconstructions of the Mausoleum. 1. C.T. Newton 2. J.J. Stevenson 3. F. Adler.

Not all architects agreed with this ratio, but the basic design was followed by all in their interpretations of the tomb (see Figure 22). The most recent and probably most accurate reconstruction is that still being assembled by Professor Kristian Jeppesen of Aarhus University in Denmark, although he emphasizes that the reconstruction attempted so far is still preliminary in several respects and that the final results are still to be published. His conclusions, which have been amended slightly by Britain's Dr Geoffrey Waywell, form the basis for the following description (see also Figure 23).

The podium was probably raised upon a platform of three giant steps each about ten feet high and faced with white marble. These levels were adorned with a variety of sculptures, complete on their own (unlike the frieze reliefs) but not intended as statues. Because they stood close against the superstructure wall the sculptors economically fashioned only those parts that would be visible and left the rear roughly shaped. The lowest level portrayed scenes from the battles between the Greeks and the Persians, a very topical subject. The second level carried portraits of members of Mausolos's family, whilst the top level represented a ritual funerary sacrifice of sheep and oxen.

The podium rose from the upper level. It too was faced with white marble and around its top was a frieze portraying the battle between the Greeks and the Amazons. It is the best preserved and most impressive of the Mausoleum friezes, carved on marble blocks three feet high and one foot thick.

Above the podium rose the colonnade with eleven columns on the sides and nine on the façades, including the four corner supports. Their base diameter was three feet seven inches, their height about thirty-three feet, and they were surmounted by a narrow entablature. Within the colonnade was the cella, itself adorned with a frieze depicting a chariot race. As we saw with the origin of the Olympian Games, chariot races were closely associated with funeral games, and it was an appropriate scene for the Mausoleum sanctuary.

Between the columns were further statues, and Jeppesen and Waywell believe that here stood the two impressive giants now preserved in the British Museum and long identified as Mausolos and his Queen. It was conjectured that these originally stood in the four-horse chariot surmounting the pyramid, but reasoning from their state of preservation and nature of sculpting (the rear was again rough) Waywell deduced they came from a lower level. There is still no reason entirely to discount the supposition that they represent Mausolos and Artemisia: the well-preserved face of the male shows all the signs of being carved from life and it bears

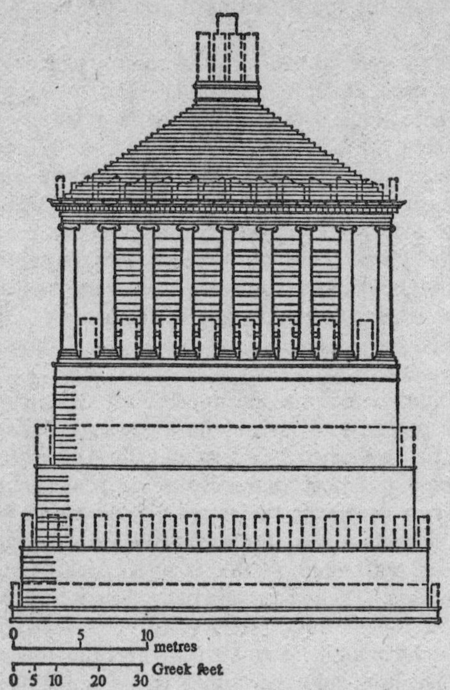

Figure 23a The Mausoleum from the East.
(based on reconstruction by Dr. G.B. Waywell)

comparison to the likeness of Mausolos on coins of his day. But it could equally well apply to his later successors Ada and Idrieos.

Rising above the colonnade was the pyramid. At its base, above the colonnade entablature, stood a series of sculpted lions, sixteen along the sides and twelve on each façade – an obvious adaptation of the Egyptian belief of the lion as guardian of the gates to the Underworld. The pyramid rose in a series of twenty-four equal steps to reach a plinth atop which stood the marble quadriga, or four-horse chariot.

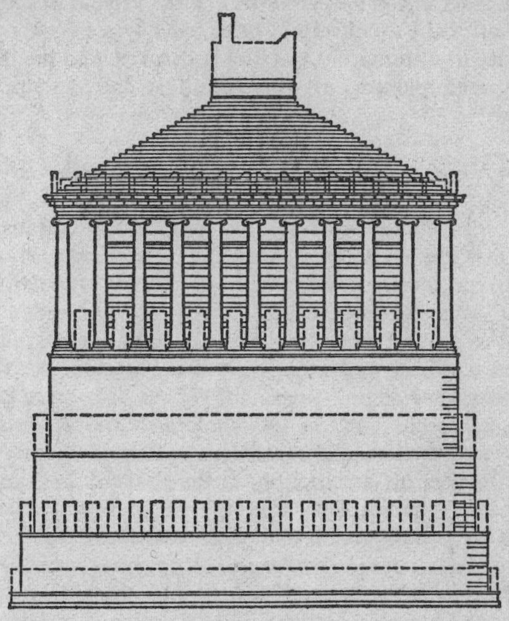

Figure 23b The Mausoleum from the South.
(based on reconstruction by Dr. G.B. Waywell)

Around the plinth was the inevitable frieze of the Centaurs and the Lapiths.

It is a generally held misconception that ancient statues and sculptures were completed only in bare stone. Originally they were gaily decorated with paints and it is only the constant weathering of centuries that has reduced them to their basic material. When Newton excavated fragments that had been buried for centuries he detected traces of the original colours preserved from exposure.

> From the examination of a number of fragments on their first disinternment I ascertained that the ground of the relief, like that of the architectural ornaments, was a blue, equal in intensity to ultramarine, the flesh a dun-red, and the drapery and armour picked out with vermilion and perhaps other colours.[8]

All of which added to the final beauty of the structure. At the outset I called it unique, and certainly in size and scope it was, but it was not quite original. The Mausoleum was rather the apex of a growing trend for such tombs amongst the Persians of which an earlier though much lesser building was the so-called 'Lion Tomb' at Knidos. However Professor Jeppesen believes that the model for the Mausoleum might well have been the Theseum, or Temple of Theseus, erected in Athens in 475 B.C. No trace of this building has been found as the whole area was cleared some time after 50 B.C. to make way for a Roman market-place. Jeppesen makes his assumption on the basis of the similarity between the Theseus cult, and the obvious cult Mausolos expected to centre about him after his death, that is as a *synoekist*, or one who brought peoples together into one state. Theseus had united several towns into the Athenian city state just as Mausolos did with Halikarnassos. Regrettably the architect of the Theseum is not known.

Surprisingly Newton's excavations did not discover the original tomb chamber beneath the Mausoleum. This was cut six feet into the bed-rock and measured about thirty feet long by twenty-six feet wide, and was entered by a wide flight of steps, which were subsequently covered to foil tomb-robbers.

The Mausoleum was set upon a wide terraced walk measuring about 265 by 115 yards. The terrace dropped away to the south to the area about the harbour, whilst beyond it to the north rose the Temple of Ares.

What of the men behind the Mausoleum? Pliny gave us their names and implied it was designed almost in the nature of a contest, with four sculptors allotted a side each, and no doubt hoping their results would outshine the others. Pliny does not mean that one artist worked solidly on each side. With the amount of sculpture known to exist, it would have been a lifetime work for all four. Neither can the artists have worked with complete independence as that would have resulted in an unevenness of style. The Greeks believed in healthy competition, but they also believed in artistic harmony. We know there were two presiding architects, Pytheos and Satyros, who would have planned the building and possibly suggested the decoration. The four artists then embellished this design, and they directed the works for the four sides, overseeing one or two pupils or apprentices and a number of assistant carvers.

We know little about the architect Satyros other than that he came from the island of Paros, like Skopas. It is possible he was already employed by Mausolos in the redesigning of Halikarnassos and consequently only assisted Pytheos marginally in the planning and execution of the Mausoleum. Pytheos, on the other hand, is of greater renown, although it is as a consequence of designs executed after the Mausoleum. In 340 B.C. he worked on the Temple of Athene Polias at Priene and may subsequently, as we have conjectured, have assisted with the completion of the Temple of Artemis. He wrote a treatise about his work at Priene in which he may have alluded to other commissions, but as the book has long since vanished we may never know.

From Pliny we learn that the great Skopas was responsible for the east side of the Mausoleum. This artist's trademark is betrayed in scenes of violent emotion and in some of the action-packed episodes of the Amazon frieze art historians fancy they have detected his hand. It is, of course, almost impossible to tell. It is only the desire to identify a sculpture as an original Skopas rather than a later copy that prompts such investigations, for alongside Pheidias and Praxiteles, Skopas was ranked as a genius. Pliny refers to a statue of Venus (Aphrodite) by Skopas that, in his estimation, surpasses the much revered Aphrodite at Knidos by Praxiteles.[4] Skopas was a native of Paros, one of the most attractive of the Cyclades group of islands in the Aegean and famed for its marble quarries. He was the son of Aristandros who worked on a number of memorials such as that at Amyklai (the ancient capital of the Mycenaeans) in Laconia. His father's connections with the Peloponnesos would probably explain the presence of Skopas at Tegea in Arkadia. Here a temple dedicated to Athene was destroyed by fire in 394 B.C. Work on a new temple did not begin immediately and although dating is uncertain it has been estimated to about 370-365 B.C. Curiously the fragment of a tablet was found in the excavations of a house near the Temple of Tegea inscribed with the names of Ada and Idrieos, the successors of Mausolos and Artemisia. It has been conjectured that as they did not begin to reign until 351 B.C., the Temple at Tegea was not commenced until after the Mausoleum, and although this theory cannot be disputed there is no reason to assume the tablet must be dated concurrently with the rebuilding of the Temple.

Skopas was both architect and chief sculptor for the Temple of Athene, a temple that Pausanias regarded as the most beautiful in the Peloponnesos. For the eastern pediment Skopas provided a dramatic scene from the Hunt of the Kalydonian Boar, another of the great sagas of Greek legend. It was particularly relevant to the Arkadian temple since, following the success of the hunt, Atalanta of Arkadia was awarded the hide of the Boar as her part of the spoils, and this was still preserved within the temple.

Pliny singles out for special mention a group sculpture by Skopas portraying Achilles accompanied by Poseidon and Thetis all riding dolphins and other sea creatures. It probably once adorned a temple in Bithynia, a region south of the Black Sea. He also sculpted a colossal statue of the war god Ares at Pergamum, and the number of his works completed in Asia Minor leads one to believe that he spent most of his life there.

Bryaxis has been assigned the dates 372-312 B.C., the latter date arising from the fact that Bryaxis cast a bronze statue of Seloukos Nikator who established himself as ruler of Syria in that year. However we should not overlook the possibility that Bryaxis could have been commissioned for this work some time between 321 and 316 B.C. when Seloukos was governor of Syria and Mesopotamia. If this was the case then we can reassign the sculptor's birthdate to about 380 B.C. This would have made him nearly thirty when he came to work at

Halikarnassos, a more likely age for eminence than a youth of twenty. According to Clement of Alexandria (*c* A.D. 150-220), Bryaxis attained such a degree of perfection that in later years his work was confused with that of Philias. The giant statue that might or might not represent Mausolos has been attributed to Bryaxis because it was found on the north side of the Mausoleum which was allotted to the sculptor. If so then Bryaxis was indeed an artist of impressive talent as anyone who has seen this statue in the British Museum will attest (see Plate 12).

Timotheos may have been the oldest of the artists at Halikarnassos. We know from the fortuitous survival of some ancient expense accounts that he worked upon the Temple to Asklepios at Epidauros in Argolis. Asklepios was the Greek god of medicine, derived from the Egyptian Imhotep, father of the Pyramids. The temple was started in about 380 B.C., and Timotheos was contracted to make the akroteria, or statues surmounting the apex and two corners of the pediment, for one façade, plus several reliefs for the pediment. As Timotheos received less money than the sculptor who provided the corresponding akroteria for the other temple façade, we can presume he was a younger and less accomplished artist at that time. On this basis we can probably place his birthdate at between 400 and 405 B.C., meaning he was in his fifties when at work at Halikarnassos.

After Skopas, Leokhares was the most distinguished sculptor working on the Mausoleum. He would later find favour with King Philip II of Macedonia and produce a series of chryselephantine statues of the king and his family for the Philippeion at Olympia. This building was founded to commemorate Philip's victory over the Athenians at Chaeronea in 338 B.C. Leokhares's probable date of birth was about 390 B.C., placing him in his forties when he designed the western side of the Mausoleum. Whilst at Halikarnassos he also made a colossal acrolithic statue (one of wood with only the extremities of stone) of Ares for his Temple. His most famous work was of Ganymede being borne aloft by an eagle, a representation of the legend whereby Zeus, taken by the beauty of the young son of King Tros of Troy, sent his eagle to bring the child to Olympus so that he might serve as his cup-bearer. Several interpretations of this work exist, all presumed to be copies of Leokhares's original, but nothing by the artist himself.

We can see therefore that the Mausoleum represented a convergence of both mature and flowering talent. Skopas, Timotheos and (possibly) Satyros had their credentials of excellent work elsewhere, whilst the more youthful Bryaxis, Leokhares and Pytheos were artists of promise, whose best work was yet to come, but who could add fresh ideas and enthusiasm to the older school.

With this concentration of talent the Mausoleum can only have been built at tremendous expense, yet it was only one of a number of major works in the new town, such as the Temple of Ares and the Palace of Mausolos. There is the story that after Artemisia died, the artists continued to work without thought of payment, and though such a sacrifice may exemplify the Greek ideal, it is not very likely that all six, not forgetting the scores of assistants, would waive their salaries. No, the money was there at the outset, or else the tomb could never have been envisaged. So let us see where Mausolos, ostensibly only a Persian governor, accumulated such riches to enable him to preserve his name for posterity, and make his tomb one of the Seven Wonders.

THE STORY OF HALIKARNASSOS

A century or so after the Ionians left Attica and founded cities like Miletos and Ephesos in Asia Minor, the Dorians followed. Three groups from Argos founded the cities of Lindos, Ialysos and Kameiros on the island of Rhodes, Lakonians founded Knidos, whilst settlers from Troezon established Kos and Halikarnassos some time around 900 B.C. These six towns formed the Doric 'Hexapolis', a league linked in the common worship of Apollo at Cape Triopium near Knidos. Here was held an annual festival with athletic contests and, at an early stage, Halikarnassos was expelled from the league because one of its citizens became a victor at the games but instead of dedicating his prize, a brazen tripod, to Apollo, he unsportingly took it home!

Halikarnassos thus had an early independence. As the northernmost of the Dorian towns it was heavily influenced by Ionia, and it is probable that the city rapidly became a fusion of Dorians, Ionians and Karians.

At the time of the Ionian revolt in 500 B.C., a Karian named Lygdamis set himself up as tyrant of Halikarnassos. The Persians had enough trouble on their hands, and as Lygdamis showed them no opposition, they let him be. In time he passed the rulership of the city to his daughter, Artemisia. It was she who excelled herself in the eyes of the Persian Great King Xerxes at the Battle of Salamis in 480 B.C. Herodotus, himself a native of Halikarnassos, was only four years old at the time of the battle, but he doubtless heard of the Queen's heroic exploits as a bedtime story.

Artemisia had advised Xerxes not to engage the Greeks in a sea battle at Salamis, but the weight of opinion was against her and Xerxes decided to fight, to his great cost. According to Herodotus it was Artemisia who advised the king to return to Asia after the battle leaving Mardonius to fight the Greeks. It was advice Xerxes readily accepted, and he entrusted some of his children to Artemisia, ordering her to take them safely to Ephesos.

Following this Artemisia was clearly in Xerxes's favour, and we can imagine that he allowed her and her son, Pisindelis, free rein in Halikarnassos. The city enjoyed privileges unlike its neighbours for, provided it maintained allegiance to Persia, its rulers were allowed to do as they wished. Naturally such freedom led to corruption, and Artemisia's grandson, Lygdamis II, governed as a despot. The epic poet Panyasis, an uncle of Herodotus's, was put to death by order of Lygdamis for supposedly treasonable activities. Herodotus fled for safety to the island of Samos where he resided for some six years. He returned to Halikarnassos some time about 450 B.C., and reputedly either led or was involved with an insurrection against Lygdamis which finally freed the city of the tyrant. The citizens now turned to Athens for security and joined the expanding Delian League.

Under the Peace of Antalkidas in 387 B.C., Halikarnassos was returned to the Persians. At about the same time a Karian nobleman called Hekatomnus set himself up as Prince of

Karia with his capital in the mountains at Mylasa. Hekatomnus had taken advantage of the renewed Persian strength by allying himself with the Great King Artaxerxes II against Evagoras, the king of Salamis in Cyprus. The Persians adopted the same attitude towards Hekatomnus as they had to Lygdamis I, that provided he remained loyal he could enjoy a certain amount of autonomy.

In 377 B.C. Hekatomnus was succeeded by his eldest son Mausolos, an ambitious and perceptive prince. He realized that for the Karians to attain identity in the world they would have to adopt the Greek way of life. For the next twenty years therefore whilst maintaining apparent allegiance to Persia he began systematically to hellenize the Karians by converting them from mountain shepherds and tribesmen to Greeks in everything but heritage. He stormed Halikarnassos and made it his new capital in 367 B.C., and joined in the various local rebellions against Persia. With the Persian defences dwindling, Mausolos was able to dominate much of the Ionian and Dorian coast, with his influence extending to Miletos, Lydia and the nearby islands. He capitalized on the satrap revolt against Artaxerxes II in 362 B.C., a revolt that he almost certainly organized, and obtained virtual autonomy. With this supremacy came vast sources of income from the profitable trade routes and Mausolos rapidly became wealthy. Although he hoarded much of his revenue, he channelled some into the rebuilding of his capital.

Mausolos was something of a paradox. Although he adopted the Greek way of life it was merely as a means to meet the Greeks on their own terms. He still retained the Karian customs, as was clear from his marriage to his sister Artemisia. He conquered Rhodes and in 357 B.C. aided them in their fight against Athens.

In keeping with the Greek ideal, Mausolos respected science and art and kept their appreciation separate from politics. Thus even when he was fighting the Greeks, he welcomed their learned and artistic to Halikarnassos. The Greeks reciprocated and although in their eyes Mausolos was a barbarian, they had no qualms in assisting the prince in building his new capital.

The conversion of Karia to a hellenized state did not

happen overnight. We know that from 377 B.C. onwards Mausolos began to spread his area of influence, but it was not until after 362 B.C. that he became a formidable power. His ability to conquer Rhodes by 357 B.C. shows how his strength had grown. This chronology enables us to place the planning and redesigning of Halikarnassos into some pattern. Although the union of the lesser towns was probably underway as early as 367 B.C., Mausolos did not control the necessary resources until after 362 B.C. We also know that Pytheos, architect of the Mausoleum and doubtless involved in the city planning, was at work at Priene after 350 B.C., so it is likely that the bulk of the rebuilding must be concentrated between these two dates.

If we regard the Mausoleum as a royal tomb along the lines of the Theseum, as Jeppesen suggests, then its construction would have been financed out of the city funds – a ploy which is in keeping with Mausolos's miserly nature. There is no reason to suppose that work was not already well under way by the time of Mausolos's death in 353 B.C., but what we do not know was whether it was built as it was originally planned. The authorities of antiquity tell us that Artemisia built the tomb in memory of her husband who, in the eyes of the Karians, clearly had been a great and magnificent king. After Mausolos's death Artemisia would have inherited his accumulated wealth, and being less parsimonious she no doubt supplied additional funds to further adorn the tomb, At this stage it may have consisted solely of the central structure, complete with friezes and quadriga, but now the three levels of sculpture about the base were added, and here we can imagine a more competitive spirit amongst the artists.

One of the friezes was certainly appropriate – that of the battle between the Greeks and the Amazons. Artemisia and her namesake of the previous century were both formidable female warriors and readily identifiable with the Amazons. Although Artemisia II only reigned two years she proved herself to be an able and ingenious commander. After the death of Mausolos, the Rhodians objected to being governed by a woman and their fleet set sail for Halikarnassos. Entering the harbour the Rhodians disembarked to capture the city, unaware of Mausolos's secret harbour. The Karian fleet now slipped into the harbour, manned the Rhodian ships, sailed back to Rhodes and recaptured that city. In commemoration Artemisia set up a victory monument of which the Rhodians were ever ashamed.

In addition to adorning the Mausoleum, Artemisia also instituted an *agon*, or contest to eulogize the name of the king. Magnificent prizes were offered, and distinguished Greeks accepted the challenge. Aulus Gellius tells us that even the renowned Isokrates may have entered the competition, but the winner was one of his pupils, the historian Theopompos of Khios (378-305 B.C.). Another entrant, Theodektes, wrote a play called *Mausolos* which unfortunately has not survived.

Another story perpetuated by Gellius tells us that, stricken by grief at her husband's death, Artemisia mixed his bones and ashes with spices, ground them into a powder, and drank them down with wine nightly. This might well have hastened her death, but there is little cause to accept the story as any more than fiction. Why go to the trouble of building a tomb-chamber complete with sarcophagus if it is only to contain ashes? Moreover, judging by her actions, Artemisia does not seem the kind of woman who would grieve for any longer than was necessary.

Artemisia died in 351 B.C., and was succeeded by her brother Idrieos who had also married his sister, Ada. Idrieos inherited an enviable estate and was known to be one of the most wealthy and powerful princes in Asia. Persia was now ruled by Artaxerxes III who allowed Idrieos his autonomy provided the prince showed no hostility and still paid homage. This was soon put to the test when Artaxerxes commanded Idrieos to supply a fleet to aid him against Cyprus, and the Karian provided over forty triremes and eight thousand mercenaries. Since he was renowned for his wealth it settled the matter of whether the Mausoleum artists finished their work without thought of financial reward. Would you in the circumstances?

Idrieos was succeeded by his wife Ada in 344 B.C., but in 340 B.C. she was expelled from Halikarnassos by her brother Pixodaros, and she took up residence at the fortress of Alinda. This family squabble seems to have turned the fortunes of

Halikarnassos, unless Pixodaros deliberately put a stop to all construction work. Archaeological evidence now coming to light reveals that the terraced area about the Mausoleum was never completed, and it is now presumed that in the troubles following Idrieos's death the artists, who had completed the Mausoleum as far as the sculpture was concerned, left Halikarnassos and found ready work elsewhere, most likely at Priene and Ephesos.

Pixodaros died in 335 B.C., and in the absence of any son, Karia passed back into Persian hands under the satrap Orontobates. It was he who ruled at Halikarnassos when Alexander, now king of Macedonia, marched into Asia in 334 B.C. The Ionian towns had already bowed to the Macedonian, but not so Halikarnassos. Orontobates called for reinforcements and Memnon, one of Persia's most capable generals, established himself in the city. The strength of Mausolos's defences were now proven. Apart from the high city walls, themselves surrounded by a wide moat, Halikarnassos contained three fortresses, two of which – Salmakis and 'the island' – were on promontories in the harbour. Alexander was without his fleet for support so that even after he finally breached the city walls he was unable to break the Persian garrison, which held out for a year. During this time Alexander had continued on his way leaving his general Ptolemy Lagus in command. Finally, Orontobates and Memnon made their escape by sea and lived to fight another day. In the meantime the exiled Queen Ada had paid homage to Alexander and was appointed governor of his new province of Karia. After her death, Karia's independence was lost in the wars for possession of Alexander's Empire.

When the Persians realized they could not hold the city of Halikarnassos and so withdrew to the fortresses, they fired the city, and it was all Ptolemy could do to save it. We can only assume that the Mausoleum suffered little damage as it was still standing in the twelfth century, fifteen hundred years later, making it the most durable of the Seven Wonders after the Pyramids. During those centuries Halikarnassos was subject to many nations, including the Romans. They revered the Mausoleum and adopted the idea of grandiose tombs to honour their famous, taking the name mausoleum into their language, by which route it finally passed into English. One of the greatest Roman mausolea was that of the Emperor Hadrian who died in A.D. 138, and was buried in Rome in a mausoleum of his own design.

For the next thousand years Halikarnassos remained in the East Roman and Byzantine Empires, whose rulers respected the tomb. It was nature that took the first toll when, some time during the thirteenth century, an earthquake toppled the *quadriga* from the summit and caused extensive damage to the rest. By this time the failing Byzantine Empire was facing extinction at the hands of the Turks, and in the name of Christianity their opposition came from the Hospitaller Knights of St John, originally founded to care for the wounded of the Crusades, but now rapidly becoming the main Church bulwark against the infidel.

In 1309 the Knights captured Rhodes and, building a large fleet, used the island as their base to patrol the Aegean. With increased power they began to expand their territories and in 1402 captured Halikarnassos, by then renamed Bodrum. Their first task was to build a strong fortress, the Castle of St Peter, and they chose as the site the harbour promontory known as 'the island' which had served as an admirable haven for Orontobates and Memnon seventeen centuries earlier. The work was clearly of the highest importance as in 1409 Pope Gregory XII issued a papal bull absolving all those who helped. Because of the necessary haste there was no time to quarry raw materials and the Knights used whatever was handy.

It is probable that much of the tomb remained untouched at this time as there were numerous ruins in the immediate vicinity. However the castle was having to be continually refortified because of the rapid advances in the development of cannon. Gradually the builders searched farther afield for materials and in 1494 used the first blocks from the Mausoleum. Over the next three decades the tomb was regularly plundered for stone, the statues smashed for lime, and by all accounts the Knights had no idea they were destroying a Wonder of the World. The French chronicler Claude Guichard was aware of the circumstances and in 1581 he detailed the passing of the Mausoleum. He tells how in 1506, the quarriers found a stepped marble platform which they demolished to reveal a small opening, leading to a room adorned with sculptures and reliefs. These were in turn broken up. In an adjacent room was a sarcophagus which was removed and though intact at the time was later plundered. The remains of Mausolos, and possibly Artemisia, were lost forever.

And all to no avail. In 1522 the Knights dismantled what remained of the Mausoleum to strengthen the castle for its most important stand. The Grand Master of the Knights, Villiers de l'Isle Adam, had learned that the Turkish sultan, Suleiman the Magnificent, had amassed an army of over 100,000 to vanquish the Knights. All fortresses were to be strengthened and no expense spared. But Suleiman's army was too vast, and the Knights were called back to defend the last stronghold on the island of Rhodes. Here the Knights were besieged for seven months but the Turks finally breached the walls, and on 1 January 1523 Rhodes was handed over to the Ottoman Empire.

Of the Tomb of Mausolos, there was nothing to be seen.

REDISCOVERING THE UNIQUE

Although the Mausoleum had survived almost intact into the Middle Ages, and its fate had been recorded by Claude Guichard, this seems to have gone unnoticed by the artists who depicted the Seven Wonders, including Marten van Heemskerck, who was a youth in the days of its destruction. The first person to identify the friezes which had been incorporated in the walls of the Castle of St Peter was a painter and engraver from Cumberland, England, Richard Dalton (1720-91). Dalton visited Italy and the Near East sketching remains and sculptures from the ancient days, finally published as *Antiquities and Views* in 1791. Despite his vocation Dalton was not especially expert at sketching,[5] but he nevertheless provided some invaluable examples of how the friezes looked before further weathering and the Turkish artillery made their mark.

The first real opportunity to investigate the remains came in 1846. The British Ambassador at Constantinople, Stratford

Canning (1786-1880) was a close acquaintance of the young Sultan Abdul-Medjid (1823-61). The Sultan presented Canning with the friezes from the castle and they were despatched to the British Museum. The Assistant Curator of Antiquities at the Museum was Charles T. Newton (1816-94) who took an active interest in the remains. In 1852 he became the vice-consul at Mytilene, or Lesbos, the island off the coast of Asia Minor, and then in Turkish hands. Canning was still Ambassador and he was able to arrange for Newton to investigate the site of the Mausoleum.

Newton's excavations began in January 1857 and continued until May 1858. During this time he and his assistants also excavated at Knidos and other centres of interest and he regretted that '. . . we were compelled to explore the site of the Mausoleum by instalments, and to cover up the excavated parts as we went on, instead of laying bare the whole area continuously, and transporting the dug earth to a convenient distance. For, though great care has been taken to record . . . every fact which seemed worthy of observation, it is probable that, if the area of the excavation had been presented to the eye as a whole, and not in detached portions, we should have remarked significance and relation in many details, which, viewed in isolation, appeared meaningless or contradictory; we might thus have been enabled to comprehend more fully the design of that monument which was the marvel of the ancient world, and of which, even after so much discovery, our knowledge is still so imperfect.'[6]

Despite these problems, most of the surviving statues and sculptures now retrieved from the Mausoleum were found by Newton, including the giant statue of 'Mausolos' and fragments of the beautiful horses that once pulled the chariot adorning the pyramid apex. Newton was able to take a number of measurements, but he had precious little to work from. What had been left by the Knights had been continually quarried by the Turks until the pit was too deep and then it had been filled in. Subsequent expeditions, like that by Alfred Biliotti, who took over from Newton in 1865, could not hope to find any treasures in bulk and had to be satisfied with valuable but painfully small fragments.

It was not until 1964 that Kristian Jeppesen, visiting the

Castle of St Peter, detected two new fragments of the Amazon frieze and several other architecturally significant blocks. This led to Danish expeditions in 1966 and 1967, and three more between 1970 and 1973, during which the entire site of the Mausoleum was re-excavated. It was discovered that the tomb had been built on the site of an ancient necropolis. Fragments of the sarcophagus cover were found together with a large sacrificial deposit of sheep, cows and poultry. Of special significance was the discovery of several beams and half-beams supporting the ceiling coffers, from which Jeppesen was able to deduce the overall dimensions of the colonnade.

Although not finalized, Jeppesen's reconstruction may at last resolve the problem that has puzzled architects and archaeologists for centuries. Even before Newton had made his discoveries, it had been a regular pastime of artists and architects to depict the Mausoleum, especially since 1750, when the revival of interest in classical and gothic styles brought about an upsurge of investigation into ancient buildings. Charles R. Cockerell (1788-1863), the foremost Victorian exponent of the classical tradition in Britain, had spent several years travelling in eastern Europe, and he produced his version of the tomb in 1856 showing a low podium, tall columns and a steep pyramid. He was followed by the Scottish architect James Fergusson (1808-86), an authority on Indian architecture. His version, published in 1862, favoured a high podium, short columns and a stunted pyramid.

That same year Newton published his findings in *A History of Discoveries at Halicarnassus* and produced the first authoritative reconstruction. He had opted for a high base approached by a series of steps, short columns and a squat pyramid. He also introduced the cella, but placed the friezes about the entablature and the cella.

There was no stopping architects now. In the fifty years following Newton's excavations, scores of Mausoleum interpretations have appeared. It is hard to imagine that any basic design could have so many variations, especially as only one can be correct. One of the most impressive was by the Scot John J. Stevenson (1831-1908) renowned for several London houses such as Kensington Court. Stevenson's model, completed in 1896, and at one time exhibited in the British Museum, favoured an extremely tall, almost sheer pyramid, surmounting a dipteral colonnade upon a small podium set within a raised platform.

Judging from current evidence, the most accurate of these early interpretations was by the German archaeologist Friedrich Adler (1827-1908), who was also responsible for the reconstruction of the Statue of Olympian Zeus. Adler's version, published in 1899, differs only in placing the frieze on the entablature instead of the pyramid plinth, and in the lack of the stepped blocks about the podium. There are other, less visible variations, but it demonstrates that not all the pioneers were on the wrong track.

Of course, we cannot be sure that Jeppesen and Waywell's conclusions will be definitive, because archaeologists are always likely to find something new and revive old theories. What is more important in these matters is not what the Mausoleum looked like but what circumstances brought it into existence. Even though his tomb has vanished, its name has passed into the language, and Mausolos achieved his desire for immortality.

NOTES ON CHAPTER VI

1. Vitruvius II.8.11
2. *Natural History* XXXVI.4.30-31
3. *Travels and Discoveries in the Levant* (London, 1865) II p. 131
4. *Natural History* XXXVI. 4.26
5. He later changed vocation completely and became Royal Librarian to George III.
6. *Further Papers Respecting Excavations at Bodrum and Cnidus*, C. T. Newton, (1859) p. 93

CHAPTER VII

THE SECOND SUN: THE COLOSSUS OF RHODES

Out to sea lies the island of Rhodes which, long ago, was submerged in the deep and which the Sun raised up to the light and demanded it as his own from the gods. Here stands the Colossus, seventy cubits high, executed in the likeness of the Sun, for it is recognized to be an effigy of the god as it bears the god's own special features. The artist used so much bronze for the work that there was almost a shortage of metals, for all the earth's mines were exploited in carrying out the project.

When the French sculptor Auguste Bartholdi was planning his statue called 'Liberty Enlightening the World' he used as his inspiration the Colossus of Rhodes, the giant statue of the Sun god Helios sculpted by Chares of Lindos in 300 B.C. Bartholdi's statue, made of bronze and 152 feet high, was unveiled on New York's Bedloe's Island in 1886 to commemorate the French and American revolutions, and has been called the Statue of Liberty ever since. Appropriately its prototype was erected to celebrate a similar freedom, the gallant stand by the Rhodians against the forces of the Macedonian conqueror Demetrios the Besieger, one of the epic struggles of the ancient world.

THE STATUE TO THE SUN

The journey from Halikarnassos to Rhodes in antiquity was only a few hours' sailing. The island, situated off the south-west coast of Karia (see Fig. 18, p. 156), was an important centre on the Mediterranean trade routes as well as a convenient port of call for travellers on longer journeys. By 408 B.C. the Rhodians were so prosperous that they founded a new city, also called Rhodes, at the northern tip of the diamond-shaped island.

Even without the Colossus, Rhodes was a beautiful city. Strabo, who visited the area nearly four hundred years after the city was founded, could not find sufficient words to praise it:

> The city of the Rhodians . . . is so far superior to all others in harbours and roads and walls and improvements in general that I am unable to speak of any other city as equal to it, or even as almost equal to it, much less superior to it. It is remarkable also for its good order, and for its careful attention to the administration of affairs of state in general; and in particular to that of naval affairs whereby it held the mastery of the sea for a long time and overthrew the business of piracy.[1]

The city spread over most of the northern apex of the island and was surrounded by a solid wall eighty stadio (or about 9.2 miles) in length. The main part of the city centred upon two harbours, still there today; the Northern known as *Mandraki* (meaning sheepfold) and the more important Commercial Harbour. They were separated by a long mole, as Figure 24 shows, and the Colossus was once believed to have stood here.

Of all the Seven Wonders, the Colossus is the only one whose location is not known precisely. The traditional view that it bestrode the Northern Harbour is no more than artistic licence – it was already a popular tradition by the fourteenth century. We know from accounts of how it was built that had it stood thus, the Rhodians would have lost the use of the harbour for twelve years, and no naval power would suffer that, even if there were other harbours. The sheer weight of the statue would make it technically impossible to build such a pose given the skill the Greeks possessed. The downward pressure from the head and trunk would crack it above the

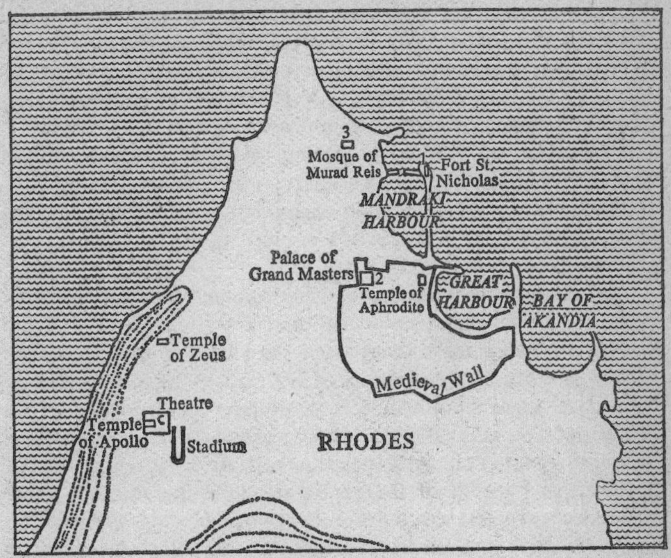

1,2,3 indicate suggested locations of the Colossus

Figure 24. Partial Plan of the City of Rhodes

knees without additional support. Most ancient accounts agree on a height for the statue of seventy cubits which would make it between 105 and 117 feet depending on which cubit is used.[2] The gap between the harbour moles is over two hundred yards today, and it was not significantly less in classical times so, if we are to accept the height of the statue as just over one hundred feet we would have to envisage it with legs entirely out of proportion straddling the harbour in a position that would bring tears to the eyes of even the most acrobatic contortionist. Finally, although the ancient authorities failed to record its location, Strabo does specify that after it was destroyed by an earthquake its remains lay 'on the ground'.[3] Had it bestrode the harbour its remains would almost certainly have crashed into the sea and would have been visible to no one.

So, having discounted the traditional view, where could the Colossus have stood, and what did it look like?

I have already mentioned one possible location, at the end of the pier between the two main harbours where Fort St Nicholas has stood since 1464. This was not only strategically imposing, but historically significant, as this mole was the first captured by Demetrios during his siege, and represented the first victory by the Rhodians when they reclaimed it. However, although this mole was wider in ancient times, the same problem of construction would apply, as well as the matter of ruins on the ground.

This leaves two other possibilities, neither supported by any more substantial evidence than tradition. South of the Mandraki harbour is the present site of the Palace of the Grand Master of the Knights of St John. A temple to Apollo originally stood here and this would have close associations with the Colossus. Apollo was regarded by the Greeks as, amongst many other things, the god of solar light, whilst Helios was the god of the sun, a subtle difference that arose more as a means to differentiate between the two deities rather than to explain their origin. Indeed some early writers call the Colossus a statue of Apollo rather than Helios, but as we shall see Helios was the patron god of Rhodes, and the Colossus was but one of many Helios statues on the island. The Temple of Apollo was erected on the highest spot in this part of the city so that the Colossus would have been in a prominent position and visible throughout the town, not just from the harbour.

The final alternative is the site now occupied by the Mosque of Murad Reis, the Turkish admiral who commanded the fleet during the siege of Rhodes in 1522. Situated on the north-west waterfront of the Mandraki harbour, it too commands an imposing view over the city and the sea but, like the other suggested sites, it awaits that vital piece of tangible evidence that will prove the location once and for all.

The exact nature of the Colossus is not known either, but as it represented Helios we can make a reasonable assumption of its likeness from the appearance of the god on ancient coins and from our knowledge of Greek sculpture of the period. An especially vital clue in this puzzle was a fragment of bas-relief found in 1932 on the site of the Apollo Temple. It shows the upper part of the god with his right hand raised to shield his eyes and the left resting on his hip. Based on this relief and Philon's own treatise, Sir Herbert Maryon (1874-1956), an expert on metals, produced his own version of the Colossus as shown in Figure 25.

Figure 25. Suggested reconstruction of the Colossus of Rhodes by Sir Herbert Maryon.

The dimensions of the statue can be judged from Pliny's description. 'Few men can embrace its thumb,' he wrote, 'its fingers are larger than most statues.'[4] It probably measured some sixty feet about the chest, and the ankles alone would have been about five feet thick. It stood upon a marble base itself higher than other statues so that in all the Colossus towered perhaps 150 feet above the harbour.

Fortunately Philon goes into more detail about the construction of this Wonder than he does with the others which probably means he left more exact notes for his copyist, who still makes his presence known. The full details are provided in appendix I, but the following are the key facts:

> The workmen fortified the statue from the inside by hewn stones joined together by iron bolts, and the bars which are used on the stones to bring the joins together seem to have been fashioned by the hammers of the Cyclops. Whatever part of the work remains hidden is greater than that which can be seen . . .
>
> A pedestal of pure marble was laid down and on this, calculating the proportion, the artist first fixed the feet of the Colossus as far as the ankle, on to which the god was to be erected, seventy cubits high . . .
>
> . . . the artist cast the rest of the statue beforehand, and it was reassembled piece by piece. One piece was fixed to the part already cast, and a third piece was added when this was finished, and then each further part, just as it had been fashioned, was completed with the same skill.
>
> . . . the artist had to preserve the shape of the work in his mind for, as parts of the Colossus were finished he poured a huge quantity of earth about the base hiding that part already completed, so that he might finish the next part from ground level. He gradually ascended to the very topmost point making a god-like image from 500 talents of bronze and 300 talents of iron . . . for in the world a second Sun stood face to face with the first.

The main support for the statue was three stone columns that extended up through the legs and drapery to the trunk and head. Stone lintels were laid across the columns and the framework was jointed by metal rods. The bronze plates were probably only as thick as a penny, which would make them easier to carry, shape and fix. Much of the Colossus was therefore hollow, and Philon tells us that Chares fortified the statue by filling it with rocks and stones, a fact supported by Pliny who noted:

> Within, too, are to be seen large masses of rocks, by the aid of which the artist steadied it while erecting it.[5]

Despite its size it was generally agreed that the Colossus was a perfect representation of the human body, the epitome of Greek art. It was for this reason, as much as its size and meaning, that the Greeks classed it as a World Wonder even though it stood for less than a lifetime.

We must also consider that behind the Colossus was a wonderful tale of courage and daring, for the statue was a consequence of one of history's most fascinating sieges.

THE FIGHT FOR FREEDOM

The city of Rhodes was not built until 408 B.C. Before then the island had three main cities, Ialysos, Kameiros and, most important, Lindos. According to legend they had been founded by Tlepolemos, the son of Herakles, who established himself as King of Rhodes. He later fought and was killed in the Trojan War. Another legend tells how Helios, the sun-god, was missing when Zeus was apportioning the earth amongst the gods, and thus received nothing. Helios was naturally annoyed over this but then discovered the newly formed island of Telchinis, named after its natives, the Telchines, a primitive tribe of sorcerers and artists (it was they who made the trident for Poseidon). The Telchines were destroyed, in one version by Apollo who slew them with his arrows, in another by Zeus, who inundated the island. Thereafter it was claimed by Helios, and ever after it remained the centre for his worship. It was here that he fell in love with the nymph Rhode, after whom the island received its new name.

In the dawn of recognizable history Rhodes was recolonized by the Dorians under Althaemenes. The three island cities combined with the Karian mainland cities of Knidos, Halikarnassos and the island of Kos to form the Dorian Hexapolis. Rhodes rapidly developed as a naval power, and as early as 690 B.C., it was sending settlers to found colonies in Sicily, of which Gela was the most important.

Apart from its early mastery of the seas, Rhodes features little in history until the time of Athenian supremacy. During the sixth century B.C. the cities were governed by tyrants, of whom the most famous was Kleobulos of Lindos. He lived in about 580 B.C. and was reckoned by the Greeks amongst the Seven Sages. He and his daughter were masters of riddles, loving both to set and to solve them. One of them was: A father has twelve children, and each of these has thirty daughters, on one side white and on the other black, and though immortal, they all die. What was he talking about? The year, with its months and days.

In 478 B.C., Rhodes joined the Delian League, having cast off the Persian yoke, and remained allied to Athens until the Peloponnesian War when, in 411 B.C., they changed their allegiance to Sparta. They reverted to Athens in 390 B.C., but, as we saw in the last chapter, revolted from Athens in 357 B.C., with the aid of Mausolos. Rhodes remained subject to the Karians until the conquests of Alexander the Great, to whom they also submitted. It was not until his death in 323 B.C., that the Rhodians were able to expel the Macedonian garrison and revel once again in the glories of independence.

By this time Rhodes, which had always been a favourable acquisition, was far more desirable, following the construction of the city of Rhodes. As I said, it was built in 408 B.C. and its design was attributed by Strabo to Hippodamos of Miletos, the inventor of formal city planning. If this was the case Hippodamos would have been an extremely old man. He was born some time before 500 B.C., and in his early days had been a physician and meteorologist before turning to city planning. This probably coincided with the rebuilding of his native city Miletos shortly after 479 B.C. Perikles summoned him to design the port of Piraeos in 450 B.C., and he later sailed with Herodotus and other Athenian colonists to Thurium in Italy in 443 B.C. It is more probable therefore that Rhodes was planned by a leading student of Hippodamos who closely followed his master's designs, but it shows in what esteem the architect was held in later years for his name to be connected with one of the world's great cities.

The city was laid out in a grid plan with broad avenues up to fifty feet wide intersecting in six-hundred-feet squares, themselves subdivided by straight, narrow lanes. There was also an elaborate system of street drainage, the earliest known in the Greek world.

Naturally the city was adorned with statues and sculptures, and the prosperity of Rhodes and the likelihood of work lured many an artist to the island. It was the home of Protogenes, considered second only to Apelles as the greatest of Greek painters, although he lived for fifty years in obscurity, and was not acknowledged until Apelles drew attention to his works by offering to buy them for fifty talents each (about £17,000). Perhaps the most famous, and certainly the most prolific artist attracted to Rhodes, was Lysippos, a sculptor from Sikyon. He lived from about 365 to 300 B.C., and it was reported that he set aside one gold piece for every statue that he sold. When his heir broke into his money-box after his death he found fifteen hundred pieces of gold.

Lysippos was attached to the court of Philip of Macedonia, and Alexander declared that no one could make his statue other than Lysippos. He was the Phidias or Skopas of his day and was acclaimed in Rhodes for his magnificent sculpture of the Chariot of the Sun, portraying Helios driving his four-horse chariot across the skies. Lysippos worked mostly in bronze, and his creations range from an exquisite twelve-inch-high statuette of Herakles, intended as a table decoration, but now alas lost, to the colossal sixty-feet-high statue of Zeus at Tarentum, in Italy. At the time of its completion it was the tallest statue known in the Greek world, but it was soon to be dwarfed by the Colossus of Rhodes, the statue of Helios made by Lysippos's own pupil, Chares of Lindos.

This brings us to the year 304 B.C., and the siege of Rhodes. To fully appreciate the situation in the Aegean at this time and thus the reason for the siege and the consequent Colossus, it is necessary to understand the state of the Greek world after the death of Alexander. As it also has some bearing on the next Wonder of the World, the Pharos Lighthouse, it does no harm to clarify a somewhat chaotic period.

Alexander the Great died in June 323 B.C. in Babylon, and

left no heir. His wife, Roxane, the teenage daughter of the Bactrian king Oxyartes, was several months pregnant. There was another son, Herakles, born to Barsine, the daughter of the Persian general Artabazus, but he was never considered a legitimate heir. Alexander had made no preparations for a successor. He was only thirty-two and had doubtless expected to survive the fever that eclipsed his life in eleven days. He may well have done had he not lowered his resistance by continual drinking bouts. As it was, it was only at the very last moment that, realizing the inevitable, he passed his ring to his general Perdikkas, and ordered him to hold the Empire together until his heir was old enough. Then he died, and the troubles began.

A son was born, also called Alexander and surnamed Aigos. However in the meantime another general, Antipatros, whom Alexander had left as regent of Macedonia in 334 B.C., when he departed upon his conquests, declared Arrhidaios, Philip II's idiot son and Alexander the Great's half-brother, co-heir with Aigos. Apart from Perdikkas and Antipatros, no other general thought much of preserving an Empire for either an imbecile or an infant who was only half-Macedonian. If any ruling was going to be done, they were going to do it. So began the Wars of the Diadokhoi – 'the Successors' – which would drag on for forty years and two generations.

The map opposite (Fig. 26) shows how the Empire was first divided amongst the generals. Antigonos the One-Eyed received Lycia, Pamphylia and Greater Phrygia, Lysimakhos obtained Thrace, Eumenes claimed Cappadocia and Paphlagonia, whilst Ptolemy Lagus took Egypt, and Seloukos Syria.

One by one the generals and regents disposed of each other as well as the remnants of the royal family, and with them out of the way, there was nothing to stop the Diadokhoi aiming for total domination. The most vigorous attempts were made by Antigonos and his son Demetrios. The old general was now in his seventies and whilst still active, it was Demetrios who commanded the forces. In 307 B.C. he conquered Athens and liberated it from the governorship of Demetrios of Phaleron who fled to Ptolemy for sanctuary, and of whom we shall hear more in the next chapter. Demetrios the Mace-

Ruled by Seloukos Nikator
Ruled by Ptolemy Lagus (Soter)
Ruled by Antigonos the One-Eyed
Ruled by Kassandros
Ruled by Lysimakhos
Original boundary of Alexander's Empire

Figure 26. Division of Alexander's Empire at the time of the Siege of Rhodes in 305 B.C.

donian restored Athenian democracy and there were festivals and games in his honour.

Antigonos now summoned Demetrios to aid him in his war against Ptolemy and his generals, one of whom, Menelaos (Ptolemy's brother) had been made governor of Cyprus. On his way to Cyprus, Demetrios stopped at Rhodes and requested the islanders' aid, but they refused, wishing to remain neutral and a common friend to all. The seeds of enmity between Demetrios and Rhodes were thus sown.

Demetrios soon defeated the forces of Menelaos sent to meet him as he landed on Cyprus, and he now laid siege to the city of Salamis. The historian Diodorus relates how Demetrios prepared siege engines of 'very great size' including:

> . . . a device called the 'helepolis' (city-taker), which had a length of forty-five cubits on each side and a height of ninety cubits. It was divided into nine storeys, and the whole was mounted on four solid wheels each eight cubits high. On the lower levels he mounted all sorts of ballistae, the largest of them capable of hurling missiles weighing three talents (180 pounds); on the middle levels he placed the largest catapults and on the highest his lightest catapults . . . he also stationed more than two hundred men to operate these engines in the proper manner.[6]

These were the formidable war machines that Demetrios brought against Salamis and which ultimately earned him his nickname of *Poliorketes*, 'the Besieger'. Demetrios also defeated a fleet sent by Ptolemy to aid his brother, and in no time Demetrios took control of the island. He sent word to Antigonos who, elated by the success, assumed the title of King of Asia, permitting Demetrios to take the same rank. Not to be outdone Lysimakhos, Kassandros, Seloukos and Ptolemy followed suit, declaring themselves kings of Thrace, Macedonia, Syria and Egypt respectively.

Antigonos and Demetrios now attempted to destroy Ptolemy at Gaza but were overcome by problems of weather, the coastal marshes, and not least Ptolemy's attempts to inveigle the troops into deserting with promises of more money. Antigonos and Demetrios therefore withdrew to survey the situation. They turned their eyes to Rhodes. Despite their declared neutrality, the Rhodians maintained close trade connections with Egypt.

Antigonos sent envoys to Rhodes requesting that the islanders ally themselves with him, but they refused. Antigonos now sent a general to waylay any merchant sailing from Egypt to Rhodes, but the Rhodians, having already rid the Aegean of pirates, prided themselves on their mastery of the sea, and soon despatched the general. Promptly Antigonos accused the Rhodians of hostile action and declared war on them. Demetrios moved in.

It had only been a year since Demetrios had proved his strength at Salamis. The Rhodians commanded a far smaller force than that mustered by Menelaos and Ptolemy and which had been so easily conquered. Naturally the Rhodians were scared, but were determined not to lose their independence. They put their faith in the city and its walls, but we can well imagine that when the war fleet of Demetrios appeared on the northern horizon, the islanders scurried to their temples and sanctuaries and offered sacrifices to Helios for help in the struggle ahead.

Diodorus tells us that Demetrios

> . . . had two hundred warships of all sizes and more than one hundred and seventy auxiliary vessels; on these were transported not quite forty thousand soldiers besides the cavalry and the pirates who were his allies. There was also an ample supply of ordnance of all sorts and a large provision of all the things necessary for a siege.[7]

The Rhodians, on the other hand, numbered about six thousand plus a thousand immigrants. In addition there were numerous slaves who were promised freedom and citizenship if they fought bravely, and the city treasury promised to support the families of all those men who fell in the defence of Rhodes.

Demetrios landed on the island and set up a fortified camp south of the city, dispatching contingents to plunder the rest of the island. Preparations continued on both fronts, Demetrios ensuring the totality of his siege and the Rhodians the impregnability of their walls. The islanders even succeeded in sending out three fast ships to intercept and capture Demetrios's supply ships. Demetrios therefore planned his first assault on the harbour, having equipped himself with several floating siege towers.

His first attempt to capture the harbour was thwarted by rough seas, but when the storm settled that night he sailed in under cover of darkness and captured the mole of the Great Harbour, which he promptly fortified. For the following eight days the battle raged, and although the Rhodians succeeded in firing several of the siege towers, Demetrios had the upper hand and destroyed the island's catapults and machines in the harbour and demolished part of the outer wall. Demetrios pressed his advantage but was unable to break through.

His next tactic was to confuse the Rhodians, and he ordered an assault on the city's walls from all sides, by land and by sea. The islanders panicked as they found themselves surrounded, but this spurred them to greater effort and the invaders were driven back.

Demetrios now withdrew his forces and for seven days both sides made what repairs they could. Then Demetrios renewed his attack upon the harbour with even greater force than before. He concentrated all his catapults and siege engines on destroying the Rhodian fleet and breaching the walls, and as the battle ensued it looked like he might succeed. His fire ships were causing havoc amongst the fleet, and the Rhodians were forced to take drastic action. All the islanders not engaged in defending the walls manned the three mightiest Rhodian triremes and forced their way out of the harbour against overwhelming odds. Under the skilful command of Admiral Exekestos, they broke through the floating boom with which Demetrios defended his siege engines and rammed the boats. Two of the siege towers were destroyed and the third withdrawn. The Rhodians, overcome with victory, pursued the tower only to find themselves surrounded by Demetrios's ships. Two of the Rhodian triremes escaped, badly damaged, but the third, with Exekestos on board, was captured.

Demetrios was not defeated. He now introduced a giant siege tower, three times the size of the others, but as he brought it to the harbour a sudden strong wind caused the tower to topple. Demetrios was forced to withdraw, and knowing he was unable to dispatch reinforcements because of the storm, the Rhodians rushed the harbour mole and recaptured it. They thus made it possible to receive further troops sent by Rhodes's allies in Egypt and Crete.

The Macedonian now decided to change his tactics and besiege the city from the landward side. He built the mightiest helepolis he had yet attempted, a forerunner of the modern tank, constructed on a scale that must have awed the Rhodians as much as it petrified them. Diodorus provided us with a long description which is worth reprinting in full because this helepolis is a direct link to the Colossus of Rhodes, and was something of a world wonder itself.

> Each side of the square platform he made almost 50 cubits in length, framed together from squared timber and fastened with iron; the space within he divided by bars set about a cubit from each other so that there might be standing space for those who were to push the machine forward. The whole structure was movable, mounted on eight great solid wheels; the width of their rims was two cubits and these were overlaid with heavy iron plates. To permit motion to the side, pivots had been constructed, by means of which the whole device was easily moved in any direction. From each corner there extended upward beams equal in length and little short of a hundred cubits long, inclining toward each other in such a way that, the whole structure being nine storeys high, the first storey had an area of 4300 square feet and the topmost storey of 900. The three exposed sides of the machine he covered externally with iron plates nailed on so that it should receive no injury from fire carriers. On each storey there were ports on the front, in size and shape fitted to the individual characteristics of the missiles that were to be shot forth. These ports had shutters, which were lifted by a mechanical device and which secured the safety of the men on the platforms who were busy serving the artillery; for the shutters were of hides stitched together and were filled with wool so that they would yield to the blows of the stones from the ballistae. Each of the storeys had two wide stairways, one of which was used for bringing up what was needed and the other for descending, in order that all might be taken care of without confusion. Those who were to move the machine were selected from the whole army, 3400 men excelling in strength; some of them were enclosed within the machine while others were stationed in its rear, and they pushed it forward, the skilful design adding greatly to its motion.[8]

This juggernaut was not the only weapon in the Macedonian's army. There were lesser towers, plus 'tortoises'–

wheeled battering rams 150 feet long, sheltered by wooden roofs, and catapults. Over thirty thousand labourers and craftsmen were employed in building the machines, clearing an area half a mile wide before the city walls, and erecting porches to protect those repairing the machines. Is it any wonder that Demetrios earned the soubriquet 'the Besieger'?

The Rhodians watched these preparations but were not idle themselves. They built a second wall within the first, demolishing houses and temples for the materials, promising the gods that all would be rebuilt if they were saved. Demetrios in the meanwhile had arranged for a contingent of sappers to dig tunnels and undermine the Rhodian walls. The islanders followed suit, checking the subterranean advance. Other minor sorties took place, the Rhodians sending nine ships to crack the Macedonian blockade of the island and succeeding in capturing soldiers and supplies. Demetrios for his part tried to bribe a Milesian general in charge of Egyptian mercenaries to betray the Rhodians, but the general, Athenagoras, double-crossed the Macedonian, and the Rhodians captured a number of Demetrios's troops who expected to take the city by surprise via the tunnels.

Demetrios was also chagrined to find that Ptolemy, Lysimakhos and Kassandros were supplying Rhodes with plentiful provisions. Envoys arrived from Knidos to mediate between Demetrios and the Rhodians, but to no avail. Demetrios, his war machines complete, hurled himself at the city. One of the biggest towers was destroyed and the Macedonians attempted to surge through the breach but were unable to break the defences of the Rhodians. That night the islanders determined to destroy the helepolis and began an unremitting rain of fire missiles. Demetrios was forced to retrieve the tower and further days were spent in its repair. The Rhodians used the time in building a further wall and digging a moat behind those parts of the wall weakened by the siege machines. Again the siege was resumed and Demetrios overthrew two curtains of the wall, but savage fighting saved the intervening turret and Demetrios withdrew.

At this moment an Athenian envoy arrived hoping to reconcile the two parties, but to no avail. Both sides had expended too much to submit, and their determination to continue was equal.

Demetrios now put into action his decisive plan. He selected fifteen hundred of his ablest and strongest men under the command of Mantias and Alkimos who crept up on the breached part of the walls in the dead of night. Then, at an order from Demetrios, there was a general assault on the entire circumference of Rhodes, from both land and sea. Demetrios hoped this would strain the limits of the defenders and allow his troops access through the breach.

At first his plan seemed to work, and daylight saw the Macedonians fighting in the suburbs of the city. Demetrios raised his ensign allowing the fleet to see his success, and they too attacked. The day saw the most savage and determined fighting of the whole siege and losses were heavy on both sides. It was at this point that a charming episode occurred, probably apocryphal, but which serves to show the Greek spirit and the nature of Demetrios. While the fighting waged in the suburbs Demetrios's soldiers came upon the garden of Protogenes where the painter was absorbed in his masterpiece *Ialysos*, oblivious of the battle about him. The fame of the artist was known to Demetrios who came to him and asked him how he could paint under those conditions and was he not afraid of being captured. Protogenes scarcely wavered. Turning to the Besieger he replied, 'I know that you are making war upon people not upon art.' Demetrios regarded the comment as a compliment and respected the artist's valour. He thereupon decreed that the painter be left unharmed and allowed to continue with his work.

The fighting continued all day without respite, but with the deaths of Mantias and Alkimos, a drop in the morale of the troops, and an increase in the determination of the Rhodians, Demetrios ordered his troops to retreat and count the costs.

Another anecdote about the siege concerns the engineer Kallias of Arados who arrived in Rhodes and claimed he could defeat the siege towers. The Rhodians promptly made him city architect, replacing the then present holder Diognetos. Kallias's scheme was to place cranes on the city walls which would hoist the helepolis up and into the city. When they came to try it however the crane merely buckled under the weight of the helepolis and took part of the tower with it.

The Rhodians now pleaded with Diognetos to resume his duties and help them, but the architect sulked and only capitulated when the Rhodians gave a procession in his honour and promised him his share of the spoils if they were victorious. Diognetos surveyed the scene and then ordered troops to dig a wide tunnel just under the surface of the earth out in front of the walls in the line of the advance of the siege tower. This accomplished, as the helepolis trundled forward for a renewed attack, the thin crust of earth gave way under the machine's hundred or so tons, and it toppled into the trench. Another version of this story maintains that Diognetos diverted the city's sewage into the plain before the walls converting the area into a quagmire in which the helepolis stuck fast.

Whatever the true nature of events Demetrios had realized by now that they were at deadlock. The Rhodians also felt that the siege could only be held at bay at the expense of their beautiful city. Antigonos wrote to his son and Ptolemy to the Rhodians requesting that the siege, which had now lasted for a year, be brought to a close. Opportunely an envoy from the Aetolians arrived and offered to mediate. Both sides agreed and a treaty was concluded. Rhodes was allowed to keep its freedom provided it allied itself with Antigonos against any enemy except Ptolemy. Demetrios was to take one hundred hostages against the assurance.

Demetrios thus sailed away from the island to continue his war against the Diadokhoi. He left behind him all the siege weapons that had been constructed, including the mighty helepolis, having instructed the Rhodians, whom he much admired, to set up some memorial to this most memorable of sieges. Diognetos proudly brought the stricken helepolis into the city and set it up in a square, dedicating it to the people. In later years it and other siege machines were dismantled and sold, the proceeds going towards the financing of the Colossus.

But first the Rhodians had to rebuild the houses and temples they had dismantled during the siege. They also honoured their promises by freeing the slaves who had fought valiantly and bequeathed prizes upon the valiant citizens. Statues were set up to Kassandros and Lysimakhos, whilst Ptolemy was remembered with a more prestigious memorial. They dedicated a square in his name and enclosed it within a portico 800 yards in perimeter, where they honoured Ptolemy as a god.

As to the fate of the hundred hostages, they were taken by Demetrios to Ephesos from where they were released two years later when Lysimakhos captured the city in his war against Antigonos. Lysimakhos and Seloukos had combined forces and the collision came in 301 B.C. when they met Antigonos and Demetrios in the Battle of Ipsos. Here Antigonos, by then eighty years old, was killed, but Demetrios lived to fight another day. Alexander's Empire was thereupon divided amongst the remainder: Lysimakhos had Thrace and Asia Minor, Kassandros Macedonia, Seloukos Syria and Persia, and Ptolemy Egypt, in which situation it remained for a period of relative peace.

While Demetrios's struggle for power continued, Rhodes was gradually rebuilt. The time came when the city was in sufficient order for the citizens to remember Helios to whom they had prayed during the siege and who had obviously helped them. A statue in his honour had to be special because there were already several such giants on the island, including five by Bryaxis. Since it was to be built, in part, from the proceeds of the giant helepolis, then clearly it would have to be a statue of equal stature. In all likelihood the commission was given first to Lysippos since he had created the largest known statue at that date. Perhaps Lysippos was too old, or died before construction could begin, but the work passed to his favourite pupil Chares who came from the artistic centre of Rhodes, the old city of Lindos. Chares had been instilled by Lysippos with all the secrets of his art and was thus his natural successor.

The generally accepted translation of Pliny's text tells us that the statue took twelve years to complete and stood for fifty-six years before it was toppled by an earthquake. The precise date for this earthquake is not known but we have an approximate idea from the names of the rulers who offered aid to the Rhodians and the two dates usually assigned are 224 B.C. or 227 B.C. If we accept 224 B.C., then we can calculate that the Colossus was completed in 280 B.C., and thus work commenced in 292 B.C. Whilst one can appreciate that the Rhodians had much to do in rebuilding the city, it does seem remiss of them that they should leave the honouring of their patron god for so long, and yet hasten to deify Ptolemy. The Rhodians were deeply religious and must surely have thought that the statue of Helios was top priority.

As we have seen in other chapters, copies of Pliny's text are not renowned for their accuracy. However, the oldest surviving copy dating from the tenth century and known as the codex *Bambergensis*, states that the Colossus stood for sixty-six years: LXVI instead of LVI. It is easier to believe copyists would omit an X rather than insert one, and with this period it shifts the starting date on the Colossus to 302 B.C., which is far more reasonable. Indeed, if we accept the 227 B.C. date for the earthquake, and allow for an overlapping of the twelve-year and sixty-six-year periods, it brings us to precisely 304 B.C., and the end of the siege. However, considering the planning and resources required work could not have started immediately, whereas a two-year pause is more practical.

There is a story perpetuated by the Greek philosopher Sextus Empiricus (*fl* 130 B.C.) that before work began on the statue, the Rhodian magistrates asked that it be made twice as high. Chares thereupon demanded twice the fee, forgetting that it would require eight times the materials; as a result he went bankrupt and killed himself, leaving the work to be completed by fellow sculptor Laches. Somehow it seems unlikely that Chares, instilled with Lysippos's secrets and capable of designing a statue of these proportions, would make such an elementary mistake. It is more feasible that Empiricus concocted the story to settle the problem raised by an all but unknown poet called Simonides who attributed the Colossus solely to Laches. Simonides was in all likelihood himself confused by names of contemporaries like Leokhares and Lachares who had no connection with the statue.

THE END OF THE COLOSSUS

The earthquake that struck Rhodes and the Aegean in 224 B.C. was devastating. It not only split the Colossus at the knees causing it to crash to the ground in a shower of rocks and bronze plates, but it also brought major damage to many of the newly rebuilt temples and buildings. By now the Diadokhoi and their sons had long since passed from the scene, and the whole of the eastern Mediterranean were allies of Rhodes. Nation after nation sent gifts to the island to help them recover, and Hieron II, tyrant of Syracuse, exempted their grain ships from payment of duty. With all this benign generosity bestowed upon a single island, one would have thought the Colossus would have risen from its ruins almost immediately. But it did not. For some reason the Rhodians consulted the Oracle of Apollo at Delphi to learn the consequences of rebuilding the statue, and the Delphic priests advised against it, warning that worse troubles would follow.[9]

So the Rhodians ploughed the plentiful donations into making the island more beautiful and prosperous than ever, but they forbade that the ruins be so much as moved. And there they lay, about the stumps of the Brobdingnagian legs and plinth, generation after generation. The remains became as much a tourist attraction as the original Colossus.

Rhodes continued to prosper as it soon allied itself with Rome, although after 166 B.C., its trade suffered when Rome made Delos a free port. The fatal blow came in 43 B.C. In the civil war that split Rome after 49 B.C., Rhodes sided with Julius Caesar but after his assassination his chief enemy, Cassius, plundered Rhodes and destroyed the fleet. Never again was it a major power, although its importance increased under the Knights of St John from 1309-1522.

It seems hard to believe that the remains of the Colossus lay untouched for nearly nine hundred years through the entire duration of the Roman Empire with such megalomaniacs as Caligula, Nero, Caracalla and Commodus, but if we are to believe the written record, such they did. Even after the Decree of Theodosius, when pagan temples were dismantled, the Colossus's remains were untouched. That was until A.D. 654.

The Arabs, gripped in the religious fervour of spreading the word of their prophet Mohammed, had suddenly become a major power in the Middle East. Following Mohammed's death in 632, the position of Khalif (or *Khalifah*, 'successor'), was hotly contested by various relatives. In 656 the prophet's son-in-law, the Khalif Othman, was assassinated and another son-in-law, Ali, received the khalifate. His right to succeed was vehemently disputed by Othman's cousin Mu'awiyah, enraged by Ali's failure to punish the assassins and thus believing that Ali had engineered the murder.

Mu'awiyah (602-680) was an extremely capable general and governor and had been given the province of Damascus by his cousin in 640. By 647 he had amassed a large Syrian army to fight the Byzantine Empire. By 649 he had conquered Cyprus, and in 654 he took Rhodes.

There he found a wealth of bronze lying at his feet, just the kind of finance he needed in his fight against Ali. Claiming the bronze he had it shipped to his native Syria, complete with what remained standing, and sold it to a Jewish merchant from Edessa. Reports say that it took over nine hundred camels to transport all the bronze, but Sir Herbert Maryon and others suspect this is a misinterpretation of the original manuscript since the tonnage of bronze that constituted the Colossus could easily have been carried by just ninety camels. However we should not overlook the fact that Rhodes still possessed many of its early treasures. When Pliny visited the island in the first century he counted over two thousand statues, many of them larger than life-size. Mu'awiyah is hardly likely to have arranged the sale of just the Colossus remains without considering the other statues, so perhaps we should not discard the nine hundred camel-loads so readily.

And so the Colossus of Rhodes was transported out of history. Absolutely nothing remains and as yet archaeologists have found no direct clue to the site where it stood. The city of Rhodes is so clustered with buildings, new and old, that archaeologists have few opportunities to search in likely regions, and we must bide our time and wish to fortune that some day, some small item that escaped Mu'awiyah may come to light.

Instead let us muse for a moment on the irony of the statue's fate. Shortly after Mu'awiyah sold the remains he succeeded in claiming the khalifate following the murder of Ali, and possibly his son Hussein. It caused a major rift in the Arab world between the Shiite followers of Ali and the Sunnite adherents of Mu'awiyah, a division that remains to this day.

Is it not bizarre that the Colossus should have come into the world through the endeavours of one Successor (Demetrios) and passed out of it because of the schemes of another Successor (Mu'awiyah)? The Colossus was made possible by converting the spoils of war into finance, and it vanished because it could be converted back into money to support further wars. It is sobering to think that the wealth of the Sixth Wonder of the World went finally not to create breathtaking beauty, but to divide man against man.

NOTES TO CHAPTER VII

1. *Geographica* 14.2.5
2. See Chapter III, Note 5
3. *Geographica* 14.2.5
4. *Natural History* XXXIV.18.41
5. ibid.
6. Diodorus XX.48
7. ibid. XX.82
8. ibid. XX.91
9. The word of the oracle still holds. In recent years the American sculptor Felix de Weldon (b. 1907), renowned for his 'Iwo Jima Flag Raising' memorial, put forward a scheme to rebuild the Colossus to a height of 308 feet, but this and similar proposals proved too costly and impractical.

CHAPTER VIII

THE WORKING WONDER: THE PHAROS LIGHTHOUSE AT ALEXANDRIA

The extremity of the isle is a rock, which is washed all round by the sea and has upon it a tower that is admirably constructed of white marble with many storeys and bears the same name as the island. This was an offering made by Sostratos of Knidos, a friend of the king's, for the safety of mariners, as the inscription says; for since the coast was harbourless and low on either side, and also had reefs and shallows, those who were sailing from the open sea thither needed some lofty and conspicuous sign to enable them to direct their course aright to the entrance . . .

(Strabo *Geographica* 17.1.6)

So we have come full circle. The first Wonder of the World, the mighty Pyramids at Giza, stand some one hundred miles south-east of the seventh and final World Wonder, the Pharos Lighthouse at Alexandria. Egypt lays claim to both the alpha and omega of Wonders.

It is full circle in another sense, for it was in Alexandria, the centre of world learning, that Philon would have set down his notes about the Seven Wonders. Yet he did not include the Pharos Lighthouse and neither did any of the other ancient authorities whose works have survived qualify the description of the Pharos by calling it one of the Seven

Wonders, something they did unhesitatingly for the Mausoleum, the Colossus and the others.

We can only assume, as I suggested in Chapter I, that either those lists which included the Pharos have perished over the centuries, or the writers of old accepted the Pharos as a World Wonder, took it for granted so to speak, and it was left for others of a later period to record the fact for posterity.

One might well be surprised that any Wonder could be taken for granted, and it was only in Alexandria that such a circumstance could arise. The city was the cultural centre of the world where the pilgrims of art and science congregated. They would look in awe at the beauty of the city and compare it to the other Greek centres – Athens, Olympia, Halikarnassos, Rhodes, Pergamon, Corinth – looking through aesthetic eyes. They could easily overlook the practical, because of all the Wonders of the World, the Pharos Lighthouse was the only one that was purely functional. It served a practical purpose, not like a tomb or a temple, where the appeal is spiritual, or a statue or gardens which are purely decorative. The Pharos actually did a job and thus was appreciated on an entirely different level. It was not a work of art, and was never intended as one. That it finally made the grade as a World Wonder was because it was the first of its kind, and even after it had spawned imitations, it was still the best.

THE CITY AND THE TOWER

The Pharos Lighthouse dominated the entrance to Alexandria harbour, warning mariners of the dangerous rocks and islets just beneath the crashing waves. The lighthouse took its name from the island upon which it stood, just one of a chain of small islands lying parallel to the coast of Egypt, protecting the western, or Canopic, branch of the Nile Delta from the prevailing north-westerly winds. A thriving port had existed here in the times of the Egyptian Twentieth Dynasty when the High Priests of Ammon dominated the pharaohs. Homer mentions the port as one of the shelters of Menelaos, king of Sparta, and of his wife, the infamous Helen, on their way back from Troy.[1]

When Alexander the Great came to this spot in 332 B.C., there was only a fishing village called Rhakotis, but in less than a generation it would become the most important city in the Mediterranean.

We visit it in the time of Eratosthenes in 235 B.C. This was a period in which one could see all the Seven Wonders, although Babylon was a sorry sight. The Colossus of Rhodes was still standing in all its glory, and four days' sailing from the island would bring one in sight of Alexandria. The Pharos Lighthouse was visible from thirty-five miles away,[2] giving the seamen ample warning, either by a fire at night or a column of smoke by day. As the ships were guided in through the narrow harbour entrance created by a breakwater jutting out towards the island of Pharos, sailors must have stared upwards in vertiginous awe at this towering edifice, fearing it might collapse at any moment.

The exact height of the lighthouse is not known today despite the painstakingly accurate measurements taken by the Moor Yusuf ibn-ash-Shaykh who lived in Alexandria in 1165. Ibn-ash-Shaykh used the cubit as his measure, as did most other chroniclers, but as we have learned, the cubit was never a consistent unit, and all we can say is that the Pharos stood between 350 and 460 feet high which makes it the greatest lighthouse of all time. The largest standing today is in Yokohama, Japan, and is 348 feet high with a visibility range of 20 miles. Excluding the Great Pyramid of Khufu, the Pharos was the tallest building in antiquity, and for that matter right through till the fifteenth century when it was finally overtaken by Lincoln Cathedral.

Whatever its size, we do know clearly the appearance of the Pharos. It rose from a platform of massive masonry about 360 feet square and 20 feet high, surrounded by an enclosed portico with columns made of the same Aswan granite as the pyramid chambers. The lighthouse base measured about 100 feet square and tapered slightly to a height of perhaps 235 feet. Within this ground storey were numerous chambers, estimates varying between 50 and 300, all identifiable by the scores of windows in the outer wall. These rooms not only housed the mechanics and attendants necessary to maintain the light, but also sheltered a garrison of troops stationed there.

The ground storey terminated in a square platform, its cornices elaborately decorated with figures of Tritons, the merman attendants of the sea-god Poseidon. The second stage, octagonal in shape, rose from the centre of this platform. It measured 55 feet across and had a total perimeter of about 220 feet. The greatest estimate for its height is 115 feet, and it was surmounted by a balcony. From the centre of this platform rose the third storey, cylindrical in shape, measuring about 30 feet across and between 60 and 80 feet high.

A wide internal ramp spiralled around the inner wall allowing horses to bring fuel to the final stage where it was lifted by windlass to the beacon which stood above the third storey within a domed shelter surrounded by eight columns and surmounted by a twenty-foot-high statue of Poseidon, complete with trident. The fire was fed by resinous wood, and it was a major operation maintaining a regular supply, even though the fire burned only at night. Installed within the dome were huge convex mirrors of polished bronze or silver which reflected the fire over thirty miles. Some maintained these mirrors could focus the sun's rays on enemy ships and set them on fire. This would be possible and was a useful rumour to be employed in the defence of the city.

The exterior of the Pharos was exquisitely decorated with carvings and statues. Recent discoveries by marine archaeologists have brought to light statues of sphinxes and one of a female figure over twenty feet high which shows that there was beauty in even this, the most functional of Wonders.

The architect of this magnificent edifice was one Sostratos, a native of the beautiful Dorian city of Knidos in Asia Minor, near Halikarnassos. In about 340 B.C. the Knidians had established a new city at the very end of their rocky promontory. It was here that Sostratos was raised, and in 300 B.C. he further embellished the city with a beautiful terraced walk supported by a sheltered colonnade, which was, according to Pliny, the first of its kind.[8]

What brought Sostratos to Alexandria we don't know, but it was almost certainly the promise of work, and quite probably a definite commission. According to the tenth-century cyclopedist Suidas, work began on the Pharos in 299 B.C., which would place it in the reign of Ptolemy I Lagus, now nicknamed *Soter* ('Saviour') after his help to the Rhodians during the great siege. This is a possible date as Alexandria was nearing completion and Ptolemy would have wished for a safe harbour, the key to his wealth. Various authorities prefer to place the Pharos within the reign of the second Ptolemy called *Philadelphos* – 'one who loves his sister' – because he adopted the old Egyptian tradition of marrying his sister. Philadelphos reigned from 283 to 246 B.C., and under him Alexandria acquired its reputation as the centre for intellectual pursuits; but the lighthouse is more akin to his father's perceptive nature. Since the Pharos took twenty years to complete, it would not have been dedicated until 280 B.C., in Ptolemy II's reign, which resolves both theories.

As with all good Wonders there is a legend concerning the origin of the Pharos which may have a kernel of truth. Apparently after Sostratos had found work in Alexandria he sent word to his betrothed in Knidos to join him. When almost in sight of the harbour a tremendous storm arose and because the captain was unable to see any guiding light her ship was blown off course and lost at sea. Heartbroken, Sostratos vowed that no such accident would happen again and, appealing to the gracious Ptolemy, he received unlimited funds to carry out the work. The kind nature of Ptolemy is noted by Pliny:

> We should not fail to mention the generous spirit shown by King Ptolemy whereby he allowed the name of the architect to be inscribed on the very fabric of the building.[4]

This was indeed unusual because kings always took the honour for any new building. It was so out of the ordinary that later chroniclers made up the story that Sostratos had originally inscribed his name on the building and then overlaid it with plaster in which he cut the customary royal inscription. Whatever the case, high at the top of the first storey, the Pharos declared:

SOSTRATOS SON OF DEXIPHANES OF KNIDOS
ON BEHALF OF ALL MARINERS
TO THE SAVIOUR GODS

The final line probably had a double meaning. The Saviour Gods were the *Dioskouroi* Kastor and Polydeukes, the twin brothers of Helen of Troy. Poseidon had given them power over the wind and waves, and they appeared to sailors during storms in the shape of what is now called St Elmo's Fire. However, at the start of his reign, Philadelphos had deified his parents, Ptolemy Soter and Berenike, and was naturally promoting their worship. Soter, as we know, meant Saviour, hence the subtle ambiguity.

Linking the Pharos Island to the mainland was a long breakwater, the *Heptastadion*, so called because it was seven stadia long, or about four-fifths of a mile. At either end was a gap, covered by a drawbridge, which enabled the free flow of the tides and thus avoided the silting of the harbours. Nevertheless this is just what happened, and over the centuries the *heptastadion* became a mile-wide peninsula.

The breakwater divided the channel into two harbours, the Eastern Harbour, which was the royal and naval port, and the Western or Eunostos Harbour, poetically dubbed 'the Harbour of the Happy Return'. Here were the important merchant docks at Kibitos, and a ship canal linked the harbour with the waters of Lake Mareotis which lay south of the ridge on which Alexandria was built. A further canal linked the lake to the Canopic branch of the Nile, twenty miles away, and thereby to the interior of Egypt, the key to Alexandria's wealth.

At the eastern end of the royal harbour was a promontory known as Cape Lochias where stood Ptolemy's Palace. Another palace was built on the islet of Antirrhodos within the harbour. Along the south bank, opposite the islet, were the spacious Palace Gardens, connected by an underground passage to the Theatre of Dionysius.

Alexandria had been designed by Alexander's royal architect Deinokrates, whom we have already encountered in the redesigning of the Temple of Artemis at Ephesos. Deinokrates was an ambitious man, and Vitruvius recorded the story of how he worked his way into Alexander's favour by submitting an astonishing scheme to the King.

Along the coast of south-east Macedonia is the triple peninsula of Khalkidike, three long fingers of rock that project over thirty miles into the Aegean. The easternmost of these fingers is called Athos and terminates in the formidable peak of Mount Athos rising 6670 feet above the sea. Deinokrates's scheme was to carve Mount Athos into a statue of the young king, supporting in its left hand a city, whilst in its right would be a bowl into which all the rivers of Athos would empty.

The scheme appealed to Alexander, and had it ever been carried out would certainly have superseded all other World Wonders. As it is the king had a deep reservoir of common sense which, unlike many other rulers was not ruled by vanity. He asked Deinokrates if the neighbourhood of Athos had sufficient fields to support food for such a city, and the architect had to admit it was unlikely. The plan was dropped, but Alexander, admiring the architect, included him in his staff.

Alexandria was therefore Deinokrates's golden opportunity. It was no Mount Athos; here were fields a-plenty. The walls, laid out personally by Alexander, enclosed a city four miles in length and between a mile-and-a-half and two miles wide, filling the ridge between the coast and Lake Mareotis. The streets were set out in a grid iron plan, with seven running parallel and roughly equidistant from west to east, and eleven intersecting at right angles from north to south. Most of the streets were about twenty feet wide except for the two principal thoroughfares. The Canopic Way, which ran the entire length of the city, was one hundred feet wide. Near the city centre it crossed the main north-south route, the Street of the Soma (the Tomb of Alexander), which was nearly fifty feet wide.

Somewhere near this intersection, or perhaps between it and the Palace Gardens, were the city's most important buildings, the Soma, the Museum and the Library.

The Museum was a cluster of buildings including a Great Hall and an Observatory, set within a beautiful park that included a zoological garden and the Library. In time the

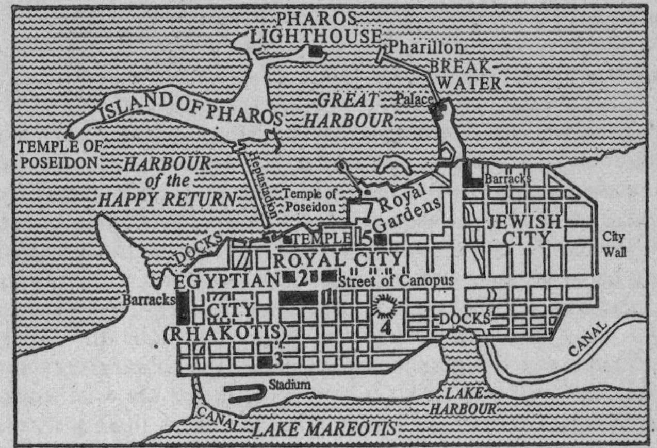

1 Tomb of Alexander (Soma)
2 University (Library and Museum)
3 Temple of Serapis
4 Sanctuary of Pan
5 Theatre

Figure 27. Plan of Ptolemaic Alexandria.

Library became overstocked and a secondary branch was opened within the Temple of Serapis in the Egyptian quarter of the city. Serapis was a deity deliberately devised by Ptolemy Soter and based on the ancient Egyptian bull-worship of Apis. His intention was to unite Greeks and Egyptians in common worship, and the god had the combined attributes of Lord Zeus the Thunderer, Asklepios or Imhotep the Healer, Osiris the Life-Giver and Apis. The Temple itself almost ranked as a World Wonder, and was so classified by the fourth-century monk and ecclesiastic Rufinus Toranius. It was built upon a raised plateau 500 cubits by 250, approached on the east by two hundred steps. These led to an entrance hall covered by a gilded dome. Surrounding the borders of the plateau were a number of buildings, including the Library through which were a series of covered colonnades leading to the Temple itself which stood in the centre of the plateau. The Temple was rectangular with gilded columns and walls overlaid with gold, silver and bronze. At the eastern end stood a giant chryselephantine statue of Serapis with outstretched arms almost touching either wall. Beneath the plateau was a honeycomb of passages, the Catacombs.

The Library had arisen from the suggestion of Demetrios of Phaleron, the Greek governor of Athens whom Demetrios Poliorketes drove from the city in 307 B.C. Demetrios fled to Alexandria and was welcomed by Ptolemy. He was given free rein by the king to acquire copies of all the world's books. It became the law that all visitors to the city had to surrender any books in their possession to the Library where they were copied and returned. Sometimes the scribes switched original and copy and the owner was frequently none the wiser. Estimates for the number of scrolls in the Library vary between 250,000 and 800,000 but either these are wild exaggerations or they include numerous copies, as there just was not that amout of literature about in those days.

At least 200,000 of these scrolls were collected by Demetrios, and although he finally fell out of favour with Ptolemy Soter over the royal succession, and was exiled, he was able to bequeath to his successor the foundation of a library that would one day contain the sum total of all the world's knowledge.

He was succeeded by Zenodotos of Ephesos, the foremost Homeric scholar who made it his life to collate and edit all the works of Homer. Through his devotion and that of subsequent Alexandrian scholars, especially Aristarkhos of Samothrake, we have the basis of the Homeric poems as we know them today. Zenodotos was also charged, by Philadelphos, with acquiring and cataloguing the works of all the Greek poets, a prodigious task, for which Zenodotos required the assistance of Lykophron of Khalkis, who had himself written an epic poem on the fall of Troy, and Alexandros Aitolos, who specialized in collating and arranging all the Greek dramas. It was also during Zenodotos's superintendency that Alexandria acquired the enviable library of the renowned Aristotle.

When Zenodotos died in *c* 265 B.C. he was succeeded by the poet Kallimakhos of Cyrene (310-240 B.C.) who catalogued the entire Library and found it contained 90,000 original scrolls and 400,000 copies. During his control the Library acquired its annex at the Temple of Serapis where a further 42,800 scrolls were housed. He was succeeded in 240 B.C. by Apollonius of Rhodes (295-230 B.C.) and he in turn by the genius Eratosthenes, whom I suggested in Chapter I could well have been the man who collated all the details on the World Wonders and produced the first official listing.

Today Alexandria is remembered more for its core of scientists than for its poets and dramatists, although the latter thrived under Philadelphos. For the furtherance of science we again trace our steps to Demetrios of Phaleron who, shortly after the founding of the Museum, summoned Eukleides (better known to us as Euclid) to start a school of mathematics. Not much is known about the life of Euclid. It has been suggested that he was born at Alexandria a year or two after it was founded, which would have made him about thirty when Demetrios called him from Athens where he had been studying and teaching. Euclid collected together all the known facts about mathematics and published them in a series of books together with innovations of his own. A number of these have survived and to this day his name is synonymous with geometry.

Euclid was succeeded by one of his pupils, Conon of Samos, who was also court astronomer. Conon in turn taught Archimedes (287-212 B.C.), without a doubt the greatest scientist and mathematician of antiquity. Clearly by his day the fame of Alexandria was known throughout the Mediterranean for Archimedes, the son of an aristocratic astronomer, hailed from Syrakuse in Sicily, and there he returned after his studies at the Museum.

The depth of scientific talent in the city over the succeeding centuries is profound, and too great to list here. Suffice it for me to list but a few individuals whose existence furthered the course of knowledge.

Aristarkhos of Samos (*c* 310-230 B.C.) was the first to measure (albeit inaccurately) the distances of the moon and the sun from the earth and also propounded that the earth revolved about the sun. Herophilos (*c* 320-250 B.C.), the first systematic anatomist, who published works on the brain and nervous system, the eyes and reproductive organs; Erasistratos (304-250 B.C.), one-time court physician to Seloukos Nikator, who founded the Alexandrian school of medicine; Ktesibios (*fl* 240 B.C.) an exceptional engineer who invented the clepsydra or water-clock, a hydraulic pump and a water organ; Hipparkhos of Bithynia (190-120 B.C.), the greatest of Greek astronomers, who lived mostly at Rhodes but studied and taught at Alexandria, and who produced the first reliable star map; and in later years, Heron of Alexandria (*c* A.D. 40-100) the inventor of a primitive steam engine; Claudius Ptolemaeus (*c* A.D. 75-165) the collator of all astronomical knowledge and the man who produced what for centuries would be the navigator's handbook; and Galenos of Pergamon (A.D. 130-200) who compiled the definitive books of his day on medicine.[5]

Scarcely without exception all the great writers of antiquity whose works I have quoted studied at Alexandria in the shadow of the towering Pharos. The lighthouse became the symbol of the city, but one day it would become the site of its downfall. The birth and downfall of Alexandria mark in turn the peak and the end of Greek domination in the Mediterranean, and with that the end of my story of the Seven Wonders.

KINGS AND CONQUERORS

We left Alexander at Halikarnassos where his general Ptolemy Lagus had finally succeeded in taking the town and driving Orontobates and Memnon out to sea. In the meantime Alexander had marched to the ancient city of Gordium in Phrygia. Before its conquest by Assyria this land had been ruled by kings called, alternately, Gordius and Midas, one of whom was the Midas renowned in legend because everything he touched turned to gold. Alexander was well acquainted with the legend of Phrygia, especially the Gordian knot. In centuries past Phrygia had been torn by civil war, and the inhabitants pleaded to an oracle for advice. They were told that a wagon would bring them a king. Sure enough moments later they espied a peasant riding his wagon into the capital, and he was promptly proclaimed king. His name was Gordius, and he dedicated his wagon to Zeus, setting it up in the acropolis. There was something extra-special about this wagon. It was attached to the yoke by an intricately tied knot of cornel bark which was so interwoven that neither end was visible. Another oracle had declared that whoever untied this knot would rule Asia.

The story of legends is one matter, the belief in them is something else. Alexander, like all Greeks, firmly believed in the oracles, and the Gordian knot was no exception. Alexander studied the knot, made a few tentative attempts to untie it, and then with customary audacity, slashed it with his sword. No one challenged him. The oracle must now prove itself, and Alexander was convinced it would.

In the summer of 333 B.C., Alexander soundly defeated the Persians at the Battle of Issus, and then marched down the Mediterranean coast, subjugating Syria including the rich port of Tyre, and conquering Gaza on the doorstep of Egypt.

Egypt opened its arms to Alexander. He was a saviour, not a conqueror, and was enthroned at Memphis as pharaoh in 332 B.C. He subsequently sailed down the Nile, intent on visiting the renowned Temple of Ammon at the desert oasis of Siwah, to see what the god predicted for Alexander. It was on this journey that he came to the fishing village of Rhakotis, and realized the potential of the site. He is said to have marked the city's boundary with barley grain, but as he trailed it behind him, so the birds swooped down for this unexpected feast. Alexander was alarmed as to what this signified, but his ever-present seer, Aristandros of Telemessos, foretold that it meant the city would be prosperous with more than enough resources for itself and others. Alexandria was to prove Aristandros right.

In 331 B.C., Alexander left Egypt, determined to destroy the entire Persian world. In his wake he left several cities named Alexandria, and it is possible he scarcely gave the Egyptian Alexandria another thought, and he would never have believed that it would be his final resting place.

He left behind him his architect Deinokrates, but in overall charge of the city was a Greek from the city of Naukratis called Kleomenes. It was not long before Kleomenes usurped his authority and set himself up as virtual dictator over Egypt.[6]

So the situation remained till the death of Alexander in 323 B.C. In October of that year Ptolemy Lagus, who had accompanied Alexander throughout his conquests, arrived in Egypt. He was aware of Kleomenes's excesses, and he had the Greek arrested and promptly executed, establishing himself as governor.

At the outset the other generals were not concerned with Ptolemy's action. The real prize was the Empire, not Egypt, which was relatively unimportant. But Ptolemy was shrewd. He had appreciated the importance of a site holding a key position on the trade routes between east and west. And he had another plan in store. The coffin of Alexander was being borne back to Macedonia, but Ptolemy re-routed it and had it brought to Alexandria. He schemed that the site of Alexander's tomb would be the capital of the Empire.

The generals might have left Ptolemy alone had it not been for this action. Perdikkas, the appointed regent, marched on Egypt, but was murdered by his own troops. Ptolemy also wished to control the lands called Coele-Syria, roughly modern Palestine, and the many Greek islands. This was what brought him to clash with Antigonos, and why he aided the Rhodians during their siege.

In the years after the Battle of Ipsos in 301 B.C., the Diadokhoi kingdoms settled down to a period of relative calm. Hence work on such large projects as the Pharos and the University would fit within this period. There were still struggles ahead, but they little affect the story of the World Wonder. Ptolemy I died in 283 B.C. at the age of 82, having secured a firm and loyal nation and a fleet that controlled the trade of the eastern Mediterranean.

Alexandria rapidly became the largest city in the world with, at its height, over 300,000 citizens, and probably as many slaves. At least a third of the population were Jews which contributed to the city's prosperity.

However, after Ptolemy II Philadelphos, the Ptolemies became rather spineless rulers dominated by their wives and advisers. By the second century B.C. the city was the scene of constant internal strife. Its trading was also suffering since the expanding Roman world now all but dominated the Mediterranean. Various factions in Alexandria allied themselves with Rome and in 87 B.C. Ptolemy Alexander, the heir to the throne, fled to Rome for protection. When Ptolemy Lathyris died in 80 B.C., Sulla sent Alexander to Alexandria where he was installed as king marrying his cousin Berenike. Within a few days Alexander had murdered Berenike and the Alexandrians, horrified at this outrage, slaughtered Alexander.

The Romans claimed that Ptolemy Alexander had bequeathed Egypt to Rome in his will but the Alexandrians, determined to remain independent, elevated Ptolemy Auletes, an illegitimate son of Ptolemy VIII, to the throne, for all that they did not like him. Auletes was in an unfortunate position as the Romans did not like him either, but he appealed to Rome who finally sent Pompey as ambassador to Egypt to support Auletes as King of Alexandria, an office recognized in Rome by First Consul Julius Caesar. The Alexandrians hated Auletes all the more now, and he fled to Rome for three years, but returned in 55 B.C. accompanied by Roman troops.

When Auletes died in 51 B.C., he was succeeded by his son Ptolemy, and his daughter Cleopatra, then a girl of seventeen. When Julius Caesar arrived in Alexandria three years later in pursuit of Ptolemy he was soon captivated by Cleopatra and she became his mistress.

The Alexandrians objected to Caesar's presence and events rapidly snowballed into the First Alexandrian War. Caesar established a garrison on the Pharos island and took over the lighthouse – which he regarded as 'a work of wonderful construction'[7] – so that he could command the Great Harbour. For several days the lighthouse was witness to a running sea battle between the Romans and Alexandrians under the command of Ganymede, the commander appointed by Cleopatra's sister Arsinoë, the newly proclaimed Regent of Alexandria.[8] The Alexandrians managed to regain the Pharos but, with their fleet weakened, were unable to hold it. By this time the Pharos was quite densely populated and its inhabitants fought bravely to defend the island, but they were finally forced to flee and Caesar, regaining the island, destroyed all the dwellings save for the lighthouse. Soon after another contingent of Romans approached the city from the south, and the cornered Alexandrian army was massacred.

Alexandria now became totally subservient to Rome. When Caesar left in 47 B.C., Cleopatra allowed him to take what he liked from the Library, which had suffered in the fighting, and he removed many thousands of scrolls to Rome. The Pharos Lighthouse had also suffered damage during the fighting and Cleopatra ensured that it was renovated. She may well have carried out some substantial maintenance (after all it was 250 years old by now), because in later years the historian Ammianus Marcellinus (*fl* A.D. 360) recorded that Cleopatra built the lighthouse.

When Caesar returned to Rome he there set up an effigy of the Pharos to commemorate his victory. The Pharos became the symbol of Alexandria and appeared on the city's coins.

Following the assassination of Julius Caesar, Cleopatra became the mistress of Mark Antony who, as one of the controlling Triumvirs, was in Cilicia. He later settled in Alexandria and plundered art treasures from all over the world and brought them to the city. Over 200,000 scrolls from the great library at Pergamon were taken to replace those removed by Julius Caesar.

The fate of the Library is enough to make one weep. It thrived in the centuries immediately after Antony and Cleopatra, but was damaged in A.D. 272, when a wealthy Egyptian merchant, Firmus, allied himself with the rebel Queen Zenobia of Palmyra and caused a riot in Alexandria which was finally quashed by the Emperor Aurelian. In 295, a Roman general stationed in Alexandria, Domitianus, declared himself Emperor, and his uprising was only settled after several years when the Roman Emperor Diocletian captured Alexandria and massacred thousands of its inhabitants.

By now the bulk of the Library was housed in the Temple of Serapis, and it was the Museum that suffered in these riots. However, the main devastation came in 391, after the conversion of Rome to Christianity. The Temple of Serapis was the last stronghold of pagan worship in the Middle East and in 389 it was decreed that the Temple be converted to a Christian church. The priests and worshippers objected and barricaded themselves within the Temple. Eventually an edict was issued declaring that the Temple be dismantled, and Theophilus, the Patriarch of Constantinople, executed the order with fanatic fervour. The Temple was totally destroyed along with all the books kept there. What books survived in the Museum were destroyed when the Arabs captured Alexandria in September 642.

Surprisingly the Pharos remained intact and working all this time, but after the Arab conquest it began to fall into disrepair. The lantern collapsed soon after 700, but the Arabs maintained a brazier at the top and in this form it continued for a further four centuries. When the Moor Idrisi visited Alexandria in 1115 he was able to report:

> This building is singularly remarkable, as much on account of its height as its solidity; it is very useful in that it is kept lit night and day as a beacon for navigators throughout the whole sailing season; mariners know the fire and direct their courses accordingly, for it is visible a day's sail away.[10]

It has been suggested that the Pharos inspired the Arabs to build minarets, adopting the staged tower, but this may be purely circumstantial. Certainly within a generation after Idrisi's visit the Pharos had ceased to function as a lighthouse and the topmost dome now housed a small mosque. There is a story that claims the Byzantine Emperor tricked the Arabs into dismantling the lighthouse so as to confuse their traders. He told the Khalif that buried beneath the Pharos was a fabled fortune, and it was not until the Arabs had already half dismantled the Pharos that they realized the trick.

Nature soon finished what the Arabs began. In 1375 an earthquake brought the top two towers crashing down and severely damaged the remainder. But, unlike the Colossus, it did not lie in ruins for centuries. The Mamelukes, or Turkish slaves of the Khalifs, had managed to overthrow their masters and in 1250 established their own sultan in Egypt. In 1477 the Sultan Qait Bey ordered that a castle be built on the site of the old Pharos as a defence against the growing danger from the Ottoman Turks. Much of the basic groundplan of the

Pharos was incorporated into the castle as well as parts of the ruined masonry, such as some of the granite columns which were built into the castle walls, and lintels were used for the doors. Some of the ruins have been discovered off the coast, but diving around the Pharos rocks is dangerous and few archaeological expeditions have been mounted.

The Pharos had more than served its purpose. The Roman engineers used it as a prototype for their own lighthouses which they established in all their harbours, including Dover. The lighthouse at La Coruña in north-west Spain, known as 'the Fire of Hercules', was built during the reign of Emperor Trajan (A.D. 98-117), and is the only lighthouse to survive intact from the ancient world, but it bears no comparison in size or grandeur to the mighty Pharos.

The word *pharos* passed into the Roman language as synonymous with lighthouse, and has so remained in many Romance tongues. Indeed, in English 'pharology' is the art of navigation by light signals.

A hundred miles to the south of Alexandria the Pyramids watched the fall of the Pharos, Seventh Wonder of the World. There they remained, the first and the last of the Wonders, waiting for their secrets to be unlocked, and the story of the Seven Wonders to be discovered.

NOTES TO CHAPTER VIII

1. It was also the legendary home of Proteus, the 'old man of the sea', who tended Poseidon's seals. He had the gift of prophecy but always evaded anyone seeking his help by rapidly assuming every possible shape.
2. *The Jewish War* by Flavius Josephus, IV.618
3. *Natural History* XXXVI.18
4. ibid.
5. There was a noticeable reduction of talent during the first century B.C. In 130 B.C. Ptolemy VII had massacred the Greeks who had sided against him in a civil war and the University was temporarily closed. It soon recovered but had to wait until the establishment of Roman rule before studies returned to normal.

6. Alexander knew of Kleomenes's tyranny but forgave him on condition he erected two memorials to Hephaestion, one of Alexander's generals and his closest friend. One was to be built on Pharos island, the other in the city, but because of subsequent events they were never erected. See Chapter III, Note 26.
7. *The Civil Wars* by Julius Caesar, III.112
8. Arsinoë was subsequently taken as captive to Rome but her life was spared and she later took sanctuary in the Temple of Artemis at Ephesos.
9. Ammianus Marcellinus XXII.16
10. Idrisi III.4

AFTERWORD

Apart from the Pyramids, the Seven Wonders of the World are no more; the men who built them and the civilizations that made them possible have vanished. It is sad to realize that cultures capable of producing such magnificent creations all, in due course, founder and perish, but what is most startling is that it was not a long process of decay but abrupt, unexpected and yet, in hindsight, inevitable.

All during my research for this book one thought became prevalent in my mind. Every one of the Seven Wonders was built at the time when the cultures that made them were at the height of their power, and in complete control of their finances, resources and peoples. But it was a double-edged sword. Those same societies also became complacent and self-indulgent. The spirit that drove them to seek supremacy was gone, and the population gave itself over to non-productive, self-centred pursuits, leaving themselves vulnerable to conquerors and tyrants. The Seven Wonders stand as testaments not only to the zenith of these nations' achievements, but also mark the start of their rapid decline. In only a relatively short period after the Wonders were completed their respective societies had ceased to exist in the same form capable of reproducing their Wonder.

The chart opposite shows this more graphically.

Some of these dates might need a little explanation, as the dates I have selected for the downfall of the culture bears no relation to the fate or longevity of the World Wonder.

The last of the kings of the Pyramid Era was Pepi II. Soon after his death in 2188 B.C. the country was divided by internal struggles and entered a period of technical decline, and the days of the great pyramid builders were over.

In 482 B.C. Xerxes despoiled Babylon to teach the inhabitants a lesson they would not easily forget, and in remov-

Wonder	Date *Completed* (B.C.)	Date of *Downfall* (B.C.)	*Period years*
The Pyramids at Giza	*c* 2500	*c* 2188	312
The Hanging Gardens of Babylon	*c* 600	482	118
The Statue of Zeus	432	365	77
The Temple of Artemis	*c* 290	*c* 64 A.D.	354
The Mausoleum	*c* 344	334	10
The Colossus of Rhodes	290	43	247
The Pharos Lighthouse	280	80	200

ing the statue of Marduk plucked the heart from the city.

The Statue of Zeus and the Olympic Games survived for centuries, but in 365 B.C., the Eleans renounced their neutrality and thereafter matters were never the same. There were certainly many major buildings and statues erected at Olympia after that date, but none in the same spirit as that which produced Zeus.

The Temple of Artemis is almost an exception to my rule since it had the good fortune to be greatly respected by the Romans as much as the Greeks and was lavished with treasures. Ephesos prospered and there is no denying that the Temple *could* have been rebuilt to as much or even greater glory during the first century A.D., but would it have been? Some time after A.D. 64 Timothy arrived in Ephesos and became the first Christian bishop of the city, and in the decades that followed further rival temples arose and the worship of Artemis declined. I doubt very much that the Temple would have been rebuilt to such a standard after this date.

The Karian state survived no longer than ten years after the completion of the Mausoleum. The Greek talent that created it remained, but the state created by Mausolos had been conquered by Alexander and rapidly lost its independence. Rhodes survived Alexander's Empire but, as we have seen, it's all-important naval power declined rapidly after Cassius plundered the island in 43 B.C. As for the Alexandrians, they were far too busy fighting amongst themselves to have the motivation to reproduce the Pharos, and after Ptolemy XII's murder in 80 B.C., the legitimate dynasty founded by Ptolemy I ended. When Cleopatra renovated the Lighthouse it was under Roman rule.

No culture survived much beyond 350 years after its zenith, and even that applies only to Ephesos where its culture was sustained by the city's religious significance. It was a case of the World Wonder keeping the city alive rather than vice versa. Without the Temple Ephesos would almost certainly have suffered far more in the early years of Roman domination. In the case of ancient Egypt we can see from the Pyramids that much of the art of their construction had been lost even before Pepi II's time, and his long reign was the final nail in the coffin. We could arguably therefore decrease the figure of 312 years by the 96 years of Pepi's reign.

So we find, using the Seven Wonders as a yardstick, that a society has difficulty in surviving much beyond two centuries past its zenith, and the reader might like to experiment with other ancient wonders such as the Great Wall of China, the Palace of Minos at Knossos or those listed in Appendix II, and see how long those cultures survived. The result is not dissimilar.

This train of thought caused me to consider our own day. Is it so different? The Egyptians, Babylonians, Greeks and Karians may have sat complacently marvelling at their Wonders much like Nebuchadnezzar boasting to Daniel, without ever realizing their days were numbered. Today we have many technological wonders to admire of which perhaps the most relevant is the Empire State Building which, ever since its completion in 1930, has been regarded as the Eighth Wonder of the World. In the years immediately following its construction the United States suffered the worst financial depression it had ever known. The country has recovered but technological advances have marched hand-in-hand with political and social unrest, and there is no reason to assume that the United States will be any more immune to its fate than the cultures of the ancient world.

The Seven Wonders of the World therefore serve as a lesson to societies never to assume they are invincible, no matter what marvels they can achieve. It was most appropriately summarized by Percy Bysshe Shelley in his poem *Ozymandias*, describing the remains of a colossal statue of the Pharaoh Rameses II who reigned during Egypt's greatest period, a thousand years after Khufu and Khafre:

> And on the pedestal these words appear:
> 'My name is Ozymandias, king of kings:
> Look on my works, ye Mighty, and despair!'
> Nothing beside remains. Round the decay
> Of that colossal wreck, boundless and bare,
> The lone and level sands stretch far away.

APPENDIX I

ON THE SEVEN WONDERS OF THE WORLD

by *Philon of Byzantium*

The following is a free translation by Jean Blackwood of the text of *De Septem Orbis Spectaculis* as it appears in *Aelianus Praenestinus* compiled by Rudolf Hercher and published in 1858.

Everyone knows of the renowned Seven Wonders of the World, but few have set eyes on them, for, in order to do so you have to arrange a long journey to the land of the Persians on the far side of the Euphrates; you have to visit Egypt; you must then change direction and go to Elis in Greece. Then you must see Halikarnassos, a city-state in Caria, and Ephesos in Ionia, and you have to sail to Rhodes, so that, being exhausted by lengthy wanderings over the Earth's surface, and growing tired from the effort of these journeys, you finally fulfil your heart's desire only when life is ebbing away, leaving you weak through the weight of years.

Thus, learning is a quality which is truly to be admired and to be treasured as a great gift because, at the same time as it gives their minds insight, it may show men, freed from the burden of travelling, the most remarkable of sights which are to be seen at home, and it designates the sight that is worthy of admiration. For the traveller who reaches these places sees them once, and as soon as he leaves, he forgets, because he has not firmly grasped the delicate beauty of the works he has gazed upon, and the individual details escape his memory. Whereas he, who by selective reading has become acquainted with a worthy sight knows the details of its form and has thus set eyes upon a complete work of art, and, because these sights have been seen in his mind's eye they remain, imprinted on his mind, each single image, never to be destroyed.

I must add something else that in no way departs from the truth. Where I have managed to describe the Seven Wonders of the World as accurately as possible, my words, surveying the scene, are associated by the listener in such a way that it may seem to him that he has looked upon them with his own eyes. For these wonders are the only things which diminish the worth and reputation of other distinguished sights, for, truly, ordinary men may *see* them in the same way as other sights, but they do not marvel at other sights in the same way. For beauty, like the sun, dazzles by its own brilliance and does not allow one to see the others.

I

The garden which is called the Hanging Garden suspends its plants in the air, having shoots which are supported away from the ground. The tree roots which hang above the ground, assuredly cover the earth and take the place of a floor. Here is a description of this work. First of all stone columns are supported on a general foundation and made firm. This is done in such a way that the engraved bases of the columns cover the whole area given over to the garden. Then beams made from palm trees are set down in different places, separated from one another by only a small space. For palm is absolutely the only kind of wood which does not rot. It is moistened so that it will bend back after being pressed upwards by weights. Moreover it feeds the fibres and tendrils of the roots which mix with the matter in its own cells and sinews.

A vast and deep mass of earth is poured over the beams; trees are planted with their broad leaves nearly touching to help foster the Garden. There are all kinds of varieties of flowers, and, so that it will be enjoyed by all, whatever is the most delightful, agreeable and pleasant to the eyes is there. The whole of the place is ploughed like a normal field and it is no less fertile than other ground. Yet it is done in such a way that the land can be ploughed above the heads of those walking amongst the supporting columns.

Whilst the upper layer of soil is trodden on underfoot, in places the deep, lower layers remain untouched, and that which lies at the bottom remains virgin ground. The waters gush forth from lofty fountains and sink right down through the ground and are then forced up high in twists and spirals, rushing and swirling through the circuits of the pipes of certain mechanical devices. And so the water having been collected on high in numerous ample containers irrigates the whole garden and, with its bountiful moisture, it bathes the roots of the trees which are pressed into the top layer of the ground and thus keeps the soil perpetually moist.

Here grow grasses which are perennially green, and trees whose leaves move in the breeze. The branches are made soft by constant moisture and so the leaves grow more densely. The roots, which are never removed, exude water continuously, and this circulates through the pores of the roots which are buried and pressed into the ground, keeping the trees naturally firm and thick. And so the cultivator, in his many ways, has created strength through nature; this certainly is a work of regal splendour giving much pleasure suspended above the heads of onlookers.

II

The construction of the Pyramids at Memphis is beyond the strength of men and their description is beyond belief, for they are mountains placed on top of mountains, and it is not easy for the mind to grasp how the huge masses of hewn stone could have been raised; and all have doubts concerning the huge force of the mechanical devices needed to bring the massive structures together.

After a quadrangular base had been laid down, those very stones needed to support the construction and keep it off the ground were interred, and, as the pyramid rises, the superstructure decreases proportionately in size and the whole work turns visibly into a pyramid, assuming a tapering shape.

The whole of the work of joining the stones together has been so cleverly and elegantly accomplished that the whole monument seems to have sprung from one hewn stone. Different kinds of stone are joined together in turns, for here is pure marble whilst there is a black Ethiopian stone. The stone which they call blood-like is not present. The one that is brought from Arabia is there, changing colour, translucently fresh and green. Some take on a radiant glossy blue colour, and there are others which, like the apple tree, turn golden. Some are a purple colour, not dissimilar to those stained with the marine purple dye of sea-shells. For the rest, delight is enhanced by astonishment, excellence of artistic inspiration by admiration, and distinction by extravagance. Climbing to the top tires one as much as a real journey, and if anyone stands at the highest point and looks down, dizziness veils his sight. Regal wealth adds splendour to the very pleasing variety of the range of colours. Let fortune smile while she believes that she can touch the very stars by spending extravagantly. For by works of this kind, either men rise to the level of gods, or the gods come down to man.

III

As Kronos is Zeus's father in heaven, so Phidias is his father in Elis. Immortal nature gave birth to the former, but the hands of Phidias, which alone have satisfied the gods, begat the latter. Blessed is Phidias who, alone, has seen the king of the world and has re-created his awesome presence for all to see. If it belittles Zeus to call him the son of Phidias, might we still not consider his mother to be Art, by which means Phidias created (Zeus's) likeness. With this in mind Nature provided the elephant, and filled Africa with abundant herds so that Phidias might fashion their curved teeth. We honour the other Wonders of the World with our admiration, but this is the only one that we venerate. For however much a work of art is to be admired, the image of Zeus is sacrosanct. If labour is worthy of praise, then an immortal being must truly be worthy of reverence.

O to the Grecian Age which will abound in works dedicated to the honouring of gods for many centuries to come, and which has had as the creator of immortality the artist whose like has not been seen again. You have been able to show mortals the features of the gods, and whoever has looked upon them will look more soberly at the works of others. For no other has been superior to Phidias in the way he laid Olympus at his feet. For as we know that evidence is preferable to opinion, and fact to fiction, so sight is superior to hearsay.

IV

Out to sea lies the island of Rhodes which, long ago, was submerged in the deep and which the Sun raised up to the light and demanded it as his own from the gods. Here stands the Colossus, seventy cubits high, executed in the likeness of the Sun, for it is recognized to be an effigy of the god as it bears his own special features. The artist used so much bronze for the work that there was almost a shortage of metals, for all the earth's mines were exploited in carrying out the project.

You will remember that Zeus deluged the Rhodians with great wealth so that they might devote it to honouring the Sun as they had undertaken to produce a statue of the god that would stretch right from the earth to the sky.

The workmen fortified the statue of the Colossus from the inside by hewn stones joined together by iron bolts, and the bars which are used on the stones to bring the joins together seem to have been fashioned by the hammers of the Cyclops. Whatever part of the work remains hidden is greater than that which can be seen; for the onlooker, transfixed in admiration, can only doubt that such vast masses of bronze could have been melted down and cast, wonder by what clamps they have been held, to what kind of blows they have been subjected and what strenuous exertions have brought them into being.

A pedestal of pure marble was laid down and on this, calculating the proportion, the artist first fixed the feet of the Colossus as far as the ankle, on to which the god was to be erected, seventy cubits high. At this (foot) level the base was already greater than other statues and it was not possible to lift the rest of the statue into place above; yet there were so many people helping that the whole rose up, in one continuous movement, like the temples of the gods, as if of its ow accord.

So, in order to achieve this, the artist cast the rest of the statue beforehand, and it was reassembled piece by piece. One piece was fixed to the part already cast, and a third piece was added when this was finished, and then each further part, just as it had been fashioned, was completed with the same skill. For whole parts of bronze could not be moved from the place where they were cast.

Seeing that the pieces were joined correctly, the artist ensured that the joins and connecting rods were secured after the statue had been made even more firm by the stone laid in place to hold the work steady.

But the artist had to preserve the shape of the work in his mind for, as parts of the Colossus were finished he poured a huge quantity of earth about the base hiding that part already completed, so that he might finish the next parts from ground level. He gradually ascended to the very topmost point of his desire making a god-like image from 500 talents of bronze and 300 talents of iron, so freeing a great work of art from the bold mind of its creator; for in the world a second Sun stood face to face with the first.

V

Queen Semiramis created majesty and regal splendour with her immense wealth, for she paid no heed to jewels and treasure and so left behind a Wonder of the World. For she surrounded Babylon with walls, the foundations of which were 360 stadia in diameter so that running around the city exhausted the daily courier. But they are to be admired not only because of their size but also truly on account of the solidity of their construction and the width achieved with the materials, for the walls have been built out of baked brick and bitumen.

The height of the wall certainly exceeds fifty cubits, and truly the width of the course is such that four quadrigas can drive along them at the same time. There are numerous multi-storeyed towers stretching in an unbroken link of sufficient size to house within them a large army. For this reason the city-state is a fortress for the Persians and, generally speaking, the city seems more or less self-sufficient, so many people live within its walls. Truly other states scarcely till as much land as Babylon covers with dwellings alone, and only at that place can the inhabitants walk about inside the walls.

VI

The unique Temple of Artemis at Ephesos is the abode of gods. Whoever has gazed upon it will believe that the heavenly world of the immortals has changed places with the earth. The Giants, or Aloidae, who undertook to conquer Olympus with mountains, have now built not a temple but a dwelling fit for gods. Just as work in progress surpasses its foundation, so art, by its boldness, surpasses the work in progress.

The artist, isolated from everyone because his work was known only to him, dug trenches to an immense depth and exhausted the mountain quarries in laying his extensive foundations. A supporting structure, solid and firm, was placed down with immense sculptured columns (*Atlantes*) to support the heavy superstructure; initially he constructed a base raised by ten steps placed outside to serve as a platform . . .

(Here the manuscript ends, and the remainder of this section, as well as that covering the Mausoleum, are missing.)

APPENDIX II

THE FORGOTTEN WONDERS

Philon's list was not the only compilation of Wonders of the World. Although not all writers restricted themselves to seven, many would specify which seven they considered supreme. I have selected just four of these lists to show the variety of choice and to give some recognition to those Wonders overlooked because they failed to make the traditional list. So as not to be inconsistent I shall look in particular at another Seven Wonders:

1. The Colosseum in Rome
2. The Palace of Cyrus at Ecbatana
3. The Temple of Jupiter Capitolinus in Rome
4. The Statue of Bellerophon
5. The Circus Maximus in Rome
6. The Baths of Caracalla
7. Solomon's Temple in Jerusalem

1. Valerius Martialis

Martialis was born in Bilbilis in Northern Spain in about A.D. 43. He went to Rome in 66, and became a renowned poet, respected in later years by the Emperors Titus and Domitian. He returned to his home town when he was about 57, and died there some time after A.D. 104. During his years in Rome he wrote a series of epigrams collectively entitled *Liber de Spectaculis* (*Book of Wonders*). Many critics feel they are spoiled by his excessive flattery to the Emperors which is revealed in the following example completed in A.D. 80 to celebrate the dedication of the Colosseum by Titus.

May barbaric Memphis not reveal the wonders of the Pyramids,
And may the diligence and toil that produced Babylon be not boastful,
May not the mild Ionians be extolled by the Temple of Diana,
May the Altar made of many horns hide its Delos,
And may the Karians not exalt by immoderate praises the Mausoleum, suspended in the empty air,
May they all yield to the glory of Caesar's Amphitheatre,
Let fame speak of this work in place of all.

The Colosseum was rated as a World Wonder by several Latin writers, and for once its ruins are still with us to testify, at least in part, to its glory.

The Colosseum was an arena or amphitheatre (literally 'a theatre on both sides') where the notorious gladiatorial combats took place and where the Christians were thrown to the lions. It was erected at the instigation of the Emperor Vespasian (A.D. 69-79) in place of the original amphitheatre that burned down during the Great Fire of Rome in A.D. 64 – the Fire in which Nero fiddled. It was built partly on the land appropriated by Nero for his own Golden Palace. He had arranged for a large artificial lake in the centre of Rome, and this was now drained and the land fortified. At the entrance to his Golden Palace Nero had erected a colossal statue of himself, 106 feet high. Vespasian subsequently had this redesigned to represent the Sun god and it was re-erected in the amphitheatre grounds. Over the years the statue became so associated with the arena that the name Colosseum followed naturally. Its correct name was the Amphitheatrum Flavianum, from the family name of Vespasian.

Since the death of Augustus Caesar, Rome had had to suffer the tyrannies and perversions of a series of incompetent emperors and their relatives, and Vespasian was determined to ingratiate himself with the citizens of Rome. There was no better way than to give them what they wanted – the largest arena ever built where they could wallow in a surfeit of slaughter.

To show that we have not entirely severed our connections with the accepted Seven Wonders, there is a link between the Pharos and the Colosseum. In A.D. 69 Vespasian was preparing for his offensive against Jerusalem to suppress the revolt of the Jews, and was stationed at Alexandria, beneath the very shadow of the Pharos. It was here that the troops, restless at the news that the gluttonous Vitellius had been declared Emperor by the legions at Cologne, entreated Vespasian to assume the imperial throne. The murder of Vitellius and accession of Vespasian returned Rome to a period of relative sanity and one of extensive rebuilding.

The Colosseum was elliptical in shape, 615 feet long by 510 feet wide, with the outer wall 160 feet high. The original consisted of three stone storeys with an upper gallery of wood, which was rebuilt in stone in the third century. There was seating capacity for 45,000 plus standing room for a further 5000.

The name of its architect is not known, Roman Emperors preferring to claim all the glory. Colosseum guides will tell you it was a Roman called Gaudentius who was later converted to Christianity and was killed in his own arena. It's a good story and was put forward by the eighteenth-century historian Giovanni Marangoni on the flimsiest of circumstantial evidence. Without a doubt it was a remarkable feat of engineering. Vespasian had ordered it be built in haste; he was already in his sixties and wished to dedicate the amphitheatre before his death. Work began soon after A.D. 72, and over the next eight years over 750,000 tons of stone, 8000 tons of marble and 6000 tons of concrete were shifted into place. It was still incomplete when, as one of his last acts of office, Vespasian dedicated it in June 79, but it was not officially inaugurated until the following year by Vespasian's son, Titus.

Titus opened the Colosseum with a festival of games that lasted for one hundred days. Over five thousand animals were killed on the first day, initiating a spectacle of slaughter that would last for over four hundred years. The games could be divided into three categories: battles between men and animals; gladiatorial combat between the *secutor* with sword and shield and the *retiarus* with net and trident; and thirdly naval battles whereupon the floor of the amphitheatre was flooded.

Later emperors varied in their enthusiasm for the games. Hadrian (117-138) tried to curb the citizens' lust for carnage but submitted when he realized how his actions affected his popularity. Commodus (180-192), on the other hand, lived for the games and was never more content than when witnessing the massacre of animals and gladiators. The games did not even suffer when Constantine converted to Christianity, for pagans were thrown to the lions instead of Christians. It was not until the reign of Honorius (393-423) that gladiatorial contests were officially forbidden, but it was another century before the last games with wild beasts were held (A.D. 523). By then Rome had long since ceased to be ruled by Emperors and was under the more civilized control of the Ostrogoth Theoderic.

Marvellous though the Colosseum was as a building, the slaughter committed within was inexcusable. We have this and similar amphitheatres to blame for the total extermination of the Moroccan elephant and the near extinction of the white rhinoceros. The barbarians who finally conquered Rome and the Colosseum were as nothing to the barbarians who revelled within.

II. Gaius Julius Hyginus

Hyginus lived nearly a century before Martialis, and was a freedman of the Emperor Augustus who placed him in charge of the Palatine Library. Unfortunately it is not known for sure if he wrote the works accredited to him, the earliest known copies dating from the second century. The one that concerns us is the *Fabularum Liber* or *Story Book*, a collection of 277 short fables and legends of which number 233 is entitled 'Septem Opera Mirabilis – 'The Seven Wonderful Works'.

> The Temple of Diana at Ephesus, which Otrera the Amazon, the wife of Mars made. The Tomb of King Mausolos, made of light-coloured stone, 80 feet high, 1340 feet in circum-

> ference. The Colossus is the brass statue of the Sun at Rhodes, 90 feet high. The Statue of Jove at Olympus which devoted Phidias made from ivory and gold is 60 feet high. The abode of Cyrus, the king, in Ecbatana, made by Memnon from stones which were both varied and pure in labour and which were fortified with gold. The wall in Babylon which Semiramis, the daughter of Dercetis made and strengthened with baked brick and iron sulphur, 25 feet wide, 60 feet high and 300 stadia in circumference. The Pyramids in Egypt whose likeness is not to be seen are 60 feet high.

Hyginus, or his copyist, erred on several facts, especially concerning the Pyramids, which he had clearly never seen. If the list was intended to be presented in order of glory, which seems possible with the esteem with which the Temple of Diana (Artemis) was held, then it gives us an idea of the Roman view of the Seven Wonders. Again the Pharos is missing, and this time so are the Hanging Gardens, though the Walls of Babylon make the grade. Instead we have a new Wonder, the Palace of Cyrus at Ecbatana.

We must turn back the clock more than six centuries from the Colosseum to a time approximately contemporaneous with Nebuchadnezzar and the Hanging Gardens. Ecbatana was the capital of the Median Empire and stood at the foot of Mount Orontes, mid-way between Babylon and the Caspian Sea. Here was raised Princess Amytis, daughter of King Kyaxares and future wife of Nebuchadnezzar. It was for her that the Hanging Gardens were built, and the connection with the Seven Wonders may be even more tangible than that, as can be seen from the description of Ecbatana given by Herodotus, which begins after Dayukku (or Deiokos) has been appointed first king of the Medes.

> Upon this he required a palace to be built for him suitable to his rank and a guard to be given him for his person. The Medes complied, and built him a strong and large palace, on a spot which he himself pointed out . . . Thus settled upon the throne he further required them to build a single great city, and disregarding the petty towns in

> which they had formerly dwelt, make the new capital the object of their chief attention. The Medes were again obedient, and built the city now called Agbatana, the walls of which are of great size and strength, rising in circles one within the other. The plan of the place is that each of the walls should out-top the one beyond it by the battlements. The nature of the ground, which is a gentle hill, favours this arrangement in some degree, but it was mainly effected by art. The number of the circles is seven, the royal palace and the treasuries standing within the last. The circuit of the outer wall is very nearly the same with that of Athens. Of this wall the battlements are white, of the next black, of the third scarlet, of the fourth blue, of the fifth orange; all these are coloured with paint. The last two have their battlements coated respectively with silver and gold. (Book I.98)

The city was clearly inspired by the Babylonian ziggurats, which also had seven stages of various colours. However Nabopolassar and Nebuchadnezzar may have been inspired in turn to rebuild Babylon after seeing Ecbatana. The Palace is attributed to the reign of Dayukku, in about 700 B.C., but it probably owed more to Kyaxares, who ruled from 625 to 585 B.C., and made Media a major power. Polybius tells us that the Palace had a circumference of seven stadia (four-fifths of a mile) and an area of two-thirds of a square mile. It was built entirely of cedar and cypress, of which there was a bountiful supply in the surrounding forests; but none of the wood was visible as it was all overlaid with gold and silver: the beams, the ceilings, the walls and the roof tiles. The Medes had no artistic culture of their own, but blended a style of Babylonian architecture along with an imitation of their own simple wooden houses on a grander scale. Thus the palace was a forest of columns, placed so as to form aisles and porches about the central courts.

Cyrus conquered Media in 550 B.C., and made Ecbatana his northern and summer capital, sharing with Pasargadae, the southern and winter capital. Cyrus naturally adopted the palace as his own and it became associated with him in later years.

Ecbatana still exists today as Hamadan, capital of the Iranian province of the same name, but the beautiful place of old has long since vanished.

As the Dark Ages began to close the curtains on the scholarly stage, facts metamorphosed into misty fable and the boundaries of truth and fiction become indeterminable. Although the lamp of learning was kept burning by the monks, they had insufficient information to separate myth from reality. Legends which sounded passably true were presented as facts as the following example reveals.

III. The 'Venerable' Bede

Bede was a Saxon monk at Jarrow near Durham who lived from A.D. 673-735. He has been called 'the father of English history', and was regarded as the most learned Christian of his day. He wrote some forty books, mostly commentaries on the Scriptures, which he translated into 'English', but his two most important books are *The Ecclesiastical History of England* – the only reliable history of this island from his time – and *De Natura Rerum* (*On The Nature of Things*) which includes the following 'Treatise Concerning the Seven Wonders of the World fashioned by the hand of men'.

1. The first is the Capitol at Rome, the citizen's salvation, greater than the State; and there, there were statues of the peoples who had been captured by the Romans, and images of the gods, and the names of the peoples who had been captured by the Romans were written on the breasts of the statues, and bells had been hung on their necks. The priests and the watchmen took turns both by day and by night and endeavoured to care for the statues in case each or any of the bells are set in motion. Should a bell ring they would know which of the people would rebel against the Romans. However, when this was known it was announced to the Roman leaders so that they might know which people they had to punish by sending an army against them.

2. The second is the Lighthouse at Alexandria which was made firm on top of four glassy pillars twenty paces under the sea. This is truly wonderful for the way in which such great pillars were able to be fashioned, and for the way they withstood being carried around without being broken; how the cement foundations have been able to adhere on top, and how the cement is able to remain firm under the waters, and how the pillars are not broken, and how the foundations which have been laid on top do not slide.

3. The third is the mighty statue of the Colossus on the island of Rhodes made from molten metal and standing a hundred and thirty-six feet high. This was wonderful for the way in which it was possible for such a great and massive weight to be either erected or for it to remain standing.

4. The fourth wonder is the iron statue of Bellerophon on his horse which is suspended above the town and which stands in the air and is not hung by means of chains, nor is it supported from above by any stake whatsoever, but huge magnets are contained in its main wings and it is borne hither and thither alternatively, although its size remains the same. Its weight however can be estimated at about 5000 pounds of iron.

5. The fifth wonder is the Circus of Heraclea that is hewn in such a way from one kind of marble with all the small apartments and dwelling places, the walls and the wild beasts' caves. It is balanced on the top of seven pillars hewn from the same kind of stone, and no one in the ring itself can speak softly either to himself or to anyone else than that those who are within the orbit of the building will not hear him.

6. The sixth wonder is the Bath House which Apollotaneus set alight with one consecration candle. He made the Baths hot by an everlasting fire which did not need any attention whatsoever.

7. The seventh wonder is the Temple of Diana. On top of four columns have been laid the first series of arches, then, gradually developing above the four arches even more prominent stones are placed above. On top of the series of four are placed eight columns and eight arches; then there developed a third line equally balanced on all sides and stones which are even more prominent are placed on top of these. Then above the eight, sixteen are laid down, on top of the sixteen are thirty-two; rows of sixty-four columns put the finishing touches to such a marvellous building.

Apart from the Colossus of Rhodes, which escapes relatively lightly, the remaining Wonders are almost unrecognizable. Yet Bede was respected for the care with which he sought out and selected reliable information. Alone in his tiny room at Jarrow, Bede never visited Rome, Ephesos or indeed anywhere outside Britain, but relied on what ancient manuscripts were available. If *he* could not find the correct facts what chance did anyone else have? Yet Bede was so venerated that his details were accepted without question, and you will find much of Bede's descriptions in some of the ancient paintings and woodcuts of the Wonders.

He introduces us to four new wonders which I shall briefly evaluate one at a time.

The Capitol at Rome. The city of Rome stood on seven hills: the Quirinal, Viminal, Esquiline, Caelian, Aventine, Palatine and Capitoline. The original city, traditionally founded by Romulus in 753 B.C., was built on the Palatine, but a century or so later the ruling kings transferred their residence to the Capitoline where they established a Citadel. One of the most important families in Rome at the time were the Tarquins, of Etruscan origin. The Etruscans were a highly civilized but rather enigmatic people who had occupied central Italy since about 900 B.C. One of their number, Lucius Tarquinius (subsequently called Tarquinius *Priscus* 'the Elder'), established himself as king of Rome, and during his reign the city underwent profound changes: it was politically and militarily organized, it began to dominate the surrounding towns, and it was improved by a number of public works, including a remarkable drainage system – some of which sewers still exist. Tarquinius vowed to build a temple to Jupiter who now, as a result of Etruscan domination, was rapidly becoming Rome's leading deity in place of Mars. Tarquinius was murdered before work on the temple could begin and its creation fell to a descendent, Tarquin II, called *Superbus* or 'the Arrogant', and the last king of Rome. Tradition ascribes the dates 535-510 B.C. to his reign, and within a year or two either way they are historically correct.

Roman territory was subject to raids from neighbouring tribes, especially the Volsci in the south, and at the start of his reign, Tarquin II soundly defeated the Volsci and captured the wealthy town of Suessia Pometia. From the spoils he had built the Temple of Jupiter Optimus Maximus – 'the Best and the Greatest' – because the Etruscans claimed it was with the help of Jupiter that Rome had become prosperous. Because it was built on the Capitoline Hill it was known as the Capitolium.

The temple was divided into three long cells so that the main altar of Jupiter was flanked by shrines to Juno and Minerva, who formed the Roman triad of divinities equal to the Greek Zeus, Hera and Athene – representing strength, fertility and wisdom.

The Capitolium, originally built in wood, was raised upon a sixteen-foot-high platform of grey volcanic stone. It was tripteral hexastyle, that is it had three rows of six columns along the front porch. There was a single row of six columns along each side and none at the rear. The total dimensions were 175 feet wide by 204 feet long, making it one of the largest temples in the Mediterranean world. The columns were surmounted by a low wooden entablature decorated with terracotta sculptures. Within the temple stood a terracotta statue of Jupiter, the work of the noted Etruscan sculptor Vulca, who hailed from the town of Veii, twelve miles north-west of Rome. This statue was originally painted red and over the years the colour became associated with authority and finally devolved into the purple robe – the robe of the Emperors.

The most treasured possession kept in the Temple was the Sibylline Books – the key to the future. They were a set of, originally, nine books which recorded prophecies of future events interpreted from some extraordinary occurrence, such as the instance when an eagle drops a wolf cub into the arms of the young Claudius which was seen as a sign that one day Claudius would rule Rome. These books had been purchased by Tarquin the Elder from the Cumaean Sibyl – the priestess of Apollo at the Greek colony of Cumae, about a hundred miles south of Rome, near modern Naples. These precious books were consulted by augurs and diviners only with the permission of the Senate.

The Temple was not dedicated until the year 507 B.C., by which time Tarquin II had been banished from Rome and the republic established. The Temple stood for over four hundred years until Rome was divided by civil war in the rivalry between Sulla and Cinna. During that period the floor had been paved with marble, the ceiling gilded, and bronze statues cast in place of the terracotta sculptures. But in 83 B.C., during the hostilities in Rome, the Capitolium was burned down, and within it the Sibylline Books destroyed. It was promptly rebuilt and now contained a colossal statue of Jupiter modelled in the likeness of Zeus at Olympia, but it again suffered at the hands of Caligula and later emperors, and burned down again in the Great Fire of Rome (A.D. 64). Rebuilt by Vespasian in A.D. 75, it burned down again five years later, and it was not until the time of Domitian, emperor from A.D. 81-96, that the Temple received its most glorious of restorations. Its plan and size remained the same but it was now approached by a flight of one hundred steps. It had giant bronze gates and the ceiling and roof tiles were coated with gold. The whole was constructed from marble.

The Temple was embellished with Greek statues and sculptures acquired from throughout the empire. It rapidly became an art museum with such treasures as a statue of Zeus by Myron (*c* 450 B.C.) which may have once stood at Samos; a Herakles by Lysippos (*c* 340 B.C.), and an Amazon by Kresilaos (*c* 430 B.C.) which may once have stood in the Temple of Artemis at Ephesos.

Like all Greek and Roman temples, the Capitolium's importance waned after Emperor Theodosius I passed his decree in A.D. 391, banning all pagan worship. Theodosius had raised the pertinent question at a full meeting of the Senate in 381 when he asked whether the worship of Christ or Jupiter should prevail in Rome. The Senate voted almost to a man to cast out the ancient cult of Jupiter, and although the Temple was not destroyed it was relegated in importance to a museum. Here stood the statues mentioned by Bede, but the story of their bells and how they betrayed the enemy is no more than a myth. They certainly did not work when it mattered. In A.D. 410, Alaric the Visigoth captured Rome, and in 455 it was sacked by Genseric the Vandal, who pillaged the Temple.

Curiously, just over a thousand years later, in December 1471, close to the site of the Capitolium, Pope Sixtus IV opened the first modern museum of art.

The Statue of Bellerophon. Bellerophon was one of those grand heroes of Greek myth who, whilst his name is less well known than that of Herakles or Theseus, was no less larger than life. According to legend, King Glaukos of Corinth had a son called Hipponous who became involved with a fellow Corinthian called Beleros, whom he killed. Hipponous was thus dubbed Bellerophon, and to be purified of his murder he fled to King Proetos of Argos, whose wife fell in love with him. Bellerophon rejected her advances, so she accused him of seducing her. Proetos, unable to kill Bellerophon himself, sent him to Iobates, king of Lycia, who sent him off to kill the dragon Khimaira, thinking that would be the last of him.

However, Iobates did not reckon on Bellerophon's fortune. Aided by Athene, Bellerophon captured the winged horse Pegasos which had sprung from the blood of the decapitated Gorgon, Medusa. With the aid of Pegasos, Bellerophon was able to hover above the Khimaira and kill it with his arrows. Disappointed, Iobates next sent Bellerophon against the savage tribes of the Solymi and the Amazons, but he was again victorious. On his return, Iobates set an ambush of the strongest and bravest Lycians, but Bellerophon slew them all. At last convinced that Bellerophon was invincible, Iobates gave him his daughter in marriage and made him his heir. And so, you might think, they lived happily ever after. But Greek myths and fairy tales have little in common. Bellerophon had incurred the wrath of the gods, and Artemis and Ares killed his two young children. Angered, Bellerophon mounted Pegasos and attempted to reach the summit of Mount Olympus to avenge himself, but Zeus sent a gadfly which stung Pegasos and caused the horse to throw Bellerophon. Pegasos reached the home of the gods and was immortalized, but Bellerophon fell to Earth and was lamed. Despised by all, he was forced to wander the earth, alone and in misery.

The statue to which Bede refers doubtless depicted either Bellerophon's attack upon the Khimaira or his attempt to conquer Olympus, both popular themes in Greek art, but unfortunately, it is one of the many lost in antiquity. Whilst it may well have existed one fact is definite: it would never have hovered in the air supported by nothing but magnets. Here Bede fell prey to a myth popular amongst the Greeks and Arabs. Ever since the lodestone's powers of attraction and repulsion had been discovered by Thales of Miletos in about 600 B.C., magnetism had been a subject of mystery amongst the ancients. Although they could not demonstrate it, they could see no reason why magnets of varying strengths built into the floors and ceilings of temples could not establish opposing forces in which an iron statue could be suspended. Pliny tells us that Ptolemy Philadelphos requested that Timokhares achieve just this effect with the statue of his sister-wife Arsinoë, in the Temple built to her honour in Alexandria, but the project was never completed as both Timokhares and Philadelphos died. We can be sure that other attempts were made, and it was through stories such as this that Bede contrived his Fourth Wonder.

The Circus at Heraclea. Here we must give Bede the benefit of the doubt. There were a number of Greek colonies called Heraclea, the most famous being in Lucania in southern Italy; but the remains of a circus, or hippodrome, have yet to be found at any of these sites. Judging by Bede's description he is confusing a circus with an amphitheatre, as he mentions caves for wild beasts. During the days of the Roman Empire most important Roman cities had their amphitheatres, usually modelled on the Colosseum but nearly all lesser creations.

For a circus to rank as a World Wonder it would have to

have been of formidable dimensions and thus seems unlikely to have escaped the notice of archaeologists. There were several renowned circuses of old, the most famous being the Circus Maximus in Rome. Traditionally ascribed to Tarquin the Elder, it was substantially rebuilt by Julius Caesar and was over 700 yards long with room for 200,000 spectators. I doubt that Heraclea produced anything superior to that.

The Bath House. Here Bede completely loses us. There were thousands of bath houses in the Roman world alone, and no record has survived of any Apollotaneus. This gives us an opportunity to attempt some detective work and see if we can reason out Bede's Wonder.

Apollotaneus may well be a corruption or contraction of Apollonius Tyanaeus, or Apollonius of Tyana, a so-called miracle worker who lived during the first century A.D. He was alleged to have travelled throughout the Near East visiting the many mystical sites such as Babylon, and learning the secrets of the sages. He rapidly became known in the Roman world for his powers of precognition and it is related that he met Vespasian at Alexandria and told him that he would soon become Emperor. Shortly after the Great Fire of Rome, Nero issued a decree banning magic and witchcraft, and condemning all wizards. Apollonius arrived in Rome just at this time and was promptly arrested, but he is alleged to have miraculously blinded the administrator Tigellinus and so was released for fear of any further retribution. Apollonius finally retired to Ephesos, where he predicted the death of Domitian hours before it happened, and he died at Ephesos aged nearly a hundred.

It is possible that Apollonius's visit to Rome soon became connected with the Great Fire. Since this was also blamed on the Christians, it was but a short step to associate Apollonius with that sect and presume him to have started the fire with a consecration candle at a bath house. However this would not be in keeping with the later legend that grew up around Apollonius, started by a writer called Hierocles during the reign of the Emperor Diocletian (A.D. 284-305). Hierocles established Apollonius in opposition to the Christians, promoting him as a pagan rival to Jesus Christ. Bede would have certainly known of this belief, and it is hard to imagine him confusing Apollonius with the Christians. One other coincidental fragment of information comes in the *Life of Apollonius* written by the Greek Philostratos in about A.D. 200. He tells us that whilst at Antioch, Apollonius chided the citizens for using hot baths, asserting that only cold baths were good for the body and soul. There were many Jews in Antioch and Paul used it as the home base for his missionary journeys. It was in Antioch that the disciples were first called 'Christians', so it would be a logical place for Bede to cite as the city from whence Christianity spread like a fire.

If any baths ranked as a World Wonder they would be those named after the Emperor Caracalla (A.D. 211-217), though construction began during the reign of his predecessor Septimius Severus and was not completed until after Caracalla's murder. To the Romans the baths were not simply a place to wash, but the social centre of the city where a major portion of the community spent many hours a day. Caracalla's Bath House had an elaborate combination of buildings with a giant cross-vaulted central hall measuring 185 by 79 feet, was over 100 feet high, and contained a swimming pool. Nearby were the main steam rooms and associated annexes with space for 1600 bathers. Surrounding the building were open-air gymnasia, a museum and garden walks.

There is a connection between Caracalla and the Christian faith, though not with his baths. Caracalla's nurse and teacher were both Christians, and during his reign he allowed the Christians to erect their own churches in the Empire, even within Rome. That is not to say Caracalla was any less savage or mad than most of his predecessors. He tried to emulate Alexander and marched off east to reconquer the old Empire, and was murdered.

The Baths marked one of the last major building phases of the Roman world, which was thereafter subject to internal strife and barbarian onslaught. Caracalla's Baths were consequently the most recent construction which could rank as one of the Wonders of the Ancient World.

IV. St Gregory of Tours

I have left till last the unannotated list supplied by Gregory, Bishop of Tours. He lived over a century earlier than Bede, from A.D. 538 to 594, and his list shows that even by his time, much of the ancient knowledge was being lost. His Seven ran as follows:

1. The Colossus of Rhodes
2. The Pharos at Alexandria
3. The Walls of Babylon
4. The Sepulchre of a Persian king (probably Mausolos)
5. Noah's Ark
6. Solomon's Temple
7. The Theatre at Heraklea.

Whether Gregory meant by the Theatre of Heraklea the same as Bede's Circus we do not know, as neither survive. I shall not dwell on Noah's Ark, though any who care to turn to the *Book of Genesis* 6.14-16, can find full details of its construction. For my final, seventh forgotten wonder, I'd like to look at Solomon's Temple at Jerusalem.

We have to go back to the year 1034 B.C. to a Wonder more ancient than any except the Pyramids. At this time the small kingdom of Israel was ruled by Solomon, the son of David and Bath-sheba. Over thirty years earlier David had succeeded in bringing the sacred Ark of the Covenant to Jerusalem but he was perturbed that the Ark resided in a tent whilst he, David, lived in a cedar palace. He thereby resolved to build a special temple to house the Ark, but was advised by his prophet Nathan that Jehovah did not wish the temple to be built by David who had waged so many wars, but that it would be built by his son during a time of peace.

In preparation David bought the land required on the site of Mount Moriah, a rocky prominence north of Mount Zion and believed to be the same place where over eight hundred years before Abraham had offered up Isaac in sacrifice. David also amassed funds equal to about £3000 million by today's standards, and drew the plans for the temple under divine instruction. All Solomon had to do was build it.

Work began in April or May of 1034 B.C., and took seven and a half years, being completed in October or November 1027 B.C. It took a further eleven months for the temple to be suitably furnished and equipped. A unique aspect about the construction was that, 'as for hammers and axes or any tools of iron, they were not heard in the house while it was being built.' (1 Kings 6.7) That cannot mean that the temple was built without using tools, since there were stones to be quarried and shaped, and fittings to be fashioned. What it means is that all the work was carried out elsewhere, and the Temple was simply assembled at the site – the world's first prefabricated building.

All the work was executed in Lebanon where Solomon was on very friendly terms with King Hiram of Tyre. Hiram supplied the necessary timber and craftsmen in exchange for wheat, barley, oil and wine. Hiram also provided a supervisory engineer, confusingly also named Hiram, who was experienced at working in gold, silver, copper, iron, wood and stone.

This was how the system worked:

> And King Solomon kept bringing up those conscripted for forced labour out of all Israel; and those conscripted for forced labour amounted to thirty thousand men. And he would send them to Lebanon in shifts of ten thousand a month. For a month they would continue in Lebanon, for two months at their homes; and Adoniram was over those conscripted for forced labour. And Solomon came to have seventy thousand burden bearers and eighty thousand cutters in the mountain, besides Solomon's princely deputies who were over the work, three thousand three hundred foremen over the people who were active in the work. Accordingly the king commanded that they should quarry great stones, expensive stones, to lay the foundation of the house with hewn stones. So Solomon's builders and Hiram's builders and the Gebalites did the cutting, and they kept preparing the timbers and the stones to build the house. (1 Kings 5.13-18)

The chapters of the *First Book of Kings* that follow on from above give a detailed description of the entire Temple complex which I shall merely summarize here.

The complex was enclosed within a wall covering an area about 850 feet from north to south and 600 feet from east to west at its widest, since it narrowed towards the southern approach. Within the complex were a number of public buildings completed by Solomon during the thirteen years following the inauguration of the Temple. Approaching the complex from the south up a wide and high series of steps and through an open archway, one first entered the House of the Forest of Lebanon, probably so named because its multitude of cedar columns, 45 in all, resembled a forest. The building served as an armoury and, depending on the cubit measure you adopted, it was 146 feet long, 73 feet wide and 44 feet high. Beyond the House was the Porch of Pillars which served as a reception area to the Porch of the Throne which lay beyond. This room, also called the Porch of Judgement, was where wise Solomon gave counsel.

These buildings were set in the Outer or Great Courtyard of the complex. Beyond the Porch of the Throne one now passed through another wall to a second Courtyard wherein stood Solomon's Palace. The Palace receives scant coverage in the *Book of Kings*, but we know from its foundation stones, which were over twelve feet in length, that it was a large building.

Beyond was a further gateway leading to the Inner Courtyard. One was immediately faced with the Copper Sea. This was a large reservoir intended to hold water especially for the priests to wash with, though some water was supplied to smaller basins for cleaning sacrificial animals. This reservoir, the work of the Phoenician craftsman Hiram, was made entirely of copper and was cylindrical, seven feet or so in height and nearly fifteen feet in diameter. It held about 17,000 gallons. The brim was shaped like a lily-blossom, whilst the base was decorated with sculptures of bulls.

Adjacent to the Copper Sea was the altar, twenty-nine feet square and over fourteen feet high, approached by a long ramp. When Solomon inaugurated the Temple in a ceremony lasting seven days, he sacrificed 22,000 cattle and 120,000 sheep.

The Temple itself followed the same plan as the original Tabernacle set up by Moses during the Exodus. There was an entrance porch, the Holy and the Most Holy. On either side of the doorway to the Porch were two copper pillars called Jachin and Boaz which names combined mean 'Jehovah will firmly establish the Temple in strength.' These were also the work of Hiram and measured twenty-seven feet high and nearly six feet in diameter. They were hollow and were surmounted by capitals over seven feet high.

Visually, the entrance porch was the most impressive part of the Temple. The *Second Book of Chronicles* tells us that it was about 27 feet wide, 15 feet deep, and nearly 180 feet high, giving the appearance of a tall tower. It was made of stone with beams of cedar wood, and the whole interior was overlaid with gold, as was the rest of the Temple. The Holy was 60 feet long and 30 feet wide whilst the Most Holy was 30 feet square. Surrounding the inner sanctum were a number of small storage chambers, and further rooms above, so that the total height was about 45 feet.

Within the Most Holy Hiram fashioned two giant statues of cherubs to stand either side of the Ark of the Covenant. They were made from the wood of the oil-tree (possibly the pine tree in this instance) and were overlaid in gold. They were fifteen feet high and their outstretched wings which touched each other and either wall were fifteen feet from tip to tip.

Solomon's Temple did not stand long unplundered. Only thirty-three years after it was inaugurated, King Sheshonk of Egypt invaded Palestine and stripped the Temple of its treasures. Subsequent kings of Judah used the Temple treasures to bribe neighbouring rulers, and only a few, notably Jehoash (*c* 860 B.C.) and Hezekiah (*c* 730 B.C.), did any restoration work. After Hezekiah the Temple was neglected and fell into disrepair. Evidently even the priests had no idea what was within for, reading between the lines of 2 Chronicles 34.14-15, it seems that the High Priest was most surprised to discover an ancient scroll law handed down from the days of Moses. It was left to King Josiah to repair and renovate the Temple.

We have met Josiah before. It was he who first came up against Nebuchadnezzar of Babylon and, as you will recall from Chapter III, Nebuchadnezzar finally besieged and captured Jerusalem in 586 B.C., plundering and dismantling the Temple. Thus it can be said that Nebuchadnezzar destroyed one Wonder of the World, but built two more.

When the Jews were released from Babylon by order of King Cyrus, they returned to Jerusalem and under the leadership of Zerubbabel rebuilt the Temple on a far lesser scale. It stood for five hundred years and was finally rebuilt by Herod the Great. It was destroyed by the Romans during the siege of Jerusalem in A.D. 70, although contrary to the orders of the commander and future Emperor, Titus. Neither Herod's nor Zerubbabel's Temples were considered World Wonders, but the magnificent splendour of Solomon's earned it a place in more than one ancient list by authorities who had never seen it but could imagine it from the detailed Biblical description.

Bishop Gregory of Tours provided another list of World Wonders, not those built by man, but ones 'created by the Hand of God': seven natural Wonders of the World which I thought might be a fitting conclusion to my own tour of Wonders:

1. The Ocean Tides
2. The growth of seeds and vegetation
3. The phoenix, a symbol of man's resurrection
4. Mount Etna
5. The Springs of Grenoble, whence fire and water flow simultaneously
6. The light and heat of the Sun
7. The Phases of the Moon

SELECTIVE BIBLIOGRAPHY

It is impossible to list all the many reference books I have consulted in the course of my researches. The following are those that I found the most useful and reliable and I recommend them to anyone wishing to read more about the Seven Wonders and their World.

I. The Writers of Antiquity

The following are available in the Loeb Classical Library published in Britain by W. Heinemann Ltd., and in the USA by Harvard Univ. Press.

Ammianus Marcellinus *History* (translated by J. C. Rolfe, 3 vols.)
Julius Caesar *Civil Wars* (trans. A. G. Peskett)
Cicero *Tusculan Disputations* (trans. J. E. King)
Quintus Curtius *History of Alexander* (trans. J. C. Rolfe, 2 vols.)
Diodorus Siculus *The Library of History* (trans. C. H. Oldfather, C. L. Sherman, R. M. Geer, F. Walton, 12 vols.)
Aulus Gellius *Attic Nights* (trans. J. C. Rolfe, 3 vols.)
Herodotus *History* (trans. A. D. Godley, 4 vols.)
Lucian *Works* (trans. A. M. Harmon, K. Kilburn, 6 vols.)
Manetho *History of Egypt* (trans. W. G. Waddell)
Pausanias *Description of Greece* (trans. W. H. S. Jones, 4 vols.)
Pliny *Natural History* (trans. H. Rackman, W. H. S. Jones, 10 vols.)
Polybius *History* (trans. W. R. Paton, 6 vols.)
Strabo *Geographica* (trans. H. L. Jones, 8 vols.)
Vitruvius *De Architectura* (trans. F. Granger, 2 vols.)
Xenophon *Anabasis* (trans. C. L. Brownson, O. J. Todd, 3 vols.)

II. General and Alexander the Great

Arrian *The Campaigns of Alexander* trans. Aubrey de Sélincourt (Penguin Classics, 1971)
Casson, Lionel *Travel in the Ancient World* (Allen & Unwin Ltd., 1974)
Cottrell, Leonard *Wonders of Antiquity* (Longmans, 1960)
De Camp, L. Sprague *Ancient Engineers* (Souvenir Press, 1963)
Eydoux, Henri-Paul *In Search of Lost Worlds* trans. Lorna Andrade (Hamlyn, 1972)
Kinder, Hermann and Hilgemann, Werner *The Penguin Atlas of World History* (Penguin Books, 1974)
Landels, J. G. *Engineering in the Ancient World* (Chatto & Windus, 1978)
Lipsius, Frank *Alexander the Great* (Weidenfeld & Nicolson, 1974)
Müller, Artur *The Seven Wonders of the World* trans. David Ash (Weidenfeld & Nicolson, 1969)
Pearson, Lionel *The Lost Histories of Alexander the Great* (American Philological Association, 1960)
Silverberg, Robert *The Seven Wonders of the World* (Macmillan, 1970)
Aid To Bible Understanding (Watchtower Bible & Tract Society, 1971)

III. Ancient Egypt

Budge, Wallis *The Mummy* (Cambridge Univ. Press, 1925)
Cottrell, Leonard *The Mountains of Pharaoh* (R. Hale, 1956); *The Lost Pharaohs* (Pan Books, 1956)
Edwards, I. E. S. *The Pyramids of Egypt* (Penguin Books, rev. 1976)
Emery, W. B. *Archaic Egypt* (Penguin Books, 1972)
Lange, Kurt and Hirmer, Max *Egypt: Architecture – Sculpture – Painting* (Phaidon Press, 1968)
Lauer, Jean-Philippe *Saqqara: The Royal Cemetery of Memphis* (Thames & Hudson, 1976)
Mendelssohn, Kurt *The Riddle of the Pyramids* (Thames & Hudson, 1974)
Montet, Pierre *Lives of the Pharaohs* (Spring Books, 1974)
Randall-MacIver, D. and Mace, A. C. *El-Amrah and Abydos* (Egyptian Exploration Fund, 1902)
Tomkins, Peter *Secrets of the Great Pyramid* (Allen Lane, 1973)

Toth, Max and Nielsen, Greg *Pyramid Power* (Warner Books, rev. 1976)
Uphill, E. P. (editor) *Who Was Who in Egyptology* by W. R. Dawson (Egyptian Exploration Fund, 1972)
Valentine, Tom *The Great Pyramid* (Pinnacle Books, 1975)
Ancient Egypt: Discovering Its Splendour (National Geographic Society, 1978)

IV. Babylon and Assyria

Champdor, Albert *Babylon* trans. Elsa Coult (Elek Books, 1958)
Koldewey, Robert *The Excavations at Babylon* trans. A. S. Johns (Macmillan, 1914)
Magnusson, Magnus *BC: The Archaeology of the Bible Lands* (The Bodley Head, 1977)
Parrot, André *The Tower of Babel* (SCM Press, 1955)
Pritchard, J. B. *Ancient Near Eastern Texts Relating to the Old Testament* (Princeton Univ. Press, 1955)
Ragozin, Zénaide A. *Media, Babylon and Persia* (T. Fisher Unwin, 1889)
Saggs, H. W. F. *The Greatness That Was Babylon* (Sidgwick & Jackson, 1962); *Everyday Life in Babylonia and Assyria* (B. T. Batsford, 1965)
Unger, E. *Babylon* (W. de Gruyter & Co., 1931)
Wellard, James *By The Waters of Babylon* (Hutchinson & Co., 1972)
Whitehouse, Ruth *The First Cities* (Phaidon Press, 1977)

V. The Greek World

Akurgal, Ekrem *Ancient Civilisations and Ruins of Turkey* trans. John Whybrow, M.A. and Mollie Emre, B.A. (Haset Kitabevi, Istanbul, 3rd ed. 1973)
Ashmole, Bernard *Architect and Sculptor in Classical Greece* (Phaidon Press, 1972)
Cook, J. M. *The Greeks in Ionia and the East* (Thames & Hudson, 1962)
Dinsmoor, W. B. *The Architecture of Ancient Greece* (Batsford, rev. 1950)
Drees, Ludwig *Olympia: Gods, Artists and Athletes* trans. Gerald Onn (Pall Mall Press, 1968)
Durrell, Lawrence *Reflections on a Marine Venus* (Faber, 1953)
Forster, E. M. *Pharos and Pharillon* (Hogarth Press, 1961)

Gardiner, E. Norman *Olympia: Its History and Remains* (Oxford Univ. Press, 1925)

Gardner, E. A. *A Handbook of Greek Sculpture* (Macmillan, rev. 1915)

Hogarth, D. G. *Excavations at Ephesus: the Archaic Artemisia* (British Museum, 1908)

Lethaby, W. R. *Greek Buildings Represented by Fragments in the British Museum* (Batsford, 1908)

Marlowe, John *The Golden Age of Alexandria* (Gollancz, 1971)

Newman, Bernard *Turkey and the Turks* (H. Jenkins, 1968)

Newton, C. T. *Travels and Discoveries in the Levant* (London, 1865)

Oman, C. W. C. *A History of Greece* (Longmans, rev. 1901)

Paradissis, Alexander *Fortresses and Castles of Greek Islands* trans. Stephen Paradissis (Athens, 1976)

Richter, G. M. A. *The Sculpture and Sculptors of the Greeks* (Yale Univ. Press, rev. 1950)

Rossiter, Stuart *Greece* (E. Benn, rev. 1977)

Stobart, J. C. *The Glory That Was Greece* rev. R. J. Hopper (Sidgwick & Jackson, 1964)

Thiersch, H. *Pharos* (Berlin, 1909)

Torr, Cecil *Rhodes in Ancient Times* (Cambridge Univ. Press, 1885); *Rhodes in Modern Times* (Cambridge Univ. Press, 1887)

Ward-Perkins, J. B. *Cities of Ancient Greece and Italy* (Sidgwick & Jackson, 1974)

Waywell, G. B. *The Free-Standing Sculptures of the Mausoleum at Halicarnassus* (British Museum, 1978)

Wood, J. T. *Discoveries at Ephesus* (London, 1877); *Modern Discoveries on the Site of Ancient Ephesus* (Religious Tract Society, 1890)

VI. The Roman World

Boethius, A. and Ward-Perkins, J. B. *Etruscan and Roman Architecture* (Penguin Reference, 1970)

Gibbon, Edward *The Decline and Fall of the Roman Empire* abridged by D. M. Low (Chatto & Windus, 1960)

Grant, Michael *History of Rome* (Weidenfeld & Nicolson, 1978)

Josephus *The Jewish War* trans. G. A. Williamson (Penguin Classics, rev. 1970)

Pearson, John *Arena, the Story of the Colosseum* (Thames & Hudson, 1973)

INDEX

Only key names and references are cited. To facilitate the use of this index it has been divided between 'People and Deities' and 'Places and Events', the latter also including miscellaneous references that are unclassifiable.

PEOPLE AND DEITIES

Ada, ruler of Karia, 190, 194, 200f
Adler, Friedrich, 130, 151, 188, 206
Alexander the Great, 20f, 29, 33n, 101, 114, 136, 154, 160, 169f, 182, 214, 215f, 232, 235, 240ff, 247n, 249
Alyattes, king of Lydia, 163
Amytis, Median princess, 96, 164, 263
Antigonos the One-Eyed, 216ff, 224, 242
Antipater, *see* Antipatros
Antipatros, general of Alexander the Great, 216
Antipatros of Sidon, 10, 16, 19, 27f, 154
Apelles, painter, 160, 215
Apollo, 155, 157, 164, 175, 210, 227, 269
Apollonios of Rhodes, poet and scholar, 18, 239
Apollonius of Tyana, 272f
Archimedes, 239
Aristobulos, general of Alexander the Great, 21f
Aristotle, 20, 238
Arsinoë, daughter of Ptolemy I, 271
Arsinoë, sister of Cleopatra, 243, 247n
Artaxerxes, three kings of Persia:
I *Makrokheir*, 168
II *Mnemon*, 198
III *Ochus*, 200
Artemis, 154, 155f, 160, 161, 162, 164, 171, 173f, 175 (*see also* Cybele)
Artemisia, two queens of Karia,
I, 197
II, 183, 186, 189, 196, 198f
Ashur-bani-pal, king of Assyria, 99, 108f, 118
Ashur-nasir-pal, king of Assyria, 96
Astyages, king of Media, 112, 164
Augustus, Roman emperor, 15, 18, 172, 179, 260, 262

Bammer, Anton, 158, 181
Bede, 265ff
Bellerophon, 270f
Belshazzar, regent of Babylon, 92, 112
Belzoni, Giovanni, 72
Berossus, historian, 95f
Brothers, Richard, 77
Bryaxis, sculptor, 183, 186, 194f, 225

Caesar, Julius, *see* Julius Caesar
Caligula, Roman emperor, 148, 168, 227, 269
Canning, Stratford, 203–4
Caracalla, Roman emperor, 227, 273
Caviglia, Giovanni, 44, 46, 71f
Champollion, Jean-François, philologist, 72
Chandler, Dr Richard, 150, 177
Chares of Lindos, sculptor, 17, 207, 212, 215, 225f

Cheops, *see* Khufu
Chephren, *see* Khafre
Cleopatra, queen of Egypt, 172, 243f
Cockerell, Charles R., architect, 205
Commodus, Roman emperor, 227, 262
Constantine the Great, 26, 149, 262
Croesus, *see* Kroisos
Curtius, Ernst, 151f
Cybele, 157, 161, 164 (*see also* Artemis)
Cyrus, king of Persia, 112f, 121n, 167, 263, 264, 278

Dalton, Richard, 203
Daniel, 102, 111
Darius I, king of Persia, 114, 117, 142, 167f
Davidson, David, 80f
Davison, Nathaniel, 47, 71
Dayukku, king of Media, 263f
Decius, Roman emperor, 175
Deinokrates, architect, 17, 170, 235f, 241
Demetrios of Phaleron, 216, 238f
Demetrios the Besieger, 207, 216–25
Demetrios the Silversmith, 173f
Diana, *see* Artemis
Diocletian, Roman emperor, 272
Diodorus of Sicily, historian, cited: 33n, 93f, 106, 120n, 135, 137, 216f, 219, 220f
Diognetos, engineer, 223f
Djedefre, pharaoh, 66f, 68, 74
Djoser, pharaoh, 35, 59ff
Domitian, Roman emperor, 175, 259, 269, 272
Dörpfeld, Wilhelm, 151

Edwards, I. E. S., 46, 60, 62, 82n
Eratosthenes, 18f, 49, 232, 239
Esar-Haddon, king of Assyria, 108
Euclid, 239

Fischer von Erlach, J., 31f, 186

Galle, Philipp, painter, 30, 120n
Gilgamesh, 103, 104, 119
Greaves, John, 71f
Gregory, Bishop, 20, 274, 278
Grotefend, Georg F., 116f

Hadrian, Roman emperor, 148, 151, 175, 262
Hammurabi, king of Babylon, 104ff
Heemskerck, Marten van, painter, 30f, 186, 203
Hekatomnos, prince of Karia, 197f
Helios, 207, 210, 213, 225f
Hemon, Egyptian vizier, 17, 54
Herakles, 123, 129, 137, 159, 160, 213
Hercules, *see* Herakles
Herodotus, historian, 42, 125, 197; cited: 42f, 52, 53, 66, 84, 86, 89, 97f, 100, 101, 109, 113, 163, 165, 169, 214, 263f
Herostratos, 169
Herschel, Sir John, 77f
Hippodamos of Miletos, 214
Hogarth, David G., 180
Horus, 56f
Howard-Vyse, Richard, 72f, 76
Hyginus, scholar, 262f

Idrieos, prince of Karia, 190, 194, 200f
Imhotep, 59–63, 74, 195, 237
Iphitos, king of Elis, 129, 139f

Jeppesen, Professor K., 188f, 192, 199, 204ff
Josiah, king of Judah, 110, 277f
Jove, *see* Zeus
Julius Caesar, 227, 243f, 272
Jupiter, *see* Temples

Ka'wab, Egyptian prince, 66f, 74
Kallimakhos, scholar, 238f
Kallisthenes, historian, 20f
Kassandros, king of Macedonia, 218, 225
Khafre (Chephren), pharaoh, 41, 67, 73
Kha-sekhemui, pharaoh, 59, 66
Khersiphron, architect, 165ff

Khufu (Cheops), pharaoh, 54, 66f, 68, 73, 74
Kircher, Athanasius, 31, 72
Kleomenes, regent of Egypt, 241f, 247
Knights of St John, 202f, 227
Koldewey, Robert, 94, 118f
Kroisos (Croesus), king of Lydia, 112, 113, 121n, 154, 164–7
Ktesibios, engineer, 29, 240
Kyaxares, king of Media, 96, 109, 162f, 264

Layard, Austin H., 109, 118
Leokhares, sculptor, 183, 186, 195f
Lepsius, Karl R., 72, 73
Lucian of Samosata, cited: 15, 33n, 102, 121n, 130
Lygdamis, two tyrants of Karia:
I: 197, 198
II: 197
Lysimakhos, king of Thrace, 171, 216, 218, 225
Lysippos, sculptor, 215, 225

Manetho, historian, 70f, 74
Marduk, 90f, 114, 115
Mark Antony, 172, 244
Martialis, Valerius, 259f
Maryon, Sir Herbert, 211
Mausolos, prince of Karia, 183, 184, 189, 192, 195, 198f, 214, 249
Mendelssohn, Professor Kurt, 52, 60, 79
Menes, pharaoh, 56, 59
Menkaure (Mycerinus), 38, 67
Metagenes, architect, 166f
Mithridates the Great, 148, 172
Mu'awiyah, khalif, 228f
Mycerinus, *see* Menkaure

Nabonidus (Nabuna'id), king of Babylon, 93, 101, 112f
Nabopolassar, king of Babylon, 85, 87, 96, 99, 101, 109, 113, 264
Napoleon Bonaparte, 43, 157
Nebuchadnezzar, two kings of Babylon:
I: 106
II: 85, 86f, 95f, 99, 102, 110ff, 112, 164, 250, 263f, 278
Nero, Roman emperor, 148, 227, 260, 272
Newton, C. T., 177f, 187, 188, 191f, 204f
Niebuhr, Karsten, 116

Oinomaos, king of Elis, 128, 137
Orontobates, satrap of Karia, 201, 240
Osiris, 56f

Paeonius, architect, 168
Panainos, painter, 131
Paul, St, 173f, 273
Pausanias, geographer, 15; cited: 16, 102, 137, 148, 194
Pelops, 128f, 137, 141
Pepi II, pharaoh, 73, 248ff
Perdikkas, regent of Macedonia, 33n, 216, 242
Perikles, statesman, 142, 145f, 214
Perring, John S., 73, 76, 83n
Petrie, Sir Flinders, 47, 53, 73f, 79
Phidias, sculptor, 17, 122, 124, 125, 126, 130ff, 141, 143–6, 152, 160, 193, 195, 255f, 263
Philip II, king of Macedonia, 33n, 136, 169f, 195, 215
Philon of Byzantium, engineer, 10, 16, 19, 22, 27, 28f; cited: 22, 35, 42, 81, 84, 89, 94, 122, 130, 154, 207, 212, 252–8
Pliny the Elder, 15, 183, 228; cited: 16, 158, 159, 160, 167, 168, 170, 182, 183, 184–7, 192, 194, 211, 213, 225f, 234, 271
Praxiteles, sculptor, 151f, 159, 193
Propertius, poet, 33n
Protogenes, 215, 223
Ptah, 57, 66f
Ptolemy, kings of Egypt:
I (called Lagus and Soter), 18, 21f, 171, 216, 217f, 224, 225, 234, 237, 238, 240, 242, 250
II (Philadelphos), 18, 234f, 238, 242, 271
III (Euergetes), 18
Pytheos, architect, 17, 171, 186, 193, 199

Rassam, Hormuzd, 118
Rawlinson, Sir Henry, 117f
Re (Ra), 57, 59, 62, 66, 68, 69
Rhoekos, sculptor, 165, 181

Sargon I, king of Akkad, 103f
Satyros, architect, 17, 193
Schliemann, Heinrich, 137, 151, 180
Seloukos Nikator, king of Syria, 115, 216, 218, 225, 240
Semiramis, queen of Assyria, 95, 101, 106f, 257, 263
Sennacherib, king of Assyria, 96, 99, 108
Serapis, 175, 237f
Seth, 56
Shamsi-Adad V, king of Assyria, 106
Shepseskaf, pharaoh, 67f, 74
Skopas, sculptor, 17, 159, 170f, 183, 186, 193f
Smith, George, 98, 118, 119
Smyth, Charles Piazzi, 73, 77f
Snofru, pharaoh, 54, 64ff, 67
Solomon, king of Israel, 274ff
Sostratos, architect, 17, 230, 233ff
Stevenson, J. J., 188, 205f
Strabo, geographer, 15, 18; cited: 16, 94, 132, 208, 214, 230
Sulla, Roman statesman, 148, 172, 243, 269

Tarquin, two kings of Rome:
I: 267f, 272
II: 268
Taylor, John, 76f
Thales of Miletos, 163, 271
Theodorus of Samos, 165f
Theodosius, two Roman emperors:
I: 149, 269f
II: 149, 175
Theopompos of Khios, historian, 169, 200
Theseus, 160, 182, 192
Timotheos, sculptor, 183, 184, 186, 195
Titus, Roman emperor, 259, 261, 278
Tuthmosis IV, pharaoh, 41

Userkaf, pharaoh, 68, 74

Vespasian, Roman emperor, 29, 260f, 269, 272
Vitruvius, Roman architect, 15; cited: 16, 166, 184f
Vyse, R. Howard-, *see* Howard-Vyse

Waywell, Dr Geoffrey, 189, 206
Wood, J. T., 172, 177–80

Xenophon, historian, 88
Xerxes, king of Persia, 114, 117, 141f, 155, 168, 197, 248

Zenodotos, scholar, 238
Zoser, *see* Djoser

PLACES AND EVENTS

Abu Roash, Egypt, 67, 73
Acropolis, Greece, 144
Alexandria, Egypt, 18f, 22, 29, 230, 234–40, 241–6, 261, 272 (*see also* Libraries)
Amphitheatres, 260, 271 (*see also* Colosseum)
Artemis, Temple of, *see* Temples
Assyria, 102f, 106–10
Aswan, Egypt, 42, 50f, 56, 82n
Athens, 141f, 214, 231
Athos, Mount, 236
ba, Egyptian spirit, 57f
Babel, Tower of, 31, 85, 97–9, 101, 116, 119, 120n
Babylon, 29, 84–121, 248, 257, 272
Hanging Gardens, 17, 19, 31, 91, 93–6, 110, 114, 118, 253f
Ishtar Gate, 90f, 93, 119
stone bridge, 101f
temples in, 86, 91, 99ff
Tower of Babel, *see* Babel
Walls of, 19, 88f, 114, 257f, 263

Battles:
Carchemish, 110; Halys, 163, 167; Ipsos, 225, 242; Issus, 241; Khaeronea, 169, 195; Marathon, 123, 142, 143; Plataea, 141, 143; Salamis, 142f, 168, 197; Thermopylae, 142
Bodrum, *see* Halikarnassos
Byzantium, 26, 29 (*see also* Constantinople)

Capitolium, *see* Temples
Centaurs and Lapiths, 129, 144, 191
Circus Maximus, Rome, 272
Colosseum, 120n, 260ff
Colossus of Rhodes, 17, 19, 31, 33n, 207–13, 221, 224, 225–9, 256f, 263, 266
Constantinople, 26, 149, 203
Cyrus, Palace of, 16, 263f
Tomb of, 21

Dahshur, 49, 65, 83n
Delian League, 143, 214
Diadokhoi, Wars of the, 147, 216, 224

Ecbatana, Media, 263ff
Elis, 123ff, 133, 137, 139ff, 145
Ephesos, 154f, 159, 161, 162f, 170, 171–81, 201, 225, 238, 249f, 272
Esagila, *see* Temples, Marduk
Etemenanki, *see* Babel, Tower of

Giza, Pyramids at, *see* Pyramids
Gordium, 240f
Great Pyramid, *see* Pyramids

Halikarnassos, 169, 184ff, 192, 196–206, 207, 231
Hanging Gardens of Babylon, *see* Babylon
Heliopolis, Egypt, 57, 66, 70
Heraclea, 266, 271f, 274

Jerusalem, 110f, 261, 274–8

ka, Egyptian spirit, 57
Knidos, 152, 192, 193, 196, 204, 213, 230, 233

Lapiths and Centaurs, *see* Centaurs
Libraries:
Alexandria, 18, 236–9, 242, 244, 246n
Ephesos, 176
Palatine, 262
Pergamon, 244
Lindos, 196, 207, 213, 214

Marathon, Battle of, *see* Battles
Marduk, Temple of, *see* Temples
mastabas, 39, 58f, 60f, 67
Mausoleum at Halikarnassos, 10, 16, 17, 171, 183–96, 199–206, 249, 262
Median Wall, 88
Meidûm, *see* Pyramids
Memphis, Egypt, 35, 56, 60, 241, 254
Miletos, 155, 162, 163, 168, 198, 214
mummification, 69

Nineveh, 87, 96, 109, 116, 118, 121n

Olympia, 122–52
Olympian Games, 122ff, 134ff, 137–41, 146–9
Olympic Games, 152

Palaces: Cyrus, 16, 263f
Mausolos, 184
Nebuchadnezzar, 91ff
Parthenon, 144f
Peloponnesian War, 146
Pergamon, 231, 244
Persian-Greek War, 142f, 168f, 197
Pharos island, 231, 235, 246n
Pharos Lighthouse, 10, 16, 17, 19f, 33n, 230–5, 240, 242, 243–6, 249f, 261, 266
Pisatis in Elis, 123f, 139ff
Priene, 155, 163, 170, 201
pyramidology, 74–81
Pyramids, 16, 17, 23, 35–83, 108, 248f, 254f, 263
'Bent', 37, 64f
Djoser's 'Step', 35, 37, 60–3, 98

Pyramids [*contd.*]
Great Pyramid (Khufu's), 37, 38f, 43–8, 49–54, 75–81
Khafre's, 37, 38f, 40, 42f, 52, 64
Meidûm, 37, 63–5, 83n
Menkaure's, 39f, 64
'Red', 37, 52, 64, 65

Rhodes, 198, 199f, 202f, 207ff, 213ff, 217, 225–9, 231, 249 (*see also* Sieges)
Rome, 26, 243, 244, 259, 260ff, 265, 267–70, 272, 273
Rosetta Stone, 72

Salamis, Cyprus, 198, 217f
Salamis, Greece, 142f, 197
Samos, 165, 167, 182, 269
Saqqara, Egypt, 49, 60f
Sardis, Lydia, 112, 155, 162, 167
seven, significance of, 25ff, 34n, 99, 175
Sieges: Babylon, 108, 112f
Halikarnassos, 201
Jerusalem, 110, 111, 261, 278
Rhodes, 203, 210, 215, 218–24, 256
Salamis (Cyprus), 217f
Sardis, 167
Solomon's Temple, *see* Temples
Sparta/Spartans, 128, 140, 142f, 146f, 170
Sphinx, The Great, 38, 41
Statues:
Amazons, 159f
Aphrodite by Praxiteles, 152, 193
Aphrodite by Skopas, 193
Athene Pallas by Phidias, 144
Athene Parthenos by Phidias, 144f, 152
Bellerophon, 266, 270f
Colossus of Rhodes, *see* Colossus
Cybele-Artemis, 161, 165, 174, 181
Ganymede by Leokhares, 195
Helios by Lysippos, 215 (*see also* Colossus)
Hermes by Praxiteles, 151f
Imhotep, 59
Jupiter, 269
Marduk, 91, 99, 114
'Mausolos' by Bryaxis, 189f
Nebuchadnezzar, 111
Nero, 260
Nike by Paionios, 128
Zeus by Lysippos, 215
Zeus by Phidias, 17, 124, 129–33, 141, 145, 147, 148f, 249, 255f, 263, 269
Susa, Persia, 105, 155, 168

Temples:
Ammon, Egypt, 241
Apollo at Didyma, 168
Artemis at Ephesos, 16, 17, 154–82; archaic, 157, 164–9, 180f; Alexandrine, 157–61, 170–81, 249, 258, 262
Asklepios at Epidauros, 195
Athene at Tegea, 194
Athene Polias at Priene, 193
Athene in Athens, *see* Parthenon
Hera at Olympia, 133f, 140, 141
Hera on Samos, 165, 166
Jupiter in Rome, 267–70
Marduk in Babylon, 85, 99f, 114, 121n
Serapis in Alexandria, 237f, 244f
Solomon's in Jerusalem, 274–8
Zeus at Olympia, 125, 126–33, 147, 149, 151f
Tower of Babel, *see* Babel

Ur, 103f

Walls, *see* Babylon and Median

Zeus, Statue of, *see* Statues
ziggurat, 84, 93, 97ff, 264